Groups, Interests, and U.S. Public Policy

Groups, Interests, and U.S. Public Policy

William P. Browne

GEORGETOWN UNIVERSITY PRESS / WASHINGTON, D.C.

Georgetown University Press, Washington, D.C.   20007
© 1998 by Georgetown University Press. All rights reserved.
Printed in the United States of America.
10   9   8   7   6   5   4   3   2   1   1998
THIS VOLUME IS PRINTED ON ACID-FREE OFFSET BOOKPAPER.

Library of Congress Cataloging-in-Publication Data

Browne, William Paul, 1945–
    Groups, interests, and U.S. public policy / William P. Browne.
        p.   cm.
    Includes bibliographical references (p.   ) and index.
    1. Lobbying—United States.   2. Pressure groups—United States.
    3. Political planning—United States.   I. Title.
    JK1118.B76   1998
    324'.4'0973—dc21
    ISBN 0-87840-681-6 (cloth)
    ISBN 0-87840-682-4 (paper)
                                                            97-41520

Dedicated to a great research scientist,
Moshe Talpaz,
who proves every day that you can follow your
own interest and still take care of the interests of others.

Contents

Acknowledgments

I can hardly thank everyone who contributed to this volume, but I'll try for the sake of informing readers. First in importance are the multitude of lobbyists and other policy players I've known over the past five decades. They rank first because my experiences with them have made the political process personally clear and real. (You can't write effectively about something you don't know.) These people also have taken the time to read and comment on my work.

Second, I'll thank four academic confidants. Bob Salisbury has helped me constantly since I was a fledgling political scientist. He helped with this book as well, and his influence on me has been enormous. John Dinse is a worthless but otherwise beloved department colleague with whom I've taught for over twenty-five years. More importantly, he knows what works for teaching purposes and he truly understands democratic theory. He helped a great deal by reading this manuscript. Chris Petras also read and commented and asked some great questions. He's now a professor, after once being my student and my wife's elementary school pupil. Ford Runge also helped by telling me to write in a more breezy style, letting my subjects speak for themselves.

Another group of scholars who study interests also made contributions. Several received and commented on selected chapters: Scott Ainsworth, Frank Baumgartner, Jeff Berry, Chris Bosso, Loree Bykerk, Connie Cook, Kevin Hula, Dave Lowery, Gary Mucciaroni, Mark Peterson, and John Tierney. Anonymous reviewers were just as useful.

Finally comes another varied but indispensable set of players. My wife, Linda, kept me going. So did numerous friends and supporters, especially EKO, my dog. She watched *every* word get written. I would particularly like to thank my medical team at the University of Texas M.D. Anderson Cancer Center and the many other Mt. Pleasant medical people who helped them. Oh yes, Jackie Robert and our departmental assistants at Central Michigan University did a great job preparing the manuscript. Deb Ervin bailed me out on it once again.

Without all of the above, this would be a less useful book. Maybe not even a book at all.

Introduction

This introduction is short, in the hope that all readers will pay it attention, using it to better follow the remaining text. Unlike most of my previous projects, this is not an empirical study based on original, systematically collected data. Rather, this is integration and modest addition to theory. It's intended to advance what political scientists understand of organized political interests and their relationship to public policy. It's also to be used for continuing education and undergraduate learning. I wrote this book because some excellent clinical empiricists kept reminding me that frequently we need to stop data collection and assemble what we have into a workable logic. The assembled theory revolves around three principles of how public policy takes place and four generally neglected questions about organized interests and where they fit into the policy-making process. These principles and the related questions are explained in the next sections.

Three Guiding Principles

The chapters that follow are my interpretation of interest politics after years of paying attention to, and sometimes playing, the policy-making game. They also rely heavily on the existing literature on both organized interests and public policy. These chapters are not meant to serve as an elegantly constructed model of what may or may not take place in politics. The ensuing chapters are my organized thoughts, after years of listening to and questioning executives, lobbyists, group activists, policymakers, and their confidants. I've seen it all at work.

Who are these people and why study their political involvement? I'll start with George Rapson. He was the first lobbyist I ever knew, back in the 1950s. My father worked for his automobile dealership so George could become a state senator and then a lobbyist. I was impressed with his swagger and style. But I was even more interested in his stories about his years of working to overcome a state ban on Sunday retail sales. These efforts were successfully aimed at changing business practices in an Iowa then imprisoned by its socially conservative culture.

What I learned, and why I mention George, are the political principles that guide this book. By the age of ten, I understood that *a small number of political players, who were just like the rest of us, could through hard work and lots of contacts, create public policy change.*[1] What these individuals did was simple. They just kept expanding their core of supporters. Moreover, it wasn't just because of the positions they held. In essence, George did the same things as a lobbyist that he'd done as a state senator, just without running for office. But he was a political interest in both instances, doing lobbying, or advocacy. This led me, as the remaining chapters will make clear, to *be very leery of labels. It's people who matter in politics.*[2] Even the label "interest group" has been used most inexactly, not really clearing up what exists or what happens in the policy process through advocacy. As used in this analysis, "lobbyists" include all the advocates—professional and volunteer—who work on behalf of all sorts of organized interests. A major intent of this volume is to see lobbying as a generic interest activity, not a job of those with specific organizational ties. "Interest groups," as commonly used, will be seen as "organized interests."

Anyway, to return to my ancient past, I was hooked on the politics of who wants what and what they do to get it. I even hung out with student anti-war radicals because I liked to watch advocacy politics. That led to academics, eventually, and to the study of the relationships among people, their interests, and public policy. I sought chances every time I could to meet people and organize my thoughts on interest politics, always doing what professors call "field research." In the late 1960s, I interviewed dozens of Iowa lobbyists.[3] The early 1970s were spent with those representing municipal government.[4] Later I conducted, with Laurily Epstein, a multistate study of policy players in the politics of aging.[5] Still later I interviewed many of the Michigan policy players.[6]

In the late 1970s, I became immersed in agriculture, which certainly affects what's in this book. I became convinced that *public policy is nearly impossible to study without understanding a great deal about its many issues and about its institutions, from which issues emerge.* So I became a policy expert.[7] From there, using my office in the U.S. Department of Agriculture, I studied systematically the many interests seeking to define and influence food and fiber policy.[8] And, finally, I spent a year with Congress, interviewing and listening to those who use and listen to the endless complaints of agriculture's private political interests.[9]

In the final analysis, what I learned through these many stops, and in doing considerable consulting lobbying of my own,[10] are three principles that guide this book on interest theory. First, organized interests—not just groups—matter in American politics. Second, these interests matter the most through the efforts of specific people working with an expanding array of other players. Third, one can't understand an interest or why it matters politically without understanding its issues and how those fit within the broader confines of public policy and policy making.[11]

Asking the Right Questions

The problem with integrating a theory by using one's own previously observed principles should be obvious: One can too easily look selectively for evidence that supports personal views and reject evidence that refutes them. As a consequence of that tendency, those who do theory need something to ground it in a reliable, scholarly exercise. The best grounding is to ask, at the onset, the right or proper questions about what needs explanation. Those questions need to be built on that entire set of studies linked to the subject matter. They need eventually to provide answers as well, ones that help sort out the many contradictions and commonalities in previous research.

In the field of interest politics, the literature is at once well-developed and in need of further work. That seeming contradiction exists because there are really two lines of inquiry followed in studying political interests. The first, and most theoretically developed approach, examines the internal organization and operation of interests.[12] Interest groups as mass membership associations are given the greatest attention.[13] Scholars like to reflect on the relations between people and their leaders, probably because these interactions are reasonably well-defined and predictable.

The second line of inquiry is developed less satisfactorily, even though it was the first addressed: that literature focuses on the public policy effects of interests and their external relationships with policymakers. This latter explanation, or lack of it, is the void that this book aims to fill, developing an integrated view of how and why interests matter.

There seem to be three main reasons why the public policy effects of interests are so unsatisfactorily understood. First, it's hard and expensive research work to do. Data need to be collected from innumerable and hard-to-reach sources.

A second reason appears to be the tendency of scholars to, as they've done successfully with the internal operation of groups, look for a well-defined and predictable explanation of who talks to whom and who follows whose lead in policy making. This search once gave rise to an emphasis on little sets of recurring participants from interests, the Congress, and executive agencies.[14] To the general exclusion of other policymakers, these iron triangles, whirlpools of activity, policy networks, subgovernments, or whatever else they've been called were seen collectively as the only people who ran things in government. The problem with this explanation is that it's just far too simple. Other people, like presidents and judges, do get involved, regularly. Nearly every policy player or institutional scholar can point to several examples where an iron-triangle or network explanation of what happens is just plain silly.[15]

Closely related to this second reason is a third one. Students of interest politics have become waylaid by a no less silly disagreement from which they've only in the past two decades broken free. Some argued that organized interests dominate national government.[16] Others in turn rejected that idea, seeing policymakers as the ones who, for personal reasons, decide whether or not to listen to interest advocates.[17] This preoccupation with who's biggest and best made much of the study of interests and public policy a dead-end effort, since the answers never satisfied anyone.

In short, my conclusion for explaining the void in interest/policy studies is that people generally have not asked the right questions, or at least have not asked the truly answerable ones. Wrong questions crop up over and over to guide interest/policy research. Common ones include: Do interests have influence? How much influence do they have? Do interests work to the common good?

It seems that any serious observer would never start with any such obvious and impossible questions. Of course interests have influence, or there wouldn't be so many Washington lobbyists. Having a lobbyist isn't just a modern-day fad; the word itself goes back to the early nineteenth century—the year 1808.[18] What then of the question about how much influence? Since influence never can be weighed or checked for size, asking how much will never bring a complete or widely accepted answer. Influence is intangible, like faith or patriotism, so it's not easily measurable from one person or group to another. Observers could never agree on a common measure if they tried. And what of the question about the common good? Right, that's why groups and firms go through such heavy expenses in having lobbyists, going to Washington, and providing information and support to policymakers. They're just there for the public interest. Sure. Let's get real, why even ask that question?

Nonetheless, those questions and similarly obtuse ones are common to interest/policy scholarship. And they create a morass from which students of political interests need to be worked free. To break that bond, this book starts with some more basic and thus more answerable questions. In that sense, it retreats to the simple as a way to clearly order thoughts on interests and public policy. The four organizing questions for the following chapters are: Where do interests fit into the policy-making process? (And, quite importantly, where do they fit within the country itself? Where do they fit what's pretty much everyday political reality? Not how do they fit our best philosophical visions.) What do they do to fit? How do they do it? And, to what degree do interests adapt and change over time and with new circumstances?

Those four questions are enough to get started. Each of them builds on the book's central assumptions that interests matter, their advocates produce, and their issues and institutions come to take on special political and social significance. While these questions and principles seem easy enough, their unraveling will be, as it must, complex and difficult. Hopefully, though, it will be easy to read. As it also must, that unraveling needs to be done with an eye to history, or to the emergence and evolution over time of American lobbying. But it needs also to emphasize the here and now. Additionally, it's a hope that the ensuing answers to the organizing questions will point readers to some understanding of those other impossible questions they want answered about influence and power. For example, does the American Dental Association matter more than does the National Association of Manufacturers? After reading this, maybe some better informed guesses can be made.

The Following Chapters

The starting point for this text is a description of interest groups and what their representatives do. Interest groups, which are the most generally recognized of politically organized interests, are seen as voluntary associations having their own memberships, of either people or institutions, that share a common purpose. By definition, interest groups lobby, or work, to structure or restructure public policy.[19]

Chapter Two turns to other and varied nonmembership interests that are active in U.S. politics: individual businesses, foundations, churches, governmental enterprises, and various personal political organizations. The intent is to explain the proliferation of demands on government from sources that are not really interest groups in a membership sense. Nonetheless, these interests do the same things—lobby on issues of public policy. They do advocacy.

After explaining the organizational structure that exists within the universe of political interests, Chapter Three examines more precisely what it is that organized interests do to influence public policy making and why they do so much. The many facets of lobbying are covered: providing information, making financial contributions, litigating, organizing protests, shaping public opinion, cultivating the media, and the host of other tasks that lobbyists can, in their creative ways, conjure up. For any interest, all of these tasks can combine to constitute an integrated issue campaign or a public affairs effort. It's that organized effort that's so unique. Lobbying activity is not randomly taking place in all directions. The different tasks are interrelated and highly selective.

By this point it should be clear to readers that both political interests as well as their activities are familiar and constant features of American society. Politics and society converge. Interest politics is not something hidden away in Washington, D.C., or in a state capital city, or something that just goes on periodically or in a crisis situation. It's something that people see daily, whether they recognize it or not.

The theory then turns to why interests are so recognizable and even valued. Chapters Four, Five, and Six focus on who it is that interests seek to influence and why each of these specific targets are selected. While the targets are different, it's important to remember that they're viewed as a common effort. The emphasis of these chapters is on the historical structure and development of the U.S. government and its lobbies. Chapter Four starts with the public as a target, emphasizing that mainstream opinion most likely moves politicians in an open, democratic, and decentralized government. Policymakers as targets are considered next in Chapter Five. The emphasis is on how many—not how few—policymakers need be considered as necessary targets in any public affairs effort. Legislators, legislative staff, administrators, other executive officials, and judges are among those covered, all of whom respond to selected publics, as interests.

Interests as targets of other interests are then addressed. The emphasis is on the need for organized interests to broaden their appeal, not be politically isolated as advocates of an unpopular or widely contentious issue. The essence of lobbying among interests is explained as coalition building and as other forms of organized mutual issue support, all of which involve considerable and skilled public affairs talents.

Yet, what public policy wins can interests gain? And how does what they win compare with what it is that their members, supporters, and fans actually want or prefer? Chapters Seven and Eight are concerned with those questions in order to demonstrate that not all potential interests emerge, that not all succeed when they do get organized, and that the politics of moderation and compromise are truly limiting factors faced by all lobbies. Chapter Seven starts by examining which issues tend to get addressed and which interests win. Chapter Eight then explains why some issues generally tend to be ignored and why other interests never quite get well-organized, why they in all likelihood lose.

The idea of policy niches is introduced in Chapter Nine as the key to long-term interest survival. The argument is that specific interests need to fit well—not just try to alter—the broader conditions of politics, policy making, and public beliefs. In other words, all successful interests need to link effectively to the political mainstream and their immediate environment, but not necessarily win majority support. Organized interests just want majority acquiescence. To get that acquiescence, they must create political and social identities that clearly distinguish each interest, one from the other, in the minds of likely targets and their supporters. Interests that survive and prosper keep marginally adjusting their identities to changing circumstances.

That conclusion brings the text to its final chapter. There the previous findings are briefly reviewed, especially the way in which interest politics so nicely fit the general fabric of American public policy making and not some nebulous idea of the "nature of man."[20] Despite this nice fit with ongoing politics, the chapter argues that organized interests do change things, in large part because they work continuously to alter the wants and wishes of large segments of the entire public and governing structure. Because the targets of public affairs are so extensive and so interdependent, successful interests that can fit or force a fit with the political mainstream truly matter. Like George Rapson once did, they even help change the course of political events. The rest of us are just along for the ride.

One warning needs to be given. This is a serious book. But it's lighthearted, written with a lot of tongue-in-cheek. Its style crosses a cultural divide that many readers won't like. Certainly my favorite nun, who taught parochial school grammar, wouldn't have liked its written style. To get its points across, this book has had to be written as fun and easy reading. It doesn't function as an itemized textbook. It unravels instead in storybook fashion and with some redundancy built into the chapters. Why the tongue-in-cheek? As they must, organized interests project their own self-importance way too much. And they like to gloss over some things. To strike a balance, they get deflated and trampled a little in the following pages. But it should be clear, organized interests and the scholars who've commented on them are both still respected in those same pages.

1

Interest Groups and Public Policy

Politicians in the United States love to complain about those notorious special interest groups, the ones that proliferate in Washington, D.C., or in the nearest state capital. But what the heck are they? Their complaints have become expected, much like other common complaints that mask poor performance. Baseball batters, when unsuccessful, complain about the bad lights. Drivers who have accidents rail against the chintzy corporations that made their cars and trucks. Of course, kids who spill milk are never to blame for their own clumsiness. Somebody or something else made them do it, maybe a startling noise or dad's hurried appearance to grab a beer from the refrigerator. Yes, everyone makes excuses, convenient ones that at least deal enough with reality to make their complaints understandable.

It's no wonder, in such a world, that special interests have a bad name. They organize things, such as demands for tax breaks, that many don't like. They seem, on one level, to be unfamiliar and slightly mysterious in their hideaways close to government. Some give away money—always a suspect act. And since politicians and the media that report on such groups denounce interests so loudly and so often, it's understandable that they're seen as a negative social and economic influence.[1]

Of course there's always some shred of truth to even the worst excuse. Bad lights, after all, do make it hard to hit a baseball. Corporations don't spare every expense to make automobiles crash resistant. Dads who hurry into the kitchen during a commercial break from a football game can be scary if a kid's in the way. Such familiarity brings knowing condemnations of outdated baseball stadia, of corporate America, of beer-guzzling fathers, of special interest groups. All are among the mythic criticisms that Americans seem bred, or at least conditioned, to routinely make.

Myths, however, are only based on partial reality.[2] In their more reflective moments Americans also know larger truths: that a .115 hitter couldn't succeed under a noonday sun, that their own friends couldn't produce better autos in their garages or neighborhood shops, that all dads aren't elbowing their children from the way, or that politicians are blameless for at least some of government's inadequacies and failures. Lousy hitters, corporations, and fathers are accepted, as well as condemned, because in the American soul, they all fit well with our view of the universe. They make baseball a sport of some balance and skill, provide desirable consumer products, and oftentimes lovingly help mop up that spilled milk.

Likewise special interest groups as well as nonpolitical groups fit the American soul, they fit the public nicely. Nowhere is that more evident than in the organizations that people join. Every time someone within that public faces a particular need, it seems that an interest group responds. When a child needs hunter safety lessons, old dad takes Tammy or Tommy to a class taught through the National Rifle Association (NRA). When an auto plant worker is chastened by a supervisor, that person goes to the United Auto Workers union for support. When the farmer down the road sees this year's crops being stunted by weather, he and his neighbors go together to their congressional office to work for disaster assistance. One old farmer said it best: "By myself, I'm nothing it seems, just spit in the wind. But when most of the folks in the area complain as a group, we get action. These are all people just like me, too, nobody special."[3]

Interest groups, in other words, do indeed fit Americans. In addition to being generally unfamiliar and vilified, they're also among the first things to which people, on their own, turn when in need. People do know them, or at least they know examples of them. Groups fit American needs: the way Americans go to government, the way they live their lives. Special interest groups then are seen as something more than just at fault, even by the worst cynics. They're also something that if people think hard enough about them are used and appreciated,[4] at least by people who are willing to join. And Americans do join. Even the anarchistic

Freemen who barricaded themselves on a Montana ranch in 1996 were a voluntary interest group.

There are then two widely understood yet conflicting views of special interests in the United States. Americans hear enough believable ideas to generally condemn organized interests. For example, groups deadlock government. Yet people also know enough from the conditions of daily life that such groups fit their own personal needs and serve them well. They just fail to understand the contradiction between the stories of selfish groups, who must be somebody else's, and the value of their own groups, the ones that help them personally.

What Are Interest Groups?

Political observers seem to call nearly everything that bothers them either an interest group or a bureaucracy. An association of citizens such as the National Rifle Association, a tobacco company, evangelical Christians, a business trade association: all are commonly referred to as interest groups.[5] That makes the term a pretty inexact one. It's loosely applied. Can a single company be a group? Can unaffiliated believers be one? All four of the above have interests in public policy, of course, but only two operate what realistically could be called interest groups: the NRA and the business trade association.

What exactly then are interest groups?[6] First, interest groups are voluntary associations of joiners. They have members, either formal ones who sign up or informal supporters who routinely show up to assist their organization. The National Education Association (NEA) is a formal group with teachers as the joiners. An informal group might organize in a neighborhood, for example, to protest the city widening their street. The joiners attend meetings, actively fight the project, and think of themselves as a common core of affiliates. Unlike the NEA, the neighbors pay no dues, select no official leaders, have no written constitution. They just show up, maybe bringing cookies and lemonade to share. When the street is finally widened, they glumly disband. Or they go on to other business because of another shared ad hoc interest. And they may formalize the group by adding dues and rules.

Second, interest groups have joiners who share a common characteristic that defines each organization's reason for existing.

People join the NRA because they like guns. Teachers teach. Neighborhoods are angry with the city because their residents will lose parts of their front yards to the expanded street and because traffic and speed will increase. Such commonalities as guns, teaching, and safety determine the content of a group's interest. Commonalities that distinguish Americans from one another factionalize society and with it U.S. politics.

Third, interest groups all have a public policy focus. They actively attempt to influence government, openly and with their members' consent. Even with declining membership, the NRA resists efforts to regulate in any way private guns or their ownership. The NEA battles for the classroom and for the collective bargaining rights of its members. Of course, the neighborhood group wants the city to abandon that street project. An interest group can't exist without issues of public policy that identify why its joiners have come or stayed together. The American Farm Bureau Federation (AFBF) of the 1920s was just an unfocused organization of farmers until the group sought government financial assistance for growers of major crops.[7] Prior to that, AFBF helped its local members improve their production capabilities—how to grow more and do it better. The Farm Bureau was initially a service group, and then, when its issue position was defined and its members mobilized around it, AFBF became one of the most important of American interest groups. As the Farm Bureau shows, interest groups are always evolving and modifying their behavior. Why? Because government and society are both always changing and so new things are wanted by joiners.

Other voluntary interest groups with various specific policy interests abound. Common Cause seeks members who support democratic change within government. It long has been identified as the main spokesgroup for lobbying and campaign finance reform. The American Medical Association tries hard to recruit all medical doctors and forcefully works for protecting their economic well-being against health and insurance policy alterations. The National Association of Manufacturers wants similar protection, especially against foreign trade inequities, for industrial firms that are their joiners. A personal favorite of many observers of politics calls itself a union. But the First National Guild for Health Care Providers of the Lower Extremities, which is ironically a single-state group, doesn't do collective bargaining. These 450 podiatrists only want to get their collective foot in the door, negotiating with businesses, government, and insurance providers as health care undergoes change. It's a lobby, and a recently organized one.

The National Milk Producers Federation (NMPF) organizes dairy cooperatives that gain from federal marketing legislation and for years, through its cooperatives, has provided dairy farmers a lucrative public policy reward by raising the price of milk. NMPF's sister organization, the National Fluid Milk Processors Promotion Board, became well-known—at least visually—by its advertisements picturing celebrities with milk on their upper lip. One of the most fascinating interest groups of recent years was the decade-long effort of the Houston Regional Mobility Association (HRMA). It organized and sought funding from road builders who stood to gain from federal support of large-scale highway construction projects. As long as the need for projects was evident, the group was well-received and very active in providing campaign donations. When most projects were completed, HRMA lost its members. Then, because groups are evolving, it died. Politics no longer made sense to the dues payers, or at least paying for politics didn't.

Let's summarize then. Interest groups are known by three necessary characteristics. One, they voluntarily bring together members and supporters, or joiners. Two, these joiners share a common characteristic that differentiates them from others. Three, the group's purpose is to represent issues of public policy that fit the joiners' common concerns. That's their interest. Without all of the three, whatever an organization is, it isn't an interest group.

When a Group's Not an Interest Group

Making that three-point distinction is important. There exists not only a need to clearly define and sort out what's going on in politics, there's also a more practical need, given the intent of this volume, to show how different forms of interests fit in different ways into politics. Interest groups fit one way. A corporation fits another. A social movement of unaffiliated, at least with each other, Christians fit in yet a third fashion. Students of interest groups, who tend to generalize and lump all advocacy interests and sometimes even the most nominally political groups together, seem to overlook one critical dictum of knowledge: Don't mix apples and oranges in an explanation.

So let's separate the oranges from the apples, or interest groups from other voluntary membership associations. It's confusing when that distinction can't be made. Americans are suspect of interest groups anyway, and they find it hard to figure one from the other in attributing blame for perceived failures of government. Accordingly, such groups as the local Rotary Club, the Knights of Columbus, the Trilateral Commission, the university alumni club, and the Detroit Engineering Society often get looked upon as terribly nasty.

Blame for this confusion should fall, indirectly at least, on Alexis de Tocqueville, who really made a quite simple observation about Americans that interest group observers took to their hearts far too closely.[8] As a French commentator on the emerging colonial republic, Tocqueville was struck that Americans were such frequent joiners. Of course, he was looking at a predominately rural society. People there were logically worried about how to farm, how to protect themselves from natives, and how to socialize in scantily populated regions. Joining with others made sense: for information, for protection, and for socializing. The same was true of trade groups of journeymen craftsmen. In a formal sense, education was otherwise unavailable. Voluntary associations were a nice neighborhood or occupational fit. All of those benefits of belonging were far less necessary in Paris or even in the well-settled French countryside.

Nevertheless, Americans were labeled from the onset as joiners. John Dewey later said of why people join, "Things are made that way."[9] As James Madison warned of factional influences, it's the "nature of man."[10] This settled, students of interest groups didn't bother for years to note where interests came from or why people joined. No one felt a need to define where interest groups fit. They were just accepted—as natural.

Also, no one bothered much with distinguishing interest groups from other social and economic associations. Tocqueville and Dewey were writing of the latter, associations that served the joiners' daily and largely nonpolitical needs. Madison hadn't a clue as to what kinds of factions would come forth and how they would organize. In Madison's view, people would just be at each others' throats without strong authorities. Nonetheless, it became the norm for scholars to dredge up one or more of these commentators as they got on with their own more trendy and inflammatory business of critiquing interest influence, explaining group power, or describing the dominance of interest groups in the United States.

Were, though, interest groups really as prolific or as natural as many envisioned? In no way.[11] Here's an example. One of the earliest formal interest groups was the Order of Patrons of Husbandry, or the National Grange. Founded in 1867, the Grange, through its locals, operated mostly like the service groups that Tocqueville observed. Fraternity was its goal. Only in the 1870s did the Grange become an interest group, as Solon Justus Buck noted, when its voluntary farm affiliates and leaders took to actively advocating government regulation of the railroads.[12] Most of the other rural farm groups of the period were still only arranging farm dances and working together to grow better crops. That is, they were service groups.

Why not call them all interest groups, or mix the apples and the oranges? The answer is simple. Those groups, like the local Rotary Club of today, were neither organizing their members around politics nor actively bringing politics to the joiners. Rotaries are, in fact, a good example. Each local club, supported by Rotary International, recruits voluntary joiners who share at least some common interests in the betterment of their own local communities. Rotarians tend to be thought of, and indeed think of themselves, as a kind of community elite, organizing to provide services and undertake projects that others can't. With their emphasis on community development and civic responsibilities, and having a bit more wealth, Rotarians are different than the grassroots citizenry. The projects that they envision often fail to find widespread public understanding, even when completed. Owning and operating a downtown hotel in Traverse City, Michigan, for example, caused many local residents to question Rotary motives. Clubs, as a result, have become thought of as elitist and suspect, as one of those dreaded special interests.

Yet Rotaries seldom, if ever, become local interest groups, even with this latent potential for active political involvement.[13] By strategy and design, they undertake their own projects and generally avoid politics. They tend not to tell their members to mobilize for political influence. The clubs shun being identified with particular local issues, such as neighborhood health care centers in a big city or a job-recruiting economic development commission in a rural county. No local Rotary Club wants to get stuck with bills bigger than it can pay or projects that demand ongoing private- and public-sector cooperation. That takes away the fun and makes involvement in the group hard work. Rotaries are community catalysts and places to make contacts but not public policy advocates as the Granges became when they finally went to Congress in 1876.

Likewise, the always present parish Knights of Columbus (KC) aren't interest groups. Their voluntary joiners *are* different: Catholic, men, service proponents. Different, though, doesn't make for an interest group. The KCs tend toward fish fries or clambakes and—in nongambling states—bingo, leaving other groups to watch the city commission or go to the state house to fight abortion. The same is true of a university alumni club. It has enough to do in order to raise private donations, stage events for maintaining alumni commitment, and entertain those visiting the campus. Alumni clubs leave public policy to the campus public affairs office and to associations of universities and their officials.

No group is more suspect or different from the grassroots, however, than the Trilateral Commission. Long a target of radical U.S. farmers and many in the labor and far right political movements, the Commission is vilified widely as a proponent of one-world government, or of destroying national sovereignty.[14] Organized to promote international understanding and cooperation, the Commission is but a small office in New York and a series of meetings around the world with its members and guests. Business and government leaders from various countries are asked to join, often on a revolving or short-term basis. The idea is that the Commission becomes a forum for understanding and advancing international awareness.[15] Networking is the buzz word, even more than for Rotary. Hopefully, its joiners go back home to their prominent jobs with renewed understanding and with useful contacts. The Trilateral Commission then is a lot like a study group, or even group therapy. It undertakes no policy agenda nor does it engage in public affairs advocacy.

The Engineering Society of Detroit (ESD) operates in a similar fashion on a far more restricted and less newsworthy scale. As a trade association of engineers, ESD secures members through conferences, technology training programs, and an assortment of other personal services. The group, especially through Michigan's automobile industry, advertises itself as the association to join for sharing state-of-the-art science and technology. ESD officials emphasize that they don't operate an interest group. Career benefits, not public policies, drive the members.

These and hundreds of other groups show that Tocqueville was indeed correct about America being a nation of joiners. However, Americans are far more likely to join other associations rather than interest groups. The public policy focus of the public isn't as strong as its focus on satisfying other wants.

Why? In fact, why don't all groups aspire to be agents of influence? Quite simply, groups such as the local Rotary and ESD find it better and more advantageous to avoid activist political identities. Politics can spell trouble. These groups have enough difficulties without being pinned down as blatantly orchestrating Traverse City development, the world economy, or technology transfer in the auto industry. The suspicions are bad enough, leading many potential joiners to reject affiliation. Many potential supporters already hear the bad stuff and refuse to help on projects. Politics would only make things worse.

But Isn't It All Politics?

Yes. But then all of life gets occasionally political. People constantly struggle over who gets what and who loses. As political scientists like to say, politics is about influencing and doing all the other things necessary to affect how society allocates its values and other things of benefit.[16] That covers a lot. Of course, the Trilateral Commission maintains an organizational belief in eliminating world trade barriers. But it doesn't send representatives to stalk the halls of Congress. Nor does ESD wander the legislature on science matters. The society does, though, hold conferences where policymakers are invited, wined and dined, and made to feel good about what science and technology can bring to society and the economy. The Commission gets the same results when members of Congress and the administration interact, or network, with true believers from the private sector.

No one, likewise, would be foolish enough to think that a local Rotary Club or a Knights of Columbus would shun *all* occasions for exercising political influence. Neither would the university alumni club. The alums may not be taking up campaign donations for those policymakers who attend a gathering at the club, nor are they sponsoring a call to blackball a graduate now serving in the legislature who voted against budget approval of a proposed university program or building, yet those folks most certainly are letting anyone who opposed the old home campus know that they are *truly* irritated. Rotarians also might make life and business difficult in town for those opposing their favored projects. People lose contracts, friends, sales, and community status. When Rotary leaders complain to the press that opponents represent Neanderthals against progress, politics *is* going on. Influence *is* being sought.

A KC chapter that champions the local Catholic grade school moves toward the same ends. Group statements about funding needs, quality education, and the importance of values learned at school all meld into the state's public policy agenda. Issues such as tuition vouchers, tax breaks for donors, and public school obligations to parochial schools for busing and special education gain momentum when the KC beats the drum about the wonderful kids, priests, and nuns from their hometown. Reporters, policymakers, and politically active citizens all take note.

So, if politics, even in these subtle forms, goes on within such groups, why not label them and others like them "interest groups"? There exists a far better answer than just saying "it's not right" or "I don't want to." Groups such as the Rotary or the Trilateral Commission are not organized around the principle of going to government or otherwise moving in politics on behalf of an issue critical to the group members' reasons for affiliating. That's not why members are there, and it would probably be a reason to stay away if the group argued for winning advocacy influence. Rotarians join to provide community service and give—and gain— hometown recognition as good folks. Trilateral Commission members join to meet, sound out, and learn from world leaders whom they previously didn't know well. The critical distinction between these groups and organized interest groups is that most joiners would never respond to either the Rotary or the Commission if the invitation read: "Let's take over the town!" or "Come dominate the world economy!"

Interest groups, on the other hand, do advertise such things. Joiners do respond to interest groups that offer similar challenges. Americans fit into service groups in one way and into their interest groups in distinctly another. As a consequence, the way in which these two groups matter in politics is very different. The former, through service work, create social sentiment, usually in subtle ways. The latter, by their direct advocacy and lobbying, are controversial and overtly contentious flag bearers.

Figure 1.1 illustrates these differences, especially in public policy involvement. Every group indeed has some political relevance. As can be seen, most groups engage in some political activity, but only interest groups are overt players in the policy process: vocal, obvious, and direct. Some examples, along with the characteristics of their members, are included in the figure.

Why People Join and Stay with Interest Groups

While everything may indeed be at least occasionally political, not every group wants or needs to be thought of as an interest group. For some, being thought of as such is their greatest fear. It's more than just trouble. As the first notable scholar to think about what makes for an interest group, David Truman was onto something important when he noted that point in rather oblique fashion. Truman felt that interest groups emerge either when other interests threaten or when there occurs some disturbance in the previous balance of politics.[17] Thus, interest groups are *about* politics while other groups may merely be involved in something political.

Unfortunately, critics of Truman never worried about that distinction. As a consequence, observers got off the track when it came to assessing where and how interest groups fit. But these critics did get waylaid and sidetracked for good ends, theoretically very important ones that did much for the study of politics. Mancur Olson, followed quickly by Robert Salisbury, began it all with a theory of group exchange.

Olson identified the legendary "free-rider problem."[18] According to Olson, joining or staying with an interest group for policy reasons is illogical, or irrational. By their nature, public policy decisions reward everyone who shares a common characteristic for which the law or regulation is intended. Those are collectively received benefits or goods. No one needs to join the group in order to win as long as enough others become joiners and make a political difference. Logical people and firms save the costs of joining: dues, energy, effort. They remain rationally ignorant or uninvolved. Resources can be used for other things—watching TV or developing a new product for sale.

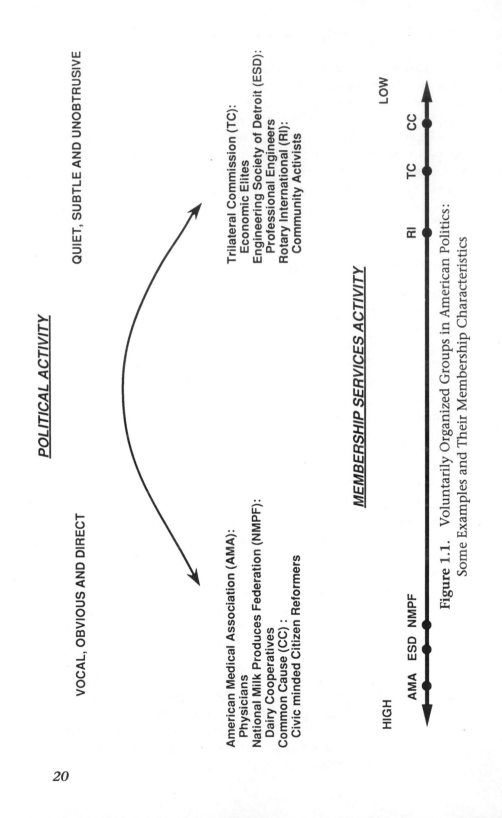

POLITICAL ACTIVITY

VOCAL, OBVIOUS AND DIRECT   QUIET, SUBTLE AND UNOBTRUSIVE

American Medical Association (AMA):   Trilateral Commission (TC):
Physicians   Economic Elites
National Milk Produces Federation (NMPF):   Engineering Society of Detroit (ESD):
Dairy Cooperatives   Professional Engineers
Common Cause (CC) :   Rotary International (RI):
Civic minded Citizen Reformers   Community Activists

MEMBERSHIP SERVICES ACTIVITY

HIGH   LOW

AMA ESD NMPF   RI   TC   CC

Figure 1.1.   Voluntarily Organized Groups in American Politics:
Some Examples and Their Membership Characteristics

To compensate for such behavior, interest groups also offer selective benefits, or goods, ones received only by those who join and which become the basic unit of exchange. These benefits are variously typed as purposive, expressive, solidarity or social, and tangible nonpolicy goods. Joiners gain such things from membership as feeling satisfaction about sounding off, sharing experiences, building camaraderie, getting current research results, buying inexpensive insurance, or any number of other things.[19] In effect, the free-rider problem came dangerously close to defining interest groups away, as just other organizations. The National Rifle Association, where members hung out with pals and took the kids to hunter safety classes, was discussed by many as little different than the Rotary or the KC.

Scholars quickly picked up on Salisbury's fine-tuning of Olson. By identifying entrepreneurs who start, organize, and market new interest groups, Salisbury was able to explain the rise of policy-based organizations when, as Truman suggested, there was no new crisis or disruption.[20] A kind of academic conventional wisdom, especially among those who only marginally studied interest groups, emerged that Salisbury never intended in his entrepreneurial theory. It goes like this: If organizers can sell interest groups for nonpolitical purposes, like the fraternal customs of the Granges, joiners are essentially not interested in public policy. That is, they really *don't* distinguish between the NRA and the Rotary.[21]

That generalization, though, is quite invalid. For one thing, research has consistently shown that large numbers of members *do* value the collective benefits of public policy work by their interest groups,[22] even if they disagree with some group positions. Sometimes, though, they like the selective benefits even more, and those may be all that some members like. Nonetheless, people claim that they expect their interest groups to be involved in public affairs and they act supportively when groups are involved. Collective goods, as a consequence, are important units of exchange—perhaps irrationally, but still ones that matter.

A second reason for distinguishing between interest groups and other voluntary associations focuses on the very characteristics of the public, those who are indeed the joiners and who seal the exchanges. People have and hold political beliefs, attitudes, and values. That's obvious. And those beliefs are held about many things, it must be added. It's also well-understood that such beliefs are easily and frequently expressed as public opinions. After all, an entire segment of the economy—pollsters—thrives from observing and measuring those views and translating the various observations into politically useful strategies and tactics. Those views then must have some importance. To deny that people and institutional representatives would never affiliate with interest groups because of their political views would be absurd. It would be like saying that people never vote, write letters to Congress, and join political parties because of their positions on issues. Of course reams of data show that they do.[23] There's more to politics than just pretty faces or appealing images: It's who's getting what that very often matters.

The public then not only cites public policy reasons as sensible ones for joining and staying with interest groups, it's also intuitively sensible, given the way individuals variously respond as political participants, that this issue-attuned citizenry behaves this way. It may be illogical and irrational, but, nonetheless, it's also expected behavior.

A third and somewhat oversimplified reason for differentiating between the NRA and the Rotary can be seen best from Paul Johnson's work.[24] Johnson points out what interest group scholars successfully, and strangely, ignored: People don't always engage in political behavior or, more specifically, join interest groups because of personal choices that, in a vacuum, strike their fancy. As Salisbury's entrepreneurial analysis reveals, interest group leaders market their organizations, recruit members, and provide people with multiple reasons for affiliating.[25] Mobilizing, as it's called, helps factionalize people by emphasizing their unique interests. It certainly pays off for interests as well. If, Johnson shows, you ask enough people who more or less believe in an interest group's issues to join, a sizable number will do it. The more that entrepreneurs ask, the more who join, which would certainly be the case in a society where people both are joiners and come to expect participation in politics. Such people find it easy, or a low-cost way, to get and stay involved. Other stuff goes on, too, of course.

So, as Steven Rosenstone and John Mark Hansen have rather elegantly demonstrated, what people do as political participants has two dimensions.[26] The first is being willing to act. The second is being asked to act, or being made more willing to do so. If potential joiners aren't asked or mobilized by entrepreneurs, issue-based membership—or most any joining—won't happen. But if entrepreneurs sell the idea of interest group membership to those in society who share policy or issue sympathies with the organization, numerous people will join interest groups for overtly political reasons.

That—politics—after all, is what interest group leaders have to sell in greatest abundance and at a low cost to the organizations in providing benefits of valued exchange to their members. As one executive director so nicely noted: "Getting members is about scaring the hell out of people." Interest groups, for that reason, become—and advertise themselves as—policy watchdogs, playing a defensive political game because more people respond out of fear of loss than out of hope for truly more advantageous public policy.[27]

For example, Ducks Unlimited tells its members and likely members that the group is watching closely for changes in federal wetlands policy, arguing against them when breeding grounds will be harmed, and fighting the bad guys who want such changes. Without DU, the idea is instilled, there would certainly be fewer ducks to shoot. Buying interest group memberships, for issue-directed consumers of politics, is also about buying a bit of peace of mind in an inexpensive way. Ducks Unlimited doesn't ask its members to boycott farm products or electrical power. Yet buying peace of mind was certainly evident when Ronald Reagan became president of the United States and, according to many activists, articulated severe antienvironmental policy positions. New members signed on. Environmental interest group membership soared for such vocal organizations as the Sierra Club and National Wildlife Federation.[28] Policy mattered to people. It wasn't because these interest groups were offering better bargains on wilderness excursions or Christmas cards or just asking for more joiners. Policy mattered because existing programs needed protection even if new ones from government seemed unlikely.

None of that negates the importance of selective benefits as units of membership exchange. Most certainly not. In Figure 1.1, it can also be seen how larger interest groups such as the AMA and NMPF provide a broader range of selective member services to their joiners than do groups such as Common Cause. With a greater scale and scope of operations in general, the larger groups have more latitude to do more for members in a nonpolicy sense. As Olson emphasized, plenty of people once joined the American Farm Bureau Federation only for its insurance. Many were even nonfarmers.[29] Stressing collective benefits only helps better explain the nature of these public policy rewards in ways that differentiate between interest groups and other voluntary membership groups. It also helps clarify the form that many selective benefits take within interest groups. For interest groups, many, and for some most, of their selective benefits are aptly political. A conference may be in Colorado yet, even amidst the scenic wilderness of Aspen, participants are learning a political purpose and a set of strategies. After all, mobilization can't be accomplished without rhetoric and even propaganda. Politics also matters in offering other selective benefits. Joiners who get the greatest attention, and often become group leaders, gain personal benefits from expressing themselves on policy issues and political failure, not a favored sonnet or a great scene from *Sleepless in Seattle*.[30] When the National League of Cities provides members tangible and low-cost research assistance on daily management problems, these services often help member communities with pressing matters of local politics: passing municipal bond issues, winning community support on fluoridation of water, and acquiring state funding for cleaning the air.

Political groups are expected then to be political. No, make that preordained to be political. What interest groups do, both collectively and selectively, serves political ends. Sometimes this happens as the group is formed. Sometimes it evolves later. And often new issues are addressed because the personal lives of the joiners are changing. Interest groups do act differently than the local Rotary, where members are reluctant to build a club's political agenda for fear of offending people or threatening the solidarity of the group. For example, it would be silly to think that a neighborhood gathering of the group attacking a city street-widening project would be mostly about swapping recipes for cookies or meatloaf. Swaps may go on, but only as a sidelight to organizing and building public affairs commitment or to lobbying. Interest groups do what used to be done in the Democratic Party clubs of central cities: capture and hold political interest among partisans.[31] People from blue-collar neighborhoods may have gone to the clubs to drink inexpensive beer. While there, however, no one forgot either that they were party members or just what that responsibly entailed at the time. Entrepreneurs and other staff were there to remind attendees why the club, and the party itself, existed. Interest groups do that, too.

The Fit between Joiners and Their Groups

Given all of the above, how do interest groups, with their volunteer members, fit the American public? Also, how well do they fit?

Unlike what might be expected from that widespread and general social condemnation of special interest groups, the fit between interest groups and the public is a nice one. Through its political institutions, the United States is decentralized into several levels and several branches where open, democratic, grassroots-based, participatory, and republican forms of government allow no absolute authorities to hold the keys to ruling. Things may be wildly complex. Public policy may be—and certainly is—hard to enact. That may indeed be discouraging to advocates. At least, however, there's nothing about the American political process that prevents nearly any group, even an occasionally odd one, from finding someone somewhere who will champion its views. Any value in America can become a political issue and usually does, just not always a likely one to win.

— In fact, as more and more public policies have added to the size and scope of U.S. government, it's quite unlikely that any value won't become political.[32] Regulating the railroads and airlines, abortion, direct financial supports for disabled workers, clean water, and hundreds of other topics get immersed in politics and, at some level, bring forward controversy and conflict. Therefore, while the complexity of politics may be discouraging, the number of issues considered willingly by some or another policymaker is extraordinarily encouraging to interest groups. So, out of discouragement with the policy process, comes an incentive to form organized interests. As a consequence, they proliferate in number. As Jeffrey Berry said, the United States has become an "interest-group society."[33]

Maybe every side of every issue on every policy doesn't have an interest group organized around it. Probably there aren't as many interest groups as some think and others might hope. The socially and economically disadvantaged are certainly underrepresented.[34] The important thing is that groups are easily formed, in large part because many Americans have come, or have been led, to believe that political participation is necessary and expected, and produces a social or personal value.

It's not hard for group entrepreneurs to point to reasons for joining and to those useful collective goods that an interest group will pursue, especially in preventing worst-case public policy losses.[35] The fit between the public and their organized interest groups, therefore, is a quite comfortable one. That fit is a lot like the way in which consumers react when they're happy with the quality of their real estate agent or their tax accountant. "Ah yes," the home owner reassures herself, "the old pro will sell that awful sucker soon, and at a good high price." When mobilized around issues that interest them, Americans willingly, and with assurance, buy into politics and into those groups that sell themselves as political and as professional about politics. That's peace of mind. Americans buy it in great numbers and much of the time, when they think it matters. That response seems to be nothing new, of course. It was observed and commented on quite well by Buck as he explained the 1876 emergence of a national interest group out of the fraternally founded, neighborly assistance Granges.[36]

In further developing exchange theory, Salisbury observed that Granges were organized by Oliver Hudson Kelly in a rather quiet period of not terribly bad farm conditions.[37] In such times, Kelly was not originally organizing or selling an interest group, just a voluntary service association. The National Grange and its locals only some years later became interest groups. They did so when business monopolies, especially the railroads, were painted black by the Grange leadership for their exorbitant and destructive fees. Farmers bought that message willingly and wholeheartedly. And they bought subsequent calls for federal regulation, even at the height of an historical period during which the government was quite unlikely to intervene in the economy and with private capital.[38]

After the transition, Granges changed radically, moving from friendly neighborhood units to intense political ones. One vision was added to another. Interest group politics had emerged only when previously affiliated farmer members believed in and followed a new public policy agenda. That, not incidentally, was the high point of Grange dominance in its recruitment and organization of large numbers of U.S. farmers. And it was the height of its political prominence. From there, after this largely unexpected success, the Granges never dropped their political identity, they just downplayed it as enemies were regulated. Accordingly, Grange membership declined dramatically. Still, however, Grange fraternity and an insistence on some low-level lobbying fit what farmer joiners wanted, at least the ones who sustained the organization for decades.

Nonpolitical groups—which interestingly enough are declining in number and in membership—fit something else: personal desires to find entertainment, be of use to the community, play games, travel, or do whatever else the organizations are inherently about. Politics may go on within these groups as, even in bridge clubs, peer interaction translates into increased individual political participation.[39] People who have the chance to talk and listen to others vote more frequently. Politics may also be a friendly and supportive by-product of these groups as policymakers are encouraged, entertained, or given forums for presenting their views. Mostly, however, politics is shunned or kept at a low level to keep from internally disrupting such nearly always tenuously maintained groups and from irritating their members. To actively play politics and try to mobilize members around issues or candidates gets too much in the way of the selective benefits on which groups of this sort organize.

Summary and Highlights

Interest groups are not well-understood by most Americans and probably are comprehended even less by those who observe the United States from beyond its borders. "Special interest groups" are widely portrayed as both frightening and horrible. Yet, despite this commonly held reputation, people still form special interest groups and others willingly join. Moreover, joiners, at least tacitly, are aware that their groups are legitimately political. That's the paradox of interest group politics: disdained in general but nonetheless valued and joined—just as politics is both disliked but engaged in by most of the public. [40]

As seen in this chapter, interest groups have three features: Their joiners affiliate voluntarily; these people share at least one common characteristic; and they seek to advance in politics the collective interest that comes as a result of that characteristic. Interest groups are about politics, articulating issue positions, and influencing public policy.

Associations of this sort find a good home in America, not simply because its complex politics are conducive to interest group advocacy. Mostly, the United States is an interest group society because Americans believe in the need for political involvement. And groups and their activists do it best, or at least most vocally. Interest groups fit quite well the tendency of Americans each to think of themselves as different from others, or to factionalize. Factions protect themselves, get actively involved in politics, create intensity about their issues among those who join, and come to have overtly political identities. Thus, even with ambivalence and disdain about special interests and politics, Americans paradoxically support both. For some things, they're important for almost all of us.

Joiners want group advocacy, value political issues, seek to protect their public policy benefits, expose themselves willingly to organizational entrepreneurs who advertise and sell groups, and rely heavily on these activists to help them win at politics. In short, interest groups—individually if not as a whole—fit well what the public feels it needs. For that reason alone, it's hard to imagine American politics without interest groups.

Interest groups are not the only interests active in politics— far from it. As seen above, other voluntary membership associations, such as the Rotary, have interests and produce their own subtle political influences. But these groups are quite different from interest groups, even as they share with them such obvious similarities as their concern with selectively received member benefits. Interest groups, though, are *about* politics while other groups might occasionally touch on the peripheries of politics. Interest groups exist to influence public policy. For their own reasons, other groups tend to publicly shun politics, usually exercising the most covert influence. Interest groups are about noise in a political sense. Other groups may whisper their political values, at least unless they, too, make the transition to organized and active interests.

Later chapters will consider the political importance and involvement of interest groups. Subtle influence will be left to psychologists. The following chapters also will examine other organized interests that are active in various ways in American politics. These do much of what interest groups do. What these other interests are, and how they, too, fit is the subject of Chapter Two.

2

Other Interests

It once was fashionable to write about interest groups as sources of "pressure." But there are many more interests around than just groups. That larger number intensifies the pressure of governing an interest group society. There are two ways to look at the pressure that all these organized interests produce. One way seems benign. Perhaps scholars such as Belle Zeller were equating interest groups with a water wellhead in a country park.[1] If you build up the pressure by priming the pump, things start to flow. Not a bad analogy, since government in the United States, on its own, so often reminds observers of being mostly unproductive. Like a well that won't give water, pressure needs to be applied to make it work.

Probably, though, early students of interest politics were thinking of something quite different, far less positive. Being rather idealistic and thoroughly democratic in values, their thoughts were more likely of pressure from outsiders disrupting the much revered slow and deliberative pace of governance.[2] Interests make government do, in terms of substance, what its officials otherwise wouldn't. That's the assumption. Because policymakers face pressure, with its resulting personal stress, government produces bad decisions.

Rather than seeing the political benefits of pressure as yielding a much needed drink of water, influence (or pressure) was portrayed as a negative and so other analogies are more apt: Pressure on government is like the pressure that produces a bad stomachache. Until one burps, built-up acidity hurts the tummy, confuses the mind, and leads to lousy judgment. That, anyway, seems to be what the old pressure group scholars were suggesting. Interests are a pain, not a satisfying drink of cold well water, for government.

Regardless of whether the result is good or bad, no one would deny that American government is subject to plenty of pressure. So much of it exists that there can be, in principle, reasons to worry. Much and probably most of that lobbying pressure doesn't come from interest groups as they were described in Chapter One. Nor does it come from those other, more subtly and less politically involved groups. A great bulk of political pressure comes, as Salisbury explained, from institutional sources.[3] These, too, are special interests, with highly specialized policy wants. Institutions are neither voluntary associations nor do they aggregate, especially in any broad way, a common characteristic that defines an interest. The organizing characteristic is singularly held by one entity such as General Motors, the United Methodist Church, or the Boy Scouts of America. At other times, a singularly focused institution such as the Ford Foundation funds and maintains another pressure organization, the National Rural Housing Coalition, for instance. All maintain a public policy interest, though, often an intense one.

In a technical sense, institutions are the rules by which people are led. They also include, or at least reflect, the interests of the organizations that keep and give life to those rules.[4] Institutions, from that perspective, are not composites of joiners who collectively and democratically set their own organizational direction. Institutions structure conformity in hierarchical ways. They constrain personal actions.[5] Therefore, a General Motors executive doesn't lobby for whatever she sees fit for the corporation. There's also not much room for fitting the private wants of a broader public, at least not very often. The public doesn't have a General Motors lobby. Groups, by contrast, practice internally some form of voluntary assembly, leaving room for group representatives to simply go rambling, one issue at a time, through the halls, or lobbies, of government. Constraints within groups are always internally judgmental and debatable, never absolute. Also, groups somewhat easily alter their interests. Institutions are clearly the more stable forms of representation. That's quite a contrast.

This chapter focuses on an analysis and description of, for one thing, institutions that pressure government. But there's more to these proliferating "other interests" in American politics than just institutions.[6] There also exist subsets of interests that break away from organized groups and, sometimes, from larger institutions. These are more personality and, often, regionally based. Corn farmers in a region with high productivity and with favorable soil and weather may develop their own public policy agendas.[7] Their interests are only marginally served by a national organization that attempts to set a balanced public policy for corn growers throughout the United States. As a result, Congress finds the National Corn Growers Association pressuring for one public policy solution while numerous individual, and often influential, corn farmers want another. Politics takes on fascinating turns when such things happen, confusing policymakers as to what really is in whose interest.

Institutions are affected a bit by organizational breakdowns of this sort. General Motors (GM) may develop a corporate message on auto safety standards that all executives and labor leaders collectively subscribe to in order to maximize sales, profits, and job security. Meanwhile, an important component of GM, such as large auto retailers in the western states, may form a dissident voice. The dealers go directly to their own states' congressional representatives, adding to the complexity of pressure and undercutting support for the institutional wants of the auto manufacturer. Despite hierarchical authority and contractual relationships, GM can do little or nothing to stop them. Unlike the way it would treat the aforementioned executive acting independently of the firm, GM's not going to fire its dealers. Who'd sell stuff?

These subsets of groups and institutions, because they do engage in such behavior, also are an important part of this chapter. Mostly they seem to matter as a result of the politics of local constituency, where regional and local American interests contrast with nationally applied public policies. Political consultants, congressional enterprises, and subsets of constituents themselves each work to sort out the required balance between the local and the national. The dilemmas that policymakers face in responding to pressure from institutions and personality interests bring up the contrast between well pressure and a great drink of water, and that of the painful stomachache. Some of these organizations, by the very nature of their self-identified policy interest and how they organize to pursue it, bring new and refreshing issues to government. These are things that otherwise wouldn't be considered. They serve as a positive, at least in a democratic sense.

Other institutions and personality-based interests do, however, speed up the policy process so rapidly that balanced and useful public policies are not seriously considered, debated, and made law.[8] Public policy decisions made in this way just rubber stamp what these interests want. The nature of their wants tend to be so narrowly self-serving and of no immediate interest to others that the policies favored by or favorable to a national following have no chance. The same also happens to some interests whose issues appear to be at first glance too far out of the political mainstream. These wants just get dumped. Both, of course, matter in quite a negative way.[9]

The following pages are more than a description of these numerous other interests and why they lobby. This chapter also includes an analysis of which types of interest demands, or pressures, are likely to produce responses from an otherwise inert government. And it covers the question of who seems most likely to speed up deliberations so rapidly that nationally aggregated interests can't be determined or, of course, ever met. The chapter also wrestles with notions of how well these interests fit the public in a normative sense.

Business Institutions

Businesses exist to make transactions or trade in some kind of a market.[10] The trades are what these firms value, the trades and the profits guaranteed by trades. Whether the market is free—or unconstrained by government—or regulated—to conform to law—takes on very secondary importance. Making money, both long- and short-term, comes first. Any idealization of the market takes a back seat unless that view merges enough with daily reality to secure profits.

One example will suffice. The U.S. Department of Agriculture, authorized by Congress, operated the popular Export Enhancement Program (EEP). EEP subsidized, among others, business firms that wished to expand their markets to new areas overseas. Gallo Winery received nearly $5 million per year in the early 1990s under that program. Other beneficiaries included Con-Agra and its Butterball turkeys, Jim Beam and its whiskeys, and Pillsbury's baking products. Even McDonalds, with its $700 million advertising budget, got into the program. Its Chicken McNuggets gained over $400,000 per year, a relatively small amount but still worth having.

For reasons such as those of EEP, corporate officials have moved more over the past few decades to engage their firms actively in their own public affairs work.[11] Executives may not like politics or really prefer not to be involved. They do it though, and the reason for their increasing participation is simple. Government moved away from its nineteenth-century laissez-faire approach of avoiding regulation of private capital, in large part through the pressure of anti-business interest groups such as the Granges. Also, as will be seen later, that move was because of pressure from western development and settlement interests. An activist and regulatory government thus emerged, found social favor, interfered more and more with the market, and created numerous and plentiful public programs that increasingly both hindered and rewarded businesses. To protect themselves, as the *National Journal* keeps reminding us, nearly every large corporation—including many foreign ones that have become U.S. corporations under law—now maintains its own independent public affairs office.[12] Rarely, except for some comfortable years under the Reagan administration in the 1980s, do they come and go. With accountants and business analysts aplenty, and with a great deal of emphasis on studying finances, corporate officials have even more convincing evidence about the value of lobbying than do most group joiners. They often know an exact payoff.

As scholars have long noted, corporations do far more than just fight government regulation, which often, in the face of media and public attention, is a futile act. Businesses have learned reluctantly for years to accept regulation and work to make its inevitable presence as favorable to corporate ledgers as possible. (They should, since the United States regulates more than any other nation.[13]) Playing the political game, if done well, is an advantage.

None of this is new, just accelerated. In 1929 and 1930, for example, industries literally flooded the halls and offices of Congress with their representatives, all of whom were trying to enact protective trade tariffs, the effect of which would be to increasingly, not decreasingly, regulate the economy. According to careful accounts, these pressure peddlers acted as if they owned Congress.[14] They ran roughshod over legislators who argued for an ideological defense of the market and for limited public intervention in the economy. What instead was important to firms was their own business problems, greater public policy protection against foreign imports, and equitable tariffs from one U.S. business to another.[15] Each business wanted as many goodies as possible and certainly as many as any of the others received.

They still want that, and sometimes, for uniquely firm-specific reasons, they want more. And sometimes they want more than merely favorable regulations. Businesses love government subsidies. Chrysler Corporation, for instance, wasn't arguing for federal loan guarantees for any business other than itself in 1979 and 1980 when its officials sought public policy help in order to keep the auto manufacturer open and operating.[16] Nor did large ethanol fuel producers, mostly Archers-Daniels-Midland (ADM), want the same federal sales rates levied against them as against competing petroleum producers. To lower ethanol costs to consumers, and therefore gain market advantage, ADM argued for tax rate relief rather than for equity from one industry to another.

To deal with larger government and its activist expectations, corporations do more than just hire a single lobbyist to represent them. When Michigan, for example, required increased reporting of all officials who met with state policymakers, Chrysler registered forty-three representatives for 1988. E.F. Hutton, a financial investment firm, registered twenty.[17]

Likewise, the public affairs tasks that firms see for these representatives are now far greater than E. E. Schattschneider found for those lobbyists merely prowling and pouncing in legislative halls during the tariff battle of the pre-Depression era. Firms of the late 1990s are amazingly far-sighted. They practice issue management, where the broad array of emerging issues and policy problems are identified and, for each, preemptive company responses are planned. To win public support, they also advertise the political views of the corporation through media-based public relations, and they engage in community service work to make the firms better appear as valued assets in their home bases. Of course, for immediate purposes, lobbyists still present proposals of the corporation to all policymakers who seem likely to listen.[18] To do all this, individual corporations hire numerous public affairs staff, not just a few. In the early 1980s, just over one-third of all those who called themselves Washington interest representatives were employed by these firms.[19] Businesses, as policy institutions, are indeed of consequence.

Why, however, don't similar businesses with similar products not just lobby together, avoiding the high costs of their own staffs and offices? After all, on the tariff conflicts of the '20s and '30s, successful lobbying was found to require substantial consensus anyway among firms in a single industry, perhaps 80 percent of them or more.[20] So cooperation did, and still does, help. Moreover, as seen in Chapter One, there are available a huge number of voluntary trade associations for single types of manufacturers, businesses, professionals, and products. Everybody seems to organize around common characteristics. When Washington representatives were counted in 1981, nearly 30 percent of those registering were employed by business trade associations, or interest groups.[21] Comparative numbers for recent years, for both individual businesses and for business trade associations, are little changed.[22]

The answer to the question of why firms don't just lobby together is, of course, a simple and rather obvious one. It also, to add complexity, requires two responses. First, firms *do* routinely join business trade associations and substantial efforts are made to identify how their own singular interests fit into a public policy consensus.[23] In addition, firms usually prefer to avoid attaching their own corporate names to highly contentious issue conflicts. To do so risks offending their consumers and the public as well as important business partners. Sales may suffer, and with them profits. For example, large, chain grocery companies like Kroger formerly let the Food Marketing Institute routinely register their unhappiness with price-increasing farm support programs, such as dairy marketing orders. By hiding in this way, Kroger avoided getting into media trouble in dairy country, with its several farming centers around the nation.

So interest group membership by corporations is indeed extensive. And it often overlaps among several trade associations. A firm like Monsanto Corporation, because of its many products, joins not one but several business trade associations. These bring together—as different interest groups—pharmaceutical producers, chemical manufacturers, farm and yard chemical producers, biotechnology research centers, patent rights advocates, plastics manufacturers, industrial petroleum users, fishing line manufacturers, and assorted other specialty businesses. All count Monsanto as an important member.

Yet what takes place within trade associations, even the wide range of them, seldom covers the gamut of what truly interests each firm in public policy. As Graham Wilson observed, business politics isn't a bed of roses.[24] That second response is really why firms maintain their own independent public affairs units. Most commonly, for most pending issues, corporations can't agree with one another on preferred policy content.[25] General Motors and Ford kept resisting stringent federal gas mileage mandates throughout the 1970s and 1980s. But not every manufacturer agreed.

With lots more small cars in its product line, Chrysler, for years, did not resist. Actually, Chrysler lent tacit support to the U.S. Environmental Protection Agency and its proposed fuel economy regulations. Support the government, screw the competition. Situations like this, which are frequent, preclude a lot of cooperative trade association lobbying. Consensus among competitors is hard, often impossible. On those divisive issues, common characteristics on a single dimension—such as being an auto manufacturer—don't produce a shared interest. A much more narrow criterion, like what size cars they manufacture, structures the various firms' policy interests. Trade associations then sit out a great many governmental issue contests, much like an injured sports team member whiling away time on the bench. Firms don't wish to be without representation, and therefore, they go on alone or with but a few allies.

Two other reasons for corporate institutions having their own lobbying offices and issue-management staffs are important as well. Government often tends to act when a crisis, or at least a sudden social or economic problem, newly appears. Getting a trade association to respond takes time, usually too much of it. Members are hard to bring together and mobilize; consensus is harder to organize among numerous joiners; and discussions over what to do and how to do it are demanding. Corporate staffs, in contrast, can be far more easily activated by those in authority within the firm. With their eyes cast to corporate gains and losses, executives like to have a ready response, sort of like their own SWAT team.

A less important, but certainly not inconsequential, reason for corporate lobbying has to do with promoting the firms' own visibility and their carefully contrived images. If a corporation lets its trade associations do all its lobbying, and make all of its contacts with policymakers, that firm comes to lack its own recognizability as well as any reputation for individual political importance.[26] Such firms never gain support as political players, forces that actually matter in public policy negotiations. Then, when problems do come up, these businesses get ignored, or at least they have a difficult time gaining access to government. It's hard for such corporations to win. Maybe, for instance, they don't get a share of EEP.

The net result is that business in America represents itself actively in public policy through both its interest groups and its own institutional structures. No wonder that Kay Schlozman chose to say that the extensive universe of U.S. political interests sings its woes with a distinct accent, one made up of praise of sales and profits.[27] Business lobbyists, as their numbers show, are ubiquitous. Hiring them for business trade associations lets individual corporations avoid many of the social stigmas of political involvement and conflict. Those associations, as a consequence, fit nicely some important corporate needs.

Corporate public affairs offices, however, fit very well those business needs that their trade associations can't address, especially quick responses or in times of conflict. That's why U.S. businesses rather paradoxically buy lots of seemingly redundant political representation. In reality, those firms are only covering all the potential policy bases, both long- and short-term.

Having both institutional representation—going it alone—and numerous interest groups—for joining—lets businesses fit nearly every contingency within the policy-making process. Firms can work together when the interests of an entire industrial sector are met by collective public policy influence. They can also enforce some degree of internal solidarity on important issues. This lets them infinitely tinker on their own with small pieces of existing or proposed public policies in order to gain something of discrete interest to their own individual corporations. And those housekeeping issues are what businesses lobby on mostly, just minor items to help profitability. That goes on, for instance, when an oil company works for new accounting standards to speed up depreciation of computers and so save on taxes. In the interest advocacy world, business has the best situation of all, a perfect if not always a winning fit.[28] That fit is costly, but with profits in mind, businesses can't help but buy it.[29]

Social Institutions

Business firms are by no means the only institutions in American society. Nor are they the only ones that, apart from interest groups, ardently chase their own political interests. Religious denominations; individual colleges and especially universities; and nonprofit organizations that do research, charity, and philanthropy work are all frequent institutional players. Some would count labor unions and farm and rural cooperatives as social institutions, but they really aren't. Both organize voluntary members, those with common characteristics who support public policy intervention.

The three non-interest group types cover most of the politically cognizant social institutions, but if others exist they probably get involved. One such institutional lobby explains why. Jonathan Rauch actually located a Washington lobbying office for the Baha'i church, a religion that forbids its members from involvement in politics.[30] Lots of ironies, of course, exist in the public policy process. Rauch's discovery may have been the biggest of those.

There can hardly be a track record, or even an accurate account, of all who represent social institutions. They either don't like to be or legally can't be called lobbyists, and so they don't register as Washington representatives. This then is very much a hidden subset of the organized interest universe, one that often quietly does its advocacy.[31] Or, as a frustrated congressional member once explained, a subset making claims that it's not advocacy that these institutions do at all.[32] That perplexed legislator remarked that he'd seen four lobbyists that morning, three of whom made it clear that they were not peddling pressure. One was from the U.S. Catholic Conference, a second from Iowa State University, and another was the Director of the International Red Cross. All wanted something. "That was why I really appreciated the fourth guy, from Sunkist Growers. He threatened me, called me names, banged his fists, and demanded protection for Florida oranges on the trade agreement. His lobbying was honest and direct. I wasn't offended. I knew where he stood very precisely, just as I really did with the innuendo from the other three smooth-talking social workers."

Playing politics can hardly be avoided by most of these social institutions, even if they don't remind anyone of General Motors, McDonalds, or Jim Beam. Yet, as the Salvation Army practically broadcast to all political observers when it hired a new executive director, that unavoidable world mandates respect. The new executive wasn't a social activist, minister, business leader, or tribal shaman. Fred Grandy had been a member of Congress and almost, but for a few votes, a state governor.

Politics matters to these institutions for all the same kinds of reasons that it has importance for business firms. In fact, politics matters to these interests because a decided component of a church, foundation, or university is clearly doing institutional business.[33] Alan Hertzke explained this well. Church denominations "own property, have employees, enjoy tax exemptions, and operate an array of schools, colleges, hospitals, nursing homes, large charitable groups, and even life insurance companies. Some churches receive government grants."[34] Much the same can be said of foundations and universities. So—like Con-Agra going after EEP funds to promote a self-basting turkey—social institutions lobby hard and often, though perhaps by promoting a different image than a Boeing or an AT&T.[35]

Like business firms, social institutions such as churches are advantaged by professional staffs that do analysis and make persuasive cases, as well as by strategic suggestions about going to government.[36] The best examples are prestigious research universities. Since 1970, when the University of Houston and the University of Oklahoma both set up Washington offices, a large number of universities have done the same thing. Over the past twenty-five years, schools such as Harvard, Michigan, Iowa, and Chicago have mastered governmental grantsmanships of a once unheard of sort. Since public money keeps many quality programs and projects alive, a heady premium exists for finding more and more of it. But such "soft money" is inherently unstable and its availability is problematic if only refereed and competitive grants are targeted. Too much competition exists. To reduce that riskiness, universities have pressured increasingly for noncompetitive grants, ones legislatively earmarked for a specific program at a single institution.[37]

Texas A&M University worked especially hard to get millions in scholarship support in the 1996–97 federal budget for its recently funded George Bush School of Public Affairs. Michigan State University went to the state in similar fashion to obtain a new livestock industry development center.

The less prestigious institutions, though, are not without their business and finance reasons for going directly to the government. With extensive and far-reaching off-campus educational programs, Central Michigan University (CMU) lobbied numerous state governments to secure licensing rights away from its home state. On another matter, again for off-campus sites, CMU lobbied both the Congress and departmental agencies when threats were being made to reduce federal educational reimbursements to employees who took university courses. This was CMU's biggest source of revenue for its profit-generating policy of carrying education to military bases, central cities, and other places where federal employees work.

Business matters of major importance for foundations also are tied to grants, especially to the grants they give.[38] Legal restrictions on philanthropic institutions that grant financial support for advocacy work are an example of a big concern. So, too, are Internal Revenue Service (IRS) interpretations, ownership of investment properties, and a myriad of other problems. The thing that charities and foundations fear most on these issues, and work hard to avoid, is loss of even a part of their tax-exempt status.[39] With so many ancillary businesses of their own, churches share the same fear. Each wants shelter from taxes far more than just the old wooden building in the meadow where Sunday services are held.

Comparatively little of the lobbying by social institutions goes into ideological and moral causes, or for that matter issues of philosophy. At least for most of them. The public policy think tanks, such as Brookings and the American Enterprise Institute, are obvious exceptions. They issue advocacy reports routinely. On special matters, some social institutions lobby, too: The Catholic Church is firmly anti-abortion, or at least its institutional representatives hold that stance. Detroit's black churches are famous for their electoral roles, almost always on behalf of Democrats. The National Center for Food and Agricultural Policy bitterly attack farm commodity programs. Another think tank, the Cato Institute, is even more vitriolic in arguing for reduced federal spending and against governmental waste. Again, though, that's why Cato as a think tank exists.

But for the most part, rather than pick up directly on most social and economic issues, these institutions, at least in spirit, leave such efforts to others. Those whom they nominally control do it. As do business firms, they affiliate with interest groups that lobby regularly on policy causes.[40] Many organized religions join the National Council of Churches. A second means of promoting issues is by organizing affiliate groups who, on behalf of parts of the institution, create policy pressure.[41] Universities are represented by a dizzying array of over three hundred higher education associations, most of which do far more service than lobbying. Catholic Charities USA and the National Jewish Community Relations Advisory Council are two examples of church associations. A third way is found when institutional leaders, often informally as part of their duties, support and become active in interest groups having a moral or philosophical purpose.[42] The Christian Coalition and its antagonist group, the liberal Interfaith Alliance, gain much of their influence this way. Bread for the World, an exponent of international food assistance, couldn't maintain itself without church support. It has few direct members so it asks for its own patronage handouts.[43]

Social institutions also follow a fourth strategy, though in a much more subtle fashion. They look for employees who have a strong background in particular social issues. The interests of the poor, rural America, and international assistance are frequent examples. After assuming leadership duties, those leaders, as experts, make regular conference and media appearances extolling their points of view.[44] Technically, their institutions aren't the ones doing the advocacy. This strategy works especially well for the policy-focused think tanks. Without being able to claim their independence from their scholars' work, these foundations would surely be in IRS trouble for their persistent advocacy of—depending on their persuasion—liberal, conservative, middle-of-the-road, free-market, or interventionist governmental practices. They irritate so many policymakers by their consistently ideological views that each of them needs such a tax shield, as well as executives who routinely flash it.[45] Universities, where this is less of a problem, simplify things and hire consultant lobbyists as well. Constance Cook, in a survey of universities, found that over half employed this strategy of buying and showing off for-hire expertise.[46]

Social institutions, thus, exercise quite a creative fit within the policy-making process. While working hard on public policy agendas, most of their recurring and routine lobbying aims at maintaining, on their own, each organization. As one executive said, "We're consumed by housekeeping work, protecting our legal status. Nobody does it for us. Our circumstances vary too much from one organization to the next."

This involvement, nonetheless, is amazingly productive. A huge array of social institutions exist over time in well-established and stable form. For most of them, this possibility only exists because they ardently promote their business needs. They lobby, that is, for exemptions from the legal restrictions that restrain and are costly for business institutions. Successes in these endeavors, while often complained about as excessively costly to institutional budgets, allow such organizations a great deal of flexibility. When it becomes useful, all of them can even find ways to advocate, one way or another, on ideological issues central to each institution's basic principles. So, while most of their lobbying seems mundane and tiresome even to institutional activists, they still manage fairly well to fit the broader expectations and wants of those who fund and manage each church, foundation, or university. That's why the Baha'i church lobbies. Yes, the fit is idiosyncratic, but it's an almost always satisfying match anyway: "I just can't say what I want every time I want. But who can?"

Governmental Institutions

Government has its institutions, its entire structure as a matter of fact. Those who represent that structure govern, but they also lobby as hard and as often as do those employed by business or social institutions. At least some of them do. Foreign governments lobby both the U.S. federal government and the states. With its multiple branches and levels of federalism, American government does the same. The organizing structure is far too cumbersome for all public-sector parts to operate in either a synchronized or even a formal fashion. The parts can't just get along. Disagreements abound, most of which reflect vastly different and competing institutional agendas.

Local governments want one thing, the states another. Of course, neither all local nor state governments want the same things. Moreover, employees of government are divided by the types of policies that each designs and implements. And different administrative jobs bring different interests. City managers usually have different issues than, say, city treasurers or building inspectors. It's not unusual to find those working for a state department of transportation to be lobbying at cross purposes with representatives of that same state's department of commerce, or for a state's transportation officials to be working against those from the U.S. Department of Transportation.

Is lobbying, or even issue advocacy for that matter, the correct way to describe these disagreements? Some would argue that these are only internally unresolved management problems, things to sort out over coffee in the office sometime before government acts. It's planning. It's also nonsense to suggest that. Anyone who's seen the process would disagree with that view. The various contestants often send scores of attorneys and other professionals for representation, all with well-developed arguments and strategies. Many come from organized public affairs offices within government. Contacts are made; promises become rhetoric; and information flows in abundance. One congresswoman said, "Those guys are from my own government?" State governments are so certain that all this is the same old lobbying as that done by interest groups and industries that they frequently require all public-sector petitioners to legally register as lobbyists.[47] Even those from their own state agencies sign up.

The routinely active institutional representatives from the American public sector tend overwhelmingly to work for individual cities, states, federal agencies, state agencies, and the courts. Others, such as administrators of the Library of Congress, are players, undoubtedly more unique ones but still involved in the complex business of their own interests. The most important thing to understand, however, is not that advocacy is their goal. That's understood. Their significance, and that of agents of foreign countries, is in the way these institutional representatives clutter the political landscape, add to the chorus of competing and unharmonious lobbying voices, and simply add to the impression in both

Washington and the state capitals that literally everyone is just out for themselves. Such are the implications of the "advocacy explosion," more pressure from what many see as unexpected players.[48]

None of this is anything new. Advocacy has just grown. "Good government" groups became organized in the early twentieth century to promote reform. All pointed to the need to improve management practices and depended on anti-machine-politics attitudes of some public officials for their sustenance.[49] Out of the good-government social networks, most notably the Louis Brownlow research groups, emerged professional associations for dozens of different types of officials and units of government, from mayors and governors to city clerks.[50] By the 1930s, directors of some of these groups were going to Washington on behalf of city needs in a Depression era. At least one openly acknowledged being a "lobbyist, politician," not just a fellow public servant.[51] Talk about coming out of the closet among one's peers.

Usually, like business and social institutions, these groups advocated on behalf of issue positions on which their members could agree.[52] In the lean years of the 1930s, not surprisingly, consensus emerged over federal programs supporting government services. They wanted them. Later, as federal intervention and financial support for local services grew, state and local officials collectively demanded more. They were still financially needy. Revenue sharing, which allocated nationally raised tax dollars directly to state and local governments, passed only when the public-sector lobby organized as a united front.[53] For years, disagreements about who would get the most and how it would come had held up the policy-making process. Each wanted the biggest share. These same groups, still later, became active proponents of increased governmental productivity and efficiency in service provision.[54] If they couldn't get more federal monies, maybe they could improve the use of what they had—with, of course, federal incentives to do so. Historically then, when the generalities of funding have been at stake, governmental institutions eventually have resolved their differences and lobbied together quite nicely as interest groups.

The problem for such institutions, though, is that the need for lobbying never ends with the generalities of enabling or appropriations legislation. At least that's how government advocates soon saw things. When that realization occurred, individual units of government began to set up their own Washington offices. Or at least they began coming regularly to town. Most large cities, such as Detroit, are now there, as are the states. The idea of spatial location became topsy-turvy. Right down the street from the Baha'i church lies Michigan, officed very close to New York and Arizona on the District of Columbia's lobbyist corridor.

Cities and states have obvious reasons for their individual institutional Washington presence. All are the recipients of earmarked federal revenues and grants. All are affected in different ways by federal regulations, particularly those governing the environment and business practices. At some other northern cities' expense, Detroit wants to be located on the international NAFTA superhighway. Constituent units, such as a state conservation department or a private industry such as Chrysler Corporation, often coordinate their lobbying with both city and state officials. That is, they lobby together. So those offices are busy places.[55]

Such offices, however, are far from the only places where representatives of government institutions hang out and transact lobbying business. On a routine and repetitive basis, more contacts involve state and federal agencies meeting on their own with congressional and other administrative personnel, usually on Capitol Hill and in departmental offices. Flying to Washington, often just overnight, happens repeatedly. Taking the Metro subway is a daily occurrence for those located closer. Within the state capitals, the same patterns of interaction dominate public-sector lobbying.

Why? The answer is quite clear. All federal and state agencies are assigned the tasks of operating their own government programs and managing their own, always tight, budgets. So each necessarily develops its own wants and funding requests. To get what's wanted, especially in an era of restrained government spending, each agency—in an executive's words—"has to outcompete and outfox the other guys." Very little of this plotting and probing can be coordinated by individual city and state lobbying offices. After all, ranking officials, such as the governor who runs that office, still haven't made up their minds about which plans to embrace. These officials are among the lobbying targets, not the coordinators of things.

Both state and federal courts are among the routine organized interest players for much the same reasons. With crime and the justice system both topics of intense political debates, court systems are buffeted by proposals for policy change. Case loads and expenses grow. Budgets, staffing, dockets, reorganization, sentencing guidelines, judicial standards, and numerous other concerns are raised by chief executives and legislators. To avoid having their businesses disrupted by arbitrary action, court officials follow the path pioneered by other institutional representatives: They lobby intensely. A judge remarked, "The bastards [legislators] won't tell us what's going on, or ask our opinions. Our only option is to campaign hard against them." To get a new building, more space, and better protection of documents, Library of Congress officials muster a similar campaign, as do Smithsonian representatives, the potentates of federal museums—and those from nearly every other federal and state institution, from prisons to highways.

For many private-sector lobbyists, the net impact of advocacy by this plethora of American governmental institutions is one of complete chaos. Many felt they once understood the U.S. Constitution. Said one corporate executive: "These people make the always unpredictable marketplace of business look tidy and well-directed." Public officials themselves tend to agree. The constitutional complexities of a decentralized and federally divided American government are nothing compared to what goes on informally as hundreds of cities, states, agencies, and court systems lobby in their own interests.

Things are no different when representatives of foreign governments come to call. Those who expect an orderly U.S. constitutional process probably also make the mistake of thinking that international relations all take place in such organized entities as the United Nations (UN) or perhaps the Organization of American States (OAS). Quite emphatically, governments don't stop—or even start—there. Foreign governments are among the largest employers of consultant lobbyists. If anyone admires the chaos of domestic governmental lobbying, they can't help but really love what goes on when foreign officials cross U.S. borders to pursue favorable treatment.

Salisbury found that just over 12 percent of Washington representatives worked for foreign interests.[56] Most of these, however, represented business rather than governmental institutions. Of course, in many cases, such as Japan, that distinction is unclear. Nonetheless, a lot of them work only for governments. Probably more than the numbers indicate are involved, since much lobbying goes on through diplomatic staff and other foreign visitors. Don't look for these people to find their way into *Washington Representatives* or any other registry of lobbyists.

The reasons for foreign government presence are even more varied than for the U.S. government's. Nigeria, for the most part, just wants to improve its image as an investment region, particularly by dispelling beliefs about its awful human rights record. For most countries, the bottom line is really the bottom line: dollars. They're present to do their own business: lobbying for foreign aid, U.S. investments, American military assistance, trade arrangements, favored nation status, and investment opportunities in the United States. A host of other things can be negotiated as well. [57] All of these matters either fall under treaties or are dealt by the U.S. Department of State.

Congress is an especially active participant in granting foreign favors. When several congressional members wish to, Congress also acts punitively. [58] That's what Nigeria fears most. Institutional lobbying hardly stops, though, on Capitol Hill. Federal departments, state agencies, governors, White House liaisons, and even local governments where foreign firms want to locate find themselves lobbied by government representatives. Designating sister cities, and thus winning local public supporters from the United States, gets a big play. And the media gets lobbied since few foreign interests are well-served when the U.S. press portrays a country's public officials back home as crooks or butchers. Better to have them appear as just misunderstood.

Foreign governments lobby very much like U.S. institutions and interest groups. [59] While most of their wants are minor, some strategies may be complex. Indeed there have been charges that foreign representatives act in a more manipulative fashion than could U.S. representatives. [60] They claim they misunderstood the culture, or the laws, or were themselves only misunderstood. Problems of U.S. strategic defense needs and foreign alliances obviously allow for some excess privileges to be granted foreign governments. That, however, seems to be a small matter. The important thing is that foreign governments find the vast and decentralized American government a perfect place to pursue small favors. As one diplomat said, "I love to shop on (Capitol) Hill." Having lobbyists in the United States provides a great fit for securing special favors. The tediousness of State Department diplomacy can be avoided. Moreover, for larger matters where greater political consensus is required, foreign interests have their own quasi-interest groups. The World Trade Organization, the UN, and OAS—as policy organizations that voluntarily organize different types of governments—have all mounted widespread opposition to U.S. issues. Lobbying, posturing on issues: those are the reasons.

The nice fit between lobbying by foreign governmental institutions and the needs of those countries should hardly be alarming. They simply find opportunities for effective representation. Smaller issues often gain attention when they otherwise might well be ignored in the far more formal world of international affairs. Many of these issues emerge because international groups won't or can't support a country's individual requests. These interests, their lobbyists find, still fit into the American public policy process just as do a wide variety of domestic government institutions. Special treatment is what all want, and within this context, public-sector representatives can at least reasonably work well to get it.

Personality-Based Interests

To this point, the discussion of other American political interests has revolved around institutions, as the organizations and rules that formally and informally influence economic and social behavior. Let's break from that and consider another set of active political interests—those that are far more personality based than they are institutional. General Motors, the Ford Foundation, the United Methodist Church, and the National Rifle Association all would surely survive if their executives died or were purged. Not so with personality interests, which disappear or are radically reorganized when leaders exit.

Personality interests are most visible in the United States through radio and television. Everyone who lives above ground, as opposed to under a rock, knows Rush Limbaugh and his electronic talk show. This very conservative media personality has always, with ardor, extolled a highly specific public policy agenda. Railing against feminists, gays, Democrats, tree huggers, moral decay, ethical breakdown, welfare, high taxes, and government budgets, Limbaugh influenced—or at least solidified—a great many political attitudes.

What was unique about Limbaugh was his nonsecular status, not his entrepreneurial ways. Operating under the guise of religion, other media personalities have done the same for decades.[61] Father Charles E. Coughlin, a Catholic priest popular in the 1920s and 1930s, took a hate-mongering, anti-Semitic, anti-communist, anti–New Deal radio program and parlayed it into a very tight national political following. Carl McIntire, another preacher zealot whose career spanned decades, was known for his much smaller but still fanatical following, as well as his great enthusiasm for launching a nuclear first strike against the Soviet Union.

With the advent of cable and satellite television, ministers such as Jim Baker, Jerry Falwell, and Pat Robertson established personal followings—followed later by their own TV networks, retail businesses, colleges, resorts, and even an amusement park. Without the public impact of these televangelists, the Christian Coalition would never have solidified and grown to political prominence as an organized interest group. The TV evangelists were the initial mobilizers. These personalities encouraged issue-directed political action among a type of citizen previously best known, not for voting, but for staying home and praying for the salvation of politicians.

Limbaugh and electronic evangelists share a near cultlike means of holding together their followers, not unlike David Koresh who, in Texas near Waco, encouraged social isolation, gun ownership, and a willingness to die for the old (new?) cause. Yet there exists very limited room on the airwaves and in society for these strong personalities. Cults are even harder than groups to get off the ground. Jim Hightower found that out when the glib former Texas Agriculture Commissioner floundered on his liberal talk show. So have numerous preachers who aimed at emulating Falwell and Robertson. As a consequence, cultlike personality interests are more an anachronism than a routine part of American politics. But they're still there.

Other personality-based interests, though, are not at all rare. Nor are they generally as fascinating or fun to watch as are those who want to be social gurus. Three sets of interests, all organized around specific people, have come to occupy such a permanent and ongoing place in politics that they need be considered recurring political interests. These are: lobbying and other political consulting firms, which are specialized businesses; congressional enterprises, which are further fragments of Congress as an institution; and local constituents, who as neighborly pieces of the public make near-daily demands through their congressional districts and states.

Lobbying and other political consulting firms most certainly are a more recent phenomenon than popular evangelists. They've also encountered an even better marketplace for their ideas. Washington and, to a lesser extent, the state capitals, have scores of offices set up by those with distinct political skills, from public opinion polling to coalition building.[62] Even specialized policy newsletters and commodity advisors on market conditions get into the fray. The ones that lobby on issues for other associations and institutions tend to be no less specialized, usually dealing with a single or closely related set of issues. Although, if a firm hires numerous personalities and supplements them with plenty of associates, they can handle several areas of public policy.

In all cases, those firms sell their reputations, not some guarantee of winning. Just a likelihood premised on expertise, that's the promise. The most controversial and publicized of lobbying firms in the 1980s was Hill and Knowlton, a large multiclient, multipurpose corporation run by Republican confidant Robert Gray.[63] Under Gray, who was a flamboyant personality and ubiquitous throughout Washington, Hill and Knowlton traded on its routine access to the White House. Another affable character who threw a great party, Tommy Boggs, did the same by emphasizing strong Democratic ties. But his firm, Patton, Boggs, and Blow, also sold to clients its bipartisan contacts and, most importantly, its extensive stable of excellent and experienced policy experts. Executives who contracted with either Gray or Boggs were buying into much the same political mystique that distinguished Coughlin, Limbaugh, and Falwell—rough-and-tumble rounders with an attitude. That, of course, was why both were essential to their very large firms' successes. Hill and Knowlton was never the same after Gray left.

No one, though, ever seriously said that it takes a dynamic personality to build a successful lobbying business. Norman Lent is inherently boring; Marvin Leath, laconic with his slow southern drawl; and Ed Jenkins, a friendly country nerd. All three former congressmen nevertheless are very bright, very skilled in single policy areas where they once worked routinely on the Hill, and operators of thriving smaller lobbying firms. Respectively, they specialize in commerce matters, defense contracting, and corporate tax policy. And they draw high wages. Also, they're far more typical of the average multiclient lobbyist. None are someone to place as the centerpiece, or at least at the center, of a really elegant Georgetown reception. None are addressing major issues of the day. Their firms, though, all would dry up and blow away if anything happened to any of them.

For those kinds of reasons, lobbyists and other political consulting firms need to actively promote themselves. They need to retain reputations for expertise. Since their leaders don't often stand out for their charisma, they must remind likely clients of their skills, contacts, and experience. Particularly important are things these lobbyists have done lately, at least as much as what once went on in their offices in the House or Senate. For that reason alone, multiclient firms follow the fortunes of their most visible partners and aim to be constantly involved policy players.[64] As one lobbyist said, "We'll do anything to be involved. We have to be active when a bill in our area comes up. If we're not, people think we've retired, yesterday's news."

Is that important? Most emphatically, yes. Firms don't merely wait on clients for their orders to march. Rather, consultant personalities are always mucking around in the policy process. For example, a pollster such as Frank Luntz, with his strong ties to the Republican leadership of the House of Representatives, works hard to maintain that linkage. He and his associates hang around policymakers, offer information and even rumors, do favors, and generally advance their firm's political interest. The emphasis, of course, is on self-promotion. They'll even go get coffee.

Former members of Congress should be more skilled than others at promoting themselves as lobbying ventures. They've been doing it for years as legislators, as the chief executives of their own well-staffed offices. And like federal agencies that take on an advocacy role, these legislative offices—or enterprises— want specific public policy results. Distinct from party caucuses, committees, and the leadership, enterprises serve the interests of individual office holders, all of whom have personal political needs. One of the first publicly prominent free agent members was Senator Joseph McCarthy with his own office's 1950s war against communists in government. Doing favors to win help from others can be seen at the congressional office as a small business.[65] That's a very accurate description.

Congressional enterprises are organized with staffs of at least fifteen and up to or over one hundred, extensive budgets for facilitating communication, franking privileges for mailings, and access to a vast array of caucus services that provide research, media, and campaign assistance. Enterprises literally reach out to be of service. Most of the reaching out goes to sets of constituents back home who have unique policy wants.[66] "'Please ask for help', I keep saying to the homefolks," said one staffer. A lot of the reaching also goes to professional lobbying interests that do much to enhance themselves by offering enterprises their advice, keeping congressional members informed as to policy events, and lending campaign assistance.

The growth in importance and independence of congressional enterprises is a result of reforms that democratized both legislative houses in the 1970s.[67] Committees and their chairs, for instance, no longer autocratically control policy agendas. Party caucuses are more open to rank-and-file member pressure. Enterprises plan their own agendas carefully.[68] The net impact is that members of Congress, and the staffs who serve them, have real reasons as well as the resources to join in a large number of policy negotiations. What they're doing often is getting small things into legislation for those homefolks, for lobbyists who've helped them, or for themselves, that they—as iconoclastic individuals— personally like. Or, to be more accurate, enterprises are mostly getting small items of often great consequence to the beneficiaries into parts of far larger bills, such as welfare reform or the budget. This works only for member enterprises that over time develop reputations for active involvement, strategic skills, and a willingness to play the game—just like it does for consultant lobbyists.

These then are truly independent policy interests. Pressure is what they do. As do personality-based consultants, congressional members as lobbyists trade largely off their reputations, their status, and their legislative voting rights. Moreover, enterprises do things for other interests, not just because they face policy pressures. Member enterprises do things quite willingly, just to keep their hands active in the game, to cultivate images of power, and to remain potentially influential in Congress.

Legislative enterprises merge with yet another important personality-based interest that needs to be included in any analysis of who best fits into American politics. As noted above, constituents who are active in congressional districts, and for the individual states with senators, both make policy demands and get policymakers to respond. After all, they *are* the homefolks, the local voters, the familiar neighbors who, if they have community respect and make a lot of noise, can lead to a member's electoral demise, or at least a good scare.

As interests, constituents matter for a very simple reason. Legislation increasingly passes the Congress, and many state legislatures, as packages written by consensus for a larger public, or at least for a type of national or state interest within that public. But all affected interests are rarely served in the same way by a national policy, or for that matter a statewide policy. Conditions within the United States vary too dramatically. African Americans in rural Georgia have different employment problems than those in central cities. The same is true of their respective racial conditions. Wheat farmers in dryland regions dependent on irrigation have considerably higher costs of production and generally greater weather risk factors than do wheat growers nationally. Iowa businesses, in that right-to-work state, can be affected in different ways by changes in federal labor laws than are firms in places such as Michigan, where unions are comparatively strong and employment is closed to nonunion workers. The overwhelming tendency among groups as interests is to at least marginally factionalize over policy proposals. Not only are constituent interests divided internally by region, they also, through congressional enterprises, have mechanisms for adjusting policy plans to local conditions. Constituents, as a result, can win: if local personalities organize them, if they influence their neighbors, if they know how to play politics, and if they've developed ties to their own legislative members and their enterprises. If they know how to lobby, they fit the policy process well.

Such district and state constituent interests often organize around their long-term relationships with those in politics. Not only are the specific personalities from these places familiar faces to legislators, many also provide good and routine advice to members and staff about conditions back home. Some are even regularly contacted by the enterprise for their opinions. In short, constituents are not only voters, a few are also close congressional confidants.[69] What these people want, of course, translates into considerable policy pressure. When the familiar faces change or disappear, however, others back home don't usually just keep unique local interests alive. The overall pattern of state and district politics goes on, but because of changing personality characteristics, resulting pressures normally alter course as well. It's not just the region of the country or the home place that matters, it's also who serves as constituent spokesperson.

What can be seen in personality-based interests is just what a great place America and its public policy processes can be. At least it is for these quite independent and entrepreneurial players who wish to promote and articulate their own interests. Real advocates do get things. When they ardently play, various personalities can create a nice fit between politics and their own narrow interests. The fit between personal wants and the structure of American governance is such that effective pressure results if an individual plans and organizes others appropriately. It doesn't, in those cases, come from the media, or from a corporate firm, or from a group, or from a political party, or even by being a voter. Entrepreneurs have significant positions in the universe of American interests just because they find ways, as personalities, to make things happen. The policy process seems to accommodate nearly anyone who plays hard and represents the political mainstream or the generally conventional. Multiple and varied interests really fit, each in their own ways.

The Problem with Pressure

Without a doubt, this is not the special interest politics described by Schattschneider in his critique of the too limited nature of American public participation.[70] Nor is it a politics that he'd like any better. Interests and their expressions of lobbying proliferate. Capitols are as crowded as Wal-Marts on Sunday afternoon. But this is still government by special interest, not by intelligent articulation of general public needs. No, despite its busy ways, Schattschneider wouldn't like it.

But, because of other deeply held values, what scholars like and dislike about politics is generally of little consequence in understanding what goes on and why. There's a big gap between first impressions and what we as a society truly believe. One example will suffice. Anyone who's ever watched a popular television talk show, such as *Geraldo* or *Jenny Jones*, has to be terrified that these guests are also part of the electorate. Even standing in line to vote, one can easily think the same thing: Isn't it scary that the scruffiest ones vote? Can they *really* sign their X in order to register? Those fleeting thoughts, though, seldom lead observers to seriously question democratic theory, desire literacy tests, or demand extremely high poll taxes. Some initial fears are easily, or at least eventually, put aside. So it may not be all that important that Schattschneider and others condemn, on questions of ideology, governing through special interests. There is some very productive pressure there, just as there is when the scruffy vote.

That point looms large in assessing the impact of America's other interests, its many institutions, and its plentiful array of personalities. It has particular significance in helping judge whether interest pressure is like, as mentioned at the onset of the chapter, either a refreshing drink of water for policymakers or a determinant of inattentiveness in an often too hasty government. To make that judgment, some objective criteria are needed, not just a sense of wounded esthetics.

Those criteria exist if one looks hard enough and long enough at the many other interests of American politics. At least, enough can be seen about those interests to suggest some preliminary thoughts before discussing them further in later chapters. The review in this chapter has detailed an amazing array of nongroup organized interests. Moreover, all of them seem to fit quite well the representational wants of their supporters, organizers, and managers. No one who brings an interest to the policy process seems overly discontent with the way that interest gains representation. All sorts can lobby nicely and effectively if, that is, they define their issues correctly.

That contentment is, of itself, telling. As will be further explored later, it suggests—but certainly doesn't prove—the existence of a government very open and responsive to numerous and varied means of organizing interests. Nearly everyone can do it, except perhaps those already too far removed from the margins of political reality. As Robert Dahl implied, nobody's a loser *if they're all playing well*.[71] To an extent, he's correct.

So, is there a problem with pressure? What are the criteria for beginning to analyze the problem, if there is one? How well are public and policy scrutiny served? Are interests all alike? Answers seem to be suggested in the organizational characteristics of these other interests. Particularly important are two of them: the elaborateness with which types of interests lobby and the social intent of their lobbying goals.

As detailed in Figure 2.1, the elaborateness of the lobby, or how much it does when it needs to, and its social intent are both scaled from complex to simple and from broad to narrow. Then the two are shown in relationship to one another. The result shows a tremendous variation in how these many other types of interests each do business. Not all do the same things to lobby in the same mix. As the earlier discussion emphasized, no single type of interest behaves exactly like another. Some examples from Figure 2.1 help illustrate this. As would be expected, lobbying firms run highly complex public affairs efforts on their own behalf. They are not, however, trying to exercise broad social impact, only to win sound reputations for themselves as policy players. Business institutions are similar, with a highly elaborate lobby that uses groups when possible and, for their own distinct purposes, employs corporate employees when group politics doesn't work out.

In contrast, prominent televangelists aim for broad social impact on moral questions affecting—or at least of general interest to—most of society. And, because these preachers have very highly developed means for reaching out, they maintain relatively complex lobbies. With their obvious public policy focus, think tanks want to have only somewhat narrower social impact; after all, few of them want to save souls. Yet, lacking their own television networks and shows, these policy research institutions are not well-organized to maintain a complex, multitasked lobby. At any rate, given what different interests both can do and want to do, their impact can be seen to vary.

That brings up the problem of pressure. There can be little doubt that policymakers are burdened with an extensive amount of interest representation. Not necessarily excessive, just extensive. As James Bonnen, William Browne, and David Schweikhardt have shown, public officials can't accommodate all interests, successfully quiet their demands, and still make comprehensive and well-developed policy.[72] Policy is what suffers, the comprehensiveness part. The rest gets done.

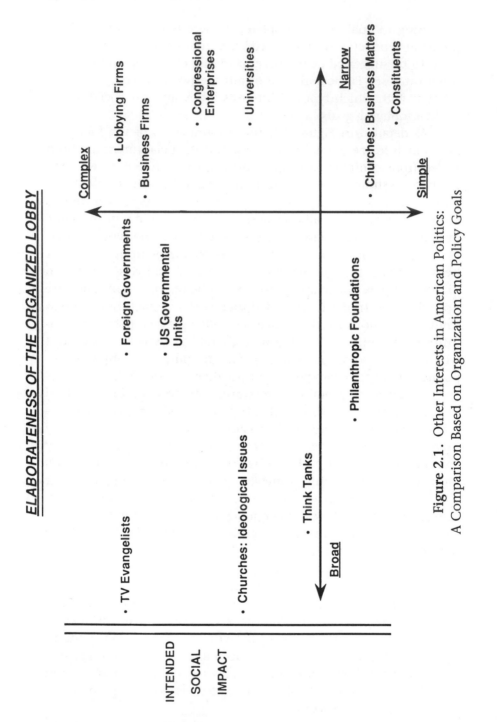

Figure 2.1. Other Interests in American Politics:
A Comparison Based on Organization and Policy Goals

There's more to the problem, however, than merely that. It's also a matter of policy inattention. Specifically, some interests make such narrow demands and are so badly lacking in broad social intent that they don't reasonably expect much systematic scrutiny of the impact of what they want. They just get accommodated and then quiet down. Interests that win with simple and less visible lobbies and with very narrow policy goals generally get what they want without the government deliberating much about their public impact. When your stomach hurts, just burp, don't think about it. That's the solution. Policymakers just do what most interests want because doing it is easier than listening. So does the public. Alternatively, they just leave these interests out without giving them due consideration. They're seen as too weird. In both those cases, the pressure of such interests, indeed, is excessive and an unpleasant burden for those who operate what was intended to be a slow, deliberate, and pensive American government. There just hasn't been much of any of that deliberation in rewriting accounting standards, funding scientific research, or assisting in foreign trade (not often at least), nor has there been much scrutiny on many social justice issues that seem remote to society, such as human rights in Kenya or prisoner rights in America.

Other institutional and personality-based pressures are less frequently found, harder to successfully mount, and a very good thing when it comes to the matter of increased public scrutiny, that is, if one discounts one's own value positions on the issues that these interests raise. These are most frequently big-issue items. Think tanks that raised questions about budget deficits, the environment, and women's rights added noticeably to the broader public's ability to know and understand things. Television ministers raised legitimate doubts about abortion, and opponents who responded by raising the issue of a woman's right of control over her own body also produced considered and thoughtful responses. In all these cases, the public responded. Although bringing forward each of these several issues has made governance more difficult and policy making more complex, doing so has nicely fit what the general public wanted to discuss. Such extensive pressures, then, have not been a problem for democratic governance. They've produced volatility and served as a refreshing drink of water from a cold and deep country well.

Summary and Highlights

One of the factors responsible for much of the misinformation about interest groups is confusion over what they are. Interest groups are one thing, service groups another, and institutions and personality-based organizations still several other things. Those distinctions count. Following Salisbury's logic as to the dominant position of institutions in policy representation, this chapter emphasizes that American interest politics logically takes many different forms.[73] So different, in fact, that some public officials may, in some capacities, work as policymakers while in others they serve as advocates and sources of interest pressure: George Rapson revisited, the guy from the introduction. Complex as it is, politics brings variable results, some positive and others negative.

These types of institutions exist, each with their own representational dilemmas. A wide range of business firms, numerous social institutions, such as churches and charities, and advocates organized by and within governments have been seen as having their own agendas and lobbying styles. Businesses are the most prevalent type, but, probably because of underreporting of advocates employed by the other two, their relative presence is somewhat overestimated. Representation by all three types, though, is even more stable and permanent than that of interest groups. That's because most of the public policy demands of institutions are defined by their own long-lived maintenance needs: keeping firms profitable or foundations and public agencies alive. Even churches, with their moral premises, need to lobby more on the basis of their business needs than on their ideals. This narrow, rarely prominent, and newsworthy advocacy is so extensive that it makes policy making both difficult and generally lacking in systematic oversight. It just doesn't fit with what titillates the public. So an advocacy issue isn't questioned much by policymakers, just enacted if it's easily done or if the claimant is especially important. Either that, or events are disregarded if the interest isn't seen as so important to the political mainstream. The costs of accommodating or rejecting institutional demands are seldom reviewed, it seems. The burden of doing so is too great and without much reward given the pressure for action.

Interest politics has yet a third component, not just groups and institutions. Personality-based interests are far less stable than either of the others, and they represent the flamboyant mobilizer as well as, far more frequently, political consultants, members of Congress, and subsets of the folks back home in districts and states. All depend heavily on who organizes the interest, and all of them tend to deteriorate badly without their leaders.

Each of these is important to the overall map of American interest politics because a substantial accumulation of political pressure comes from their advocacy, often as various organizations work together. Consultants work with enterprises, which in turn are trying to understand the most important problems of constituents. The general narrowness of most of these interests and their policy demands serve mainly to add to the problems of effective public policy making. And, as it should be clear, these narrow and usually boring issues make up the bulk of lobbying demands in American politics. Interest groups are only a wee bit less prone to address small issues. So in that regard they, too, are to blame for the problems of limited policy scrutiny, just not quite as much to blame.

As with institutions, though, some of these institutional and personality interests occasionally do a great deal to rouse the general public into greater political scrutiny. There *are* big issues, which is great for democratic rule. TV preachers and the issue of abortion, even if distasteful, are a good example of the positive effects of personality-based influence. Think tanks, and occasionally, organized religions are institutions that sometimes do the same thing, as do voluntary membership lobbies.

There exists more than just other interests in America's interest politics, and that politics brings both problems and prospects. This brief look at what interests there are, whom they represent, and how, in general, they lobby reveals quite a bit about both the problems and the virtues, or prospects, of special interest politics even if, so far, the definition of lobbying purposely has been avoided. There's been little consideration of exactly what's being done that leads either to attentiveness problems or to public scrutiny. Chapter Three turns to an inventory and an evaluation of the many tasks that, done together, make up lobbying or advocacy.

3

The Meaning of Lobbying

A great deal of attention has been given so far to understanding the organization of groups and other political interests. Considerable mention has been made of their lobbying, pressure, advocacy, or just the plain working of policymakers. However, what are interest representatives doing as actual tasks when they pressure government? Or, as British lobbyist Charles Miller put it, what are the precise "techniques of advocacy?"[1]

Part of the answer can be found in a description by Jeffrey Birnbaum of a large lobbying firm. Hill and Knowlton, while under Robert Gray's care, housed people who contacted policymakers as well as a varied assortment of "researchers, economists, political analysts, publicists, graphic artists, speechwriters, and managers of campaign contributions."[2] There was even an instructor who coached clients and staff on press interviews. Part of Hill and Knowlton's facilities included a broadcast studio, one that not only created electronic media spots but also broadcast them to commercial radio and TV stations to use as they wished. Quite literally, Hill and Knowlton made news.

Lobbying involves a lot, as this example suggests. Depending on the job, lobbyists may do a lot as well. Their techniques are many. This certainly seems a big change, at least at first glance, from the early days of American government when lobbyists were named for their simple penchant for hanging out in congressional lobbies—the halls—waiting to corral a passing legislator.[3] Modern lobbying involves far more.[4] In reality, it always did—more than most people realize. Its techniques include not only the contacts made to advocate issues, and the research needed to make any deal, there's also a great amount of what might best be called lobbying foreplay. Tommy Boggs has been a master of that. He maintained a house on the Chesapeake where policymakers went to party, hunt, and sometimes fish. To make sure communications didn't flounder because of growling and irate duck hunters among the attending members of Congress, Boggs's caretakers surreptitiously clipped the wings of some of the area's waterfowl. Shots were easy, members were happy—at least until a few were finally ticketed by conservation officers—and the techniques of lobbying advanced nicely.

Lobbyists and lobbying cover all the bases of effective communication on public policy. It's not just talking things over, or at least attempts are made to make it so. For instance, at the height of farm protests in the 1980s, one multiclient lobbying firm proposed a joint venture to the volatile American Agriculture Movement (AAM). The firm wanted to coordinate the protests, thus maximizing the effectiveness and eliminating bad publicity from ill-timed events.[5] The temperamental AAM joiners were insulted, even amazed, and flatly turned down the offer.

Perhaps the protesting farmers were too hasty. One thing that this chapter conveys is that lobbying is rarely anything other than doing several interrelated things, particularly for interests that wish to win. Protest is rarely enough. Nor is any other one task. Moreover, to make things more complicated, most of the tasks overlap but broadly fit three functions of lobbying: getting attention for interests, making contacts with public officials, and reinforcing what was accomplished through these contacts. That's not to imply that any organized interest is always doing all the tasks of lobbying on any one of its issues. Nor is it even to imply that pressure is being used as a constant, kept up on a continuous basis by each lobby. But that does very frequently tend to be true.

It's just that American politics and government present numerous bases to cover, from the mood of the public to the whims of specific legislators, and on through questions of what existing policies will allow. At the right time, on the right issue, all lobbyists need to be ready to cover every base. There exists much for interests to fit. It's much more than just a pleasant interlude between a lobbyist and a public official. As a result, as the following pages will detail, the techniques of advocacy, especially in the modern era, are necessarily multidimensional, multifaceted, and linked to one another. This is especially true in the modern era, where lobbying has become more sophisticated and refined. But it's also true that most lobbying tasks have been used in America for decades, even hundreds of years. Lobbying has simply evolved, not been newly invented. So lobbyists, as a generic name for those who represent interests, are nothing more than advocates, ones who use their variable skills in numerous ways in lots of directions—sometimes in all directions.

The Contact Game

Yet Alan Rosenthal indicates that lobbying is mostly about the contact game. As he says, "[m]uch of what happens . . . comes down to basic human relationships."[6] He's correct, as long as the emphasis on "much" remains.

It's easy to understand Rosenthal's need to attach that caveat rather even than say "most." Certainly not "all." In the first place, the traditional interaction between policymakers and lobbyists most efficiently communicates information. The contact game, where an interest representative meets personally with his or her target, gets information across. So tons of this goes on. Information certainly is the stuff of lobbying. It's right at the center of things. It's truly necessary for a complete experience, and many look forward to it with great enthusiasm. Without information, policymakers know little about what interests want. They also lack details of problems, proposed solutions, workability of the ideas at hand, and likely public reaction. And, without information from policymakers, interest representatives don't generally find out important aspects of what's going on within the policy process. Who wants what? Why do they want it? What are they doing to get it? For both components of the interaction, information sharing makes the representative process more operational.[7] Or at least it's more efficient than buying lottery tickets, dunking for apples, or calling the psychic hotline.

On the other hand, there's an omission in this logic. Just as theories of pluralism were flawed by the inability of all groups to organize their interests, and just as Truman's disturbance theory was flawed by the proclivity of many groups to organize without a threat, the theory of lobbying-as-a-communications-process lacks something.[8] While, as Rosenthal hints, communication and relationships are important in understanding lobbying, a lot of successful interest representation largely disregards the contact game. Numerous cases have been permanently advanced long before anyone suggested talking things over. The prominence of the Christian Coalition was not a product of chats with public officials. That group worked the faithful, played the media, argued before the general public, and, in doing those things, scared the hell out of politicians.[9] Nobody sat down representatives of the religious right in a congressional office to judge exactly what it was that they wanted. Those other actions had, so to speak, spread the word long before meetings were set. A long-time congressional committee chair said much the same thing. "I don't meet with staff from the American Association of Retired Persons," he concluded. "I always know what they think. Letters from home and personal visits from the elderly convinced me long ago to cooperate on whatever AARP suggests."

What then goes on within the contact game? Why is it played so often? And why not always as a priority technique? The answers to the first two questions are truly unexciting, even boring, but explain why there are precious few action movies and TV series about lobbyists. Describing the interaction is reminiscent of the family story of how Aunt Gladys became president of the garden club: "Why, she knew everyone in town. Of course not in a biblical sense!" There really isn't, despite one's hopes, a juicy part of the story. Nor is there with the many other versions of the contact game. Legislators know that best. Contacts involve listening and more listening, with maybe a quick question thrown in.

Even early accounts of lobbyists, none of which were praising of the profession, emphasized interaction, information sharing, personal relationships, and contact.[10] Even with innovations, the contact story is always a uniform one. First, lobbyists get policymakers' attention, basically by creatively fitting into the political scene. Tommy Boggs and several other prominent Washington lobbyists once formed the Washington Discussion Group (WDG), holding meetings over gracious dinners with congressional members who were reluctant to visit for long with lobbyists, one at a time, in the office. Second, lobbyists fit in by interacting in a pleasant and nonthreatening fashion, enjoying with policymakers their common interests. Issues as well as wine glasses were always raised by the WDG. Third, the intent of these pleasantries is to gain and maintain personal entry, the ability to walk into an office or call on the phone and be heard. After getting a legislator's attention over dinner, WDG participants won entry. When they demonstrated that they had something useful to say, keeping the door open was easy. In a classic analysis, Raymond Bauer and his associates explained that successful transactions of this kind bring mutually satisfactory exchanges of benefits between public officials and private interests.[11] Information, or at least what can be done with it, is the primary unit of such exchange.

This brings up point four. What everyone in the policy process needs daily are precise ideas that help them avoid risks. The best way to get ideas is by interacting with the players, people who know far more than merely who, what, and why. Policymakers need to know exactly what it is that they're proposing, supporting, and voting on. They want to know what will happen to them, both back home and in Washington, if advice is either taken or ignored. That's where an interest's researchers, economists, and political analysts fit. In contrast, lobbyists need to know the current and projected status of a bill or rule, the importance of each of those who want something in the legislation, the deals already brokered, those compromises that still can be made, and how much is in the budget for policy options. These and dozens of other things matter for both sets of players.

The need to avoid risk leads to point five. Interaction only continues when the relationship is honest, when both sides tell each other the truth, when, that is, lobbyists and policymakers provide accurate, if not perhaps complete or unbiased, information. The emphasis is on verifiable data, but a good rumor that another trusted player can confirm will often do. Sixth, to make certain that valued relationships are productive over time, and that new ones are worthwhile, policy players look for accountability, or in Rosenthal's words, they subject each other to an ongoing "trial by fire."[12] They continuously test one another. Legislators do it, but so do lobbyists. As one advocate said, "I want to see if one of these geeks can deliver." Policymakers say the same, asking, "Can this lobbyist put things together?" In politics there's precious little reason to support a loser.

In summary, the contact game aims at politics on the inside, durable relationships, sharing an understanding of process problems, credible information, trust among effective politicians, and keeping one another current and knowledgeable. Rosenthal adds that the players need also to exercise good judgment as inoffensive, circumspect, and respectful people.[13] All of this, of course, is a pretty idealized picture of lobbying. Who could turn anyone down given all that? It begs for more details in order to be complete and not so easily practiced. Or so it seems. But then, perhaps Aunt Gladys may well have done it that way: just got to know everyone in town!

But how does anyone get to know them all? A very good lobbyist once told a great story about his first advocacy venture. It illustrates perfectly how idealized the contact game has been made to appear, conceived as it is as a kind of one-on-one scrimmage between two players. The new lobbyist was asked by a client to explain to a public agency just what an unfair, arbitrary, and even unsafe ruling they'd promulgated. But nobody in the agency would talk to him, pay him even the slightest bit of attention. He really didn't know whom to confront, why they really should care enough to listen to him anyway, or why they'd go to the embarrassing trouble of reversing or modifying the ruling. All the careful information that had been accumulated by the lobbyist meant nothing without an audience: "I couldn't get them out to play, damn it."

In the end, though, this aspiring lobbyist won. He called an old friend who staffed for another old friend who was an influential senator. The staffer friend said he didn't need any of the carefully accumulated information. He'd just scream into the phone to the agency's legislative liaison, yelling threats about public responsiveness and accountability. The regulators indeed looked at their own records after that, decided that the case wasn't worth fighting, and reversed the rule. "I won," said the lobbyist, "but it had nothing to do with my skill or knowledge, just my own dumb luck. I felt like a slob."

He also knew that there was far more to his new profession than playing the contact game. And he understood that he'd have to find out about those other techniques of advocacy. He wasn't going to build a career based on two friends in one Senate office. That was clear. "They woulda gotten tired of me really soon."

This lobbyist shouldn't have been so surprised, even without much experience. Many interest scholars understand all too well that lobbying is more than just contacts and close relationships, the idealized story that everyone repeats ad nauseam. Even in surveying the techniques of advocacy, observers ask about a wide range of lobbying tasks and whether or not interests use them. Kay Schlozman and John Tierney, for example, constructed a wonderful questionnaire.[14] They listed twenty-six specific tasks in addition to contact work. At least 20 percent of all interests did each one. A majority did twenty-one or more.

Moreover, the contact work of those surveyed was hardly restricted to policymakers with whom lobbyists had nice, cozy relationships. Respondents listed contacts in thirteen specific types of public- and private-sector positions, all of whom were sometimes very important to their work.[15] Nobody's going to know them all well. So, while the contact game is a nice place to start in understanding lobbying, there remains plenty more to consider about the demands of advocacy work.

Lobbying as Winning Attention

Where do things generally start? Maybe there's no real beginning at all. Political scientists seem to have a special place in their hearts for the word "access."[16] In an analytical sense, it does convey a lot by getting to the core of lobbying. First lobbyists open doors by winning access, or what was earlier called entry, and then and only then do they get to play the contact game, that is, to win influence. This sequenced explanation is so nice and neat. Too neat. Winning access is far from being such a tidy process. The two-stage approach itself is very artificial, even though it remains analytically useful.

John Mark Hansen did a fantastic job in illustrating one case of an interest group, the American Farm Bureau Federation (AFBF), winning access.[17] What was so rich and clear about Hansen's analysis was the way in which he revealed one example of what seems necessarily to be an idiosyncratic approach for getting attention from all the necessary players. Within the reasonable bounds of limited human imagination, every interest has to win access its own way. No rigid formula exists. Resources are too varied. Likewise, Hansen shows that winning access can't be completely separated from making contacts and negotiating with policymakers. One function merges with the other.

Hansen explained the following:[18] In a first for groups of this type, the Farm Bureau organized farmers nationally. Not only did farmers express their opinions, AFBF kept its members knowledge-able. By 1921, congressional recognition of this unparalleled feat was so complete that legislators were uncomfortable, even irri-tated, that those back home knew rather well what was actually going on in the nation's capital. Recognition was not won simply by happenstance. If farm state legislators seemed unlikely to sup-port bills desired by the Farm Bureau, its lobbyists showered them with supportive farmer opinion polls and, for those still reluctant, arranged numerous messages to be telegraphed from home. As contact game players, AFBF lobbyists were middlemen, far from being the entire stuff of the group.

Even with such lobbying strategies, however, Farm Bureau access was not completely won. More pressure was necessary. That didn't come until the 1930s. In the 1920s, AFBF's access was restricted mostly to the geographically wide-ranging midwestern members of Congress. A troubled Midwest farm economy, angry heartland farmers, and farm policy issues that proved to be ongoing meant constant contact between area legislators and AFBF lobbyists. The Grange and the National Farmers Union, respec-tively stronger in the Northeast and West, similarly expressed the same farmer anger.

Yet southern congressional members paid the Farm Bureau and other groups little mind. Access to the South wasn't gained until the farm cotton economy also collapsed, anger spread to farmers of all classes throughout that region, and their members of Congress realized that issues of public policy protection wouldn't go away for them either. The result was twofold: first, an alliance of AFBF and the respected and now troubled cotton cooperatives, and second, a willingness of both midwestern and southern con-gressional members to put aside differences and work together. Access for AFBF was finally complete, and resulting contact work by lobbyists led, in Congress, to a successful rank-and-file revolt against party leaders who had few farm sympathies. Along with its allies, AFBF achieved a new status because its information was nationally important and it made sense for a wide range of legisla-tors to build relationships with its lobbyists. Most importantly, AFBF created a situation where it became more risky for individual members of Congress to ignore lobbying contacts than it was to overlook the legislative leadership demands of their parties. Until

AFBF won this competitive advantage over the leaders, access to Congress was incomplete.[19]

There was certainly nothing preordained about the rise of the Farm Bureau. Lobbyists helped set its political emergence in motion, but very little of what happened could have been planned in detail in advance. Economic circumstances affecting farmers were both too unpredictable and too variable for lobbyists to predict just how they'd win meaningful access to the contact game. The group had to adjust to these conditions, changing as they were. At best there was just a hope, predicated, of course, on mobilizing the grassroots, creating a national alliance, and frightening legislators. Lobbying and, for that matter, American public policy making don't lend themselves well to carefully laid-out conspiratorial designs. Both are adaptive and often ad hoc acts, put together as pieces of puzzles are discovered. Conspiracies are not. Things like the Washington Discussion Group and the Farm Bureau's lobby come together as pragmatic solutions when other means of reaching out pay no dividends. There's a great deal of trial and error, which is why lobbyists keep a large bag of tricks and bring out different ones as needed.

Two flaws in the theory of the contact game are its repetitive emphasis on the value of communications and its corresponding neglect of how hard it is to win access. Point one of the contact game, or fitting into the political scene, is so incredibly difficult that it consumes vast amounts of the resources that for most interests go into their politics. There is no magic. Compared to its years of winning access, negotiating final deals on farm legislation of the 1930s was relatively easy for the Farm Bureau. Likewise, the hard work was figuring out a format for the Washington Discussion Group, enhancing its status, and then getting inaccessible members of Congress to show up to be wined and dined (frequently whined and dined). Tossing out an issue that one of these guests was known to find important, such as rapid rail transit for Senator Daniel P. Moynihan (D-NY), and then later getting him to share information about it was easy.[20] Policymakers love to talk about their work if they love the issues.

Much of the confusion that leads to separating access from acts of influence comes from a widely held view of American government as its own proactive policy machine.[21] Somewhere in their hearts Americans believe that government can identify and solve all their problems for them. This view holds that policymakers sit around thinking up issues and waiting to turn them into law. Or at least they should be doing that. It's the old slow-and-deliberate governance notion again. Adherents to this proactive idea of government see interest access as pretty simply earned, often even welcomed, with the arms of public officials enthusiastically opened for that all too needed information. But there's much more to contend with than a few nice chats. A member of Congress explained: "When I came here, I was going to legislate, all by myself. I figured to throw my doors open to invited interests, all of whom I'd use, and work like hell to craft bills." He continued, "You know what happened? I didn't know who among the thousands of lobbyists to invite inside. Of greater importance were the time constraints. I couldn't take time to see numerous lobbyists. When I saw any of them, sitting around talking and listening just made me nervous. I had way too much to do to visit. They only irritated me."

This member and other policymakers, especially in Congress, explained that their work is far more reactive than proactive.[22] It's rarely public officials who think things up and develop the policy agenda. It's those from different organized interests who bring issues, proposals, and programs to government—that and, of course, sudden crises and important events that gain clamorous attention. As a consequence, there are precious few ongoing legislative events where interest representatives, after the fact, are invited in to help sort things out.

Certainly this type of invitation happens, though not often. Policymakers expect organized interest input on appropriations bills and on all renewable or omnibus enabling acts. Certain interests are expected to be present and get in from the lobby. And when interests of one distinct policy preference advance a bill, competing interests are welcomed in order for officials to hear another side. Again, doing so avoids risks. Invitations aren't, however, a very large part of the process. Expected players exist but rarely invited ones. Any interest whose lobbyists wait diligently for their invitations from government to arrive in the mail are either hopelessly naive or just ignorant. Interest information isn't that valued or respected.[23] "Anybody who doesn't bring me a message," continued the congressman above, "I just say screw 'em."

For those reasons, lobbyists have long grappled with how to stand out, gain attention, and get in the door when they show up in the halls. A favored, and most direct trick of the nineteenth century was bribery, a great way to corral attention in the hallway.[24] Lobbyists later took to buying drinks, dinners, and presents for bored legislators.[25] Capitals then were mostly geographically isolated, not centers of social and economic life, and without much entertainment value. So lobbyists found willing legislator attention. Conditions, though, have changed. Standing around in a purple striped suit, lugging a huge cigar and a sack of money, no longer lets a grossly overweight lobbyist fit appropriately into the political scene. Laws, ethics, political reporting, and other watchfulness, as well as norms of conduct, all militate against that stereotyped cartoon character of robber baron days.[26] And it's quite difficult today to get legislators not to pay for their own lunch with a lobbyist, if they'll even go out. It's the new ethics.

Accordingly, modern lobbyists find gaining access more complicated. They also tend to find it especially intriguing since it's so hard to master, and that's what makes lobbying such a fascinating political game. It's one that gets plenty of public and media attention because access tasks can rarely be done in a boring way (not at all like the tedium of playing that idealized version of the contact game). Attention-getting gimmicks, in fact, could make for a popular movie or TV lobbyist series.

A plethora of lobbying techniques help interests gain attention and access. Not all, of course, use each one, yet most could. Elections are peak events for gaining access. Of course, the favorite task is donating political action committee (PAC) funds to an electoral campaign.[27] Legislators need to raise considerable revenue to run for office. Agency officials, especially the political appointees, understand that their favorite chief executives—and patrons— need the same financial support. Many organized interests or their employees operate a PAC as a result. If not, they otherwise contribute at campaign fundraising events or through mailing requests. Sometimes they give in all these ways. Another widely undertaken lobbyist task is volunteering personal assistance in campaigns. Unions are particularly adept at getting their own members knocking on doors and doing campaign minutia: putting up signs, handing out bumper stickers, doing polling. They've also mastered the public relations gimmick—without endorsing—of taking out campaign-tied advertisements that praise the policy stances of their preferred candidates. Lobbyists, in addition, offer their own personal advice and consultation, as well as that of other interest staff, as unpaid campaign volunteers. All this gets attention, since rank-and-file workers, free media ad blitzes, and politically talented advisors are always in short supply in elections. While they don't make a big splash, group or institutional endorsements also are always well-received and policymakers do use them in campaigning. The National Education Association has such a huge base of teacher members that the group easily mastered all of the above.

Elections are but one venue for getting attention. Lobbying techniques also favor taking out an organization's own advocacy advertisements in those media sources that policymakers watch or read. Holding a well-publicized and likely hot press conference works, too. Ralph Nader was a master of that. Reporters flock to such contentious media events. Lobbyists also plant news stories with both national and local reporters.[28] Not infrequently they work to get stories about issues and legislators on such news programs as *Dateline* or the numerous political talk shows. To generate public concerns, some have even placed people on popular TV talk shows.

Making it known throughout the capital that a group or an institutional office is always available for publicity, research, or technical assistance also gets attention. Offers of help in drafting legislation or regulations are widely accepted. Encouraging group members or institutional supporters to write letters, complain about issues, and personally contact policymakers all open doors as well. This is the old grassroots at work, or perhaps, more accurately, it's astroturf because it's a synthetic version of what may or may not be real local political interest. Even with the synthetics, the grassroots work especially well when respected constituents from back home are the ones mobilized. To the same end, interests hold local and regional meetings where policymakers gain the opportunity to mingle with the homefolks.[29] Local business groups are masters of these techniques.

Interests also increasingly bring legal suits.[30] These get media coverage and, as a result, policymaker attention. It's routine for environmental interests to advertise their capacity to muck things up and make politics difficult by litigating. Filing amici curiae, or friendly and supportive litigant briefs, gets less attention, but this technique is widely used. Lobbyists also may encourage leading legal authorities to write an advocacy piece for a law journal, hopefully influencing court cases. Sometimes interests just threaten litigation that may complicate, impede, or even force the policy process. "When that happens on my issues," said a legislator, "I invite those people right in for a talk. Right now! That lawsuit business makes a lobbyist really stand out from the crowd."

Other attention or access winners range from strategies of what many call "insider politics" to ones that call attention to an interest's outsider political status, or its much ballyhooed claims of being too long neglected by that awful old government. This insider-outsider dichotomy is really quite an artificial distinction. No matter. Lobbyists still make a big deal about it in trying for access. A traditionally used insider technique occurs when interest representatives volunteer to serve on institutional governing boards, government advisory commissions, and local civic organizations. These things obviously are for the already prominent, and appearing in this capacity communicates prominence. Lobbyists go to such places, sometimes work hard, become recognized faces, and not infrequently meet policymakers who either also serve the organization or appear with it. A less subtle insider approach is simply hiring a widely known and respected multiclient, for-hire lobbyist, or even several of them. The consultants already have access and drag a group's or firm's unknown or unloved lobbyists inside along with them. Joining a coalition with widely respected other interests works to the same ends.

The classic outsider, or "poor us," technique is the organized protest or demonstration. Lots of upper income groups use it, such as sportsfishing organizations that ring a state capitol with expensive boats. So protest isn't just for the poor and downtrodden, and using it makes a statement. The American Agriculture Movement (AAM) mobilized farmers entirely around tractorcades and protests in 1977 and throughout the mid-1980s, even though these activists were hardly without other interest group ties or personal wealth. They just believed that, in their words, "the squeaking wheel gets the grease," which led them to charge other farm groups with being too timid to win what farmers really wanted.[31] The demands of these farmers, both before and after the protests, weren't treated by agricultural observers as very credible. In fact, they were seen generally as hopelessly outdated. So AAM acted as an outsider interest. Its joiners, however, quickly won access when farmers appeared, rather surprisingly, to be in open revolt. AAMers were then able to present their case in nearly every public office in

Washington, D.C., throughout 1978. People for the Ethical Treatment of Animals try to work in much the same way, but these folks are much less successful because they seldom surprise policymakers; they usually just get in the way for a short time and then go away.

Access then is gained in many ways, through numerous lobbying techniques and by use of some artificial distinctions such as insider and outsider claims. In almost infinite combinations, these techniques can be used as means of moving lobbyists from the hallways into offices where deals can be brokered. What's important of all these techniques and mixes of tasks is that public officials are caught, at least slightly, off-guard by them, not surprised, necessarily, but just suddenly aware that an interest and its lobbyists seem to matter—aware, in fact, that the access-seeking lobby, at least for the moment, may well fit appropriately into ongoing events in the political process. If the access game is played creatively enough, lobbyists are seldom left out of the ensuing contact game. Even the religious right representatives now are welcomed routinely in numerous offices of public officials after years of being ignored.

Reinforcement: Same Techniques, Different Purpose

Even when lobbyists get to play the contact game, though, attention can be lost quickly. Policymakers easily drop those who once felt they'd made it. Success can be so very fleeting, as AAM found out when their tractor protests ripped up the Mall and irritated Washingtonians in 1979. They lost their access, promptly.

This problem has been noted by several observers. Miller, the British lobbyist, warned: always *maintain* your liaisons.[32] Rosenthal said it better: "Lobbyists have to work at more than *building* relationships."[33] Hansen gave the generic prescription: Lobbyists need to ensure that their issues, and presumably the interests that they represent, have recurrence.[34] That means lobbyists keep coming back, showing their issues are still alive, reinforcing both their access and previously discussed policy matters. It means that radio and television preachers, as well as other flamboyant organizers, don't take long sabbaticals from their political agendas. They'd be forgotten if they did. It means that constituent confidants keep providing useful local information or they get abandoned by congressional enterprises.[35]

So how does reinforcement work? One answer to that is not easily, and certainly not successfully for all interests. Reasons for the difficulty are numerous and interdependent.[36] First, even with trials by fire, interests are suspect for the quality and accuracy of their information. "Everyone always presents a spin," concluded one member of Congress, "you just don't know what it is, so take heed." Second, interests are seldom organized or integrated enough internally to present a united front. Certainly policymakers know this. Interest groups, for instance, have splits and differences of opinion between joiners and the lobbying or management staff. And, of course, splits among joiners are unavoidable. Institutional cleavages are often found between what politically astute lobbyists wish to agree on with public officials and what business, church, or charity leaders insist on as their mandatory wants from government.

Third, interests often lack their unique appeal over the long term. Public policymakers just see no reason for paying attention any longer. Lots of facts become irrelevant. There are no longer any risks for ignoring what lobbyists who peddle the facts say. Fourth, of course, there are just so many interests out there.[37] As political conditions change, somebody just isn't going to continue to get into the all too crowded policymaker door, even when public officials might like to let them in. Things are often just too crowded.

For instance, the issue agenda of government may have been altered by a new event, policy changes may have made some interests appropriate only to an earlier era, or dominant political philosophies and ideologies may shift within the capital. Examples include the replacement of farm commodity programs in the 1995 farm bill, as well as the sudden and unexpected election of a conservative Republican congressional majority in 1994. Some once prominent interests were for both reasons back in the lobby, wishing for their former access and attention. As one of them said, quite astonished at his predicament: "I couldn't get in once friendly doors. Not even to see staff." Food stamp advocates and farm commodity interests were only two of many examples. A long-time congressional staffer phrased the partisan transition nicely: "I didn't have to listen to those bastards any longer. It made losing the (legislative) majority almost worth it!"

To offset some of the difficulties in keeping attention, there exists what policymakers call a kind of protocol that mandates that some interests retain access. But it extends only to a limited range of officials, and it's in effect only when these lobbyists continue to represent issues still important to policy deliberations.[38] Representative Dick Armey (R-TX), the House majority leader, saw no reason to listen to food stamp interests in 1994 and 1995, even when their legislation was up for renewal and they'd enjoyed routine access to congressional leaders since 1973. So protocol, or having to listen, doesn't mean a lot. It's subject to alteration, and it certainly guarantees nothing.

Nearly every organized interest that wants to stay politically active, as a consequence, strives to perfect reinforcement techniques. Consultant lobbyists don't want to be seen as out of the loop. A business firm such as Dow Chemical wants policymakers to understand that its lobbying office is still open and watching. The Sierra Club sometimes mobilizes letters from its joiners even when no legislation is pending. A favored tactic for keeping doors open is when lobbyists unexpectedly drop by simply to hand out useful tidbits of information. Just saying hello is too bothersome. But a nice juicy tip about events back home, what another congressional enterprise is doing, or a likely media story are always welcome if they potentially affect the lobbyists' policymaker targets. Such are the primary ingredients of maintaining relationships, even in a crowded and hectic capital.

Obviously, most of the other techniques of advocacy can be used for reinforcement, just as they were for winning access or peddling information. The exceptions tend to be threatening actions that may tear down relationships and create distrust among policymakers. The threat of a disruptive legal suit or the staging of a large-scale, media-seeking protest have such effects. Court action demonstrates that political friends are insufficient and unuseful. Protests too often embarrass government officials, making them look unresponsive and ineffective to the public. Most interests with ready access usually tend to avoid these techniques as ways of reinforcing attention. Not all, however. Jesse Jackson's Rainbow Coalition understood that its access in Washington was only grudgingly and tentatively won. Relationships were far from solid. Jackson reminded policymakers that the Coalition was still at work by chasing after media events, threatening several legal cases, and occasionally staging protests—just so no one forgot. As one of his supporters joked, "Jesse never met a camera he didn't love." In reality, he had to behave that way in order to succeed.

Every other technique seems fair game for any interest that has the internal resources to use it. In practice, tasks that are undertaken to win access or further the contact game can be used later to keep both going. Some of these things may be practiced in odd reversals. For instance, campaign funds are given to help win attention. But then, when elections are near, policymakers routinely call established interests to give them some more assistance. These lobbies can seldom say no: "I'd be afraid of being left out." The process of lobbying comes full circle as a consequence, metaphorically both starting and ending with variations on different attention-getting measures. Interest advocates do a great many things, producing a complex game that they generally intend to play over the long term. And they keep playing even when it's not obvious that their desired issues aren't up for grabs. They reinforce, reinforce, reinforce.

The result is that PAC dollars flow like water from a fountain; consultant lobbyists spread like fire; constituents are mobilized like crazy; interest group coalitions proliferate; and, where it's possible, wining and dining still pays off. These are the fun-to-watch things, the strategic options that lobbyists, the media, and the public all find unavoidably intriguing. So, too, do the targets, even if things get a bit irritating.

But Does This Busy Game Fit?

Fit? Or, one could ask, is this any way to run a railroad? Clamor, clamor, clamor! The generally painted picture of interests is that they impose unrelenting and awesome pressures on policymakers. The negative kind. That's not just a recent view. Matthew Josephson reflected on Grover Cleveland's long-ago presidential administration: "The pressure at times seemed intolerable."[39] As they had at least as far back as President William H. Harrison, finance capitalists demanded federal development policy. Sympathizing with

Cleveland, Harrison, and especially today's policymakers is easy to do. It's oh-so-much-trouble to do the job.

Yet making a public official's job difficult is no sound reason for objecting to organized political interests. Retail clerks work long hours during the Christmas season, but few businesses wish that customers would disappear. And they don't try to shorten the holiday buying spree. As the earlier sections indicate, lobbyists come at policymakers from every corner and with every technique for gaining and holding attention. So what? Lobbyists, who clearly work hard at difficult and varied tasks, have little sympathy for their policymaker targets. Why then should anyone else? As a multiclient lobbyist angrily retorted, "You think we should let legislators sit around on their dead butts? Give me a break. Their job is to listen. I work much harder as a lobbyist than I ever did as a [state] senator."

His point is well taken. The Washington governing community of the very early 1800s, before the finance capitalists developed policy interests, has been criticized extensively for its lack of pressure and interests.[40] Without organized interests and therefore without much attention from citizens, policymakers governed poorly and their institutions usually were dormant. Not much happened. Social and economic problems were often totally ignored. Jane Mansbridge makes the same case in two of her most thought-provoking works.[41] As interests come to U.S. capitals, deliberation intensifies. More things are considered, such as the ethical treatment of animals. Policymakers lose—or have stripped away—their inclination to do either little or nothing or otherwise too much when more interests are organized and lobbying. Interests then compete and gain attention. Collaboration with them is frequent and largely unavoidable. Representation of both people and ideas increases.

As Elisabeth Clemens so aptly demonstrated regarding the politics of 1890–1925, lobbying came to fit American public policy making better than did parties and elections.[42] By organizing interests, groups of regular people institutionalized participation and brought accountability to daily politics. So lobbyists made this fit, got it to work.

Active interests may make governing cumbersome under these circumstances. The benefits are generally quite extensive, however, especially for a democratic society that takes pride in its open and representative structure. Interest politics then fits very well both the public and theoretical expectations of American government precisely because so much goes on. Interests that lack access don't give up: Their lobbyists devise many creative techniques for getting attention, doing new things in new ways. Often they find the right mix. They also stay concerned that they and their ideas aren't forgotten. Irrelevant ideas that win no followings, of course, mercifully lose out. Some interests are disadvantaged by the losses, but at least no conspiracy explains their demise. Resource limitations are at the center of their representative problem. So, too, are mainstream values, the things that define winners. That's pretty much what democratic theorists such as Robert Dahl envisioned.[43] It's not perfect, but it's still a nicely deliberative process. At worst, the lobbying process offends sensibilities and a sense of equality. Not all interests and issues can win.

The strength of lobbying in the United States is that the contact game is not the only means of playing interest politics. That strength is in its busyness and its continuing pressure, in its dynamic nature. Lobbying is not all cozy relationships between friendly policymakers and advocacy activists, thank the stars! If the contact game truly were all there is to lobbying, or if access were permanent, then far more interests and policy ideas would effectively be without representation. Public officials would talk only to their prominent friends. Society would be poorer for that, not enriched. Politics would be much less democratic, even less equitable. There would, for example, have been no civil rights movement and no Voting Rights Act.

In that sense, lobbying seems to be evolving over time. And indeed the evolution enhances rather than falls short of democratic expectations. A more pleasing adaptation now exists. Unlike in President Harrison's time, today there are more than just finance capitalists from Wall Street swarming over the capital. Today's interests fit the political expectations of the United States in a better, not a worse, way. Lobbying was once as much corruption as it was information. Later, interests that really were on the inside of cozy political relationships retained their access through old-boy networks of wining, dining, and gift giving. As advocacy exploded and as technology changed both methods of communications and analysis, however, bribery and political coziness lost much of their appeal. Every modern interest has access to reporters, which means publicity. The truly left out have learned to litigate and organize protests. Society's evolution means, first of all, that more interests can play politics well; second, that more of them have quite reasonable chances of getting access and relaying their information; and third, that any of them might lose their status if they lose their competitive edge. All they need to do is pick the right issues and employ the properly useful tasks.

Summary and Highlights

If the organization of American interests is generally misunderstood by most casual political observers, and many scholars, too, of course, lobbying suffers even more from an inaccurate perception of what it entails. Lobbying is merely engaging in the techniques of advocacy, at least on the one hand. The techniques are many and varied because interests, circumstances, the personal skills and other resources of each interest representative, and creative responses all vary. So lobbying is all-directional. Interests and lobbyists, as a result, need to master many tasks beyond only a glib and persuasive rhetoric. There aren't just more interests around, there are also more and more activities from these interests,[44] particularly because more improved avenues for communication are always evolving.

On the other hand, lobbying is more about function than it is about the bag of numerous advocacy techniques mastered by interest representatives. The techniques, in fact, are pretty standard, even though always evolving.[45] This chapter has emphasized that lobbying, as a process, has three functions: getting attention, communicating with contacts about mutual information needs, and reinforcing for lobbying targets the value of their continuing to give the lobbies attention. Access isn't enough. Making contacts is insufficient. Reinforcement of the impression that interests and their issues recur over time also matters. But only in some idealized, analytically intended way do these three functions form a linear sequence. Most interests have various targets in mind and ongoing lobbying enterprises in which they've invested. As a result, most organized lobbies nearly constantly attend to each of the three functions even as they direct their resources to the tasks appropriate to the moment, issue, and problem.

The techniques of lobbying are not only numerous for that reason, they're also interrelated, one to the other. Surveys of organized interests tend to miss that point;[46] they proceed too much as inventories of tasks and targets. Taken together, techniques form a strategy. Strategies are both necessarily complex in a multifunctional process, and they emphasize, at least to some degree, the long term. Being able to put strategies together from a bag of available techniques gives lobbyists and other interest specialists their needed identities as useful political professionals, as desirable contacts.

That's why the contact game very inadequately summarizes the means and processes of effective interest representation. Even the most respected and resourceful interests don't just cultivate favor from their targets. They also challenge and confront policymakers, disrupting things when other means of winning and keeping access fail. Things are always as predictable as observers expect. Business interests frequently litigate against government, and no interests have more favorable political circumstances than businesses. Higher education associations, as another example, encouraged campus protests when colleges and universities seemed to have too little congressional access in 1995 and 1996.

As a bag of gimmicks and lobbying tools, techniques are not only blended together, they also are used in finding access, making contact, and in establishing recurrence—all three, all simultaneously. Even at what may seem the oddest moments. As John Heinz and his associates concluded, that's why interests that do more win more.[47] As John Wright contended, organized interests direct themselves to those tasks most likely to pay off[48] and not to mere convention. Doing so, without question, makes the public policy making arena an even busier setting than that suggested by the sheer numbers of organized interests in an exploding universe of advocates. These representatives are all scurrying about, working frantically to both elicit attention and not be forgotten. Farm commodity lobbyists don't want to be forgotten for long, even if their programs have been replaced. As one stated: "But they could be needed again." Farmers still beat the drums for them as a consequence. Congress keeps its options open. There is then a tremendous amount of political noise in the United States.

Neither the noise nor the hectic pace that it precipitates should be faulted. At least, that is to say, neither should be faulted for making governance cumbersome. Fault can be assigned for lots of other reasons, such as fairness and equity. A busy process of interest representation, played in variable ways, still helps to create a larger number of viable groups and institutions, a proliferation of important policy ideas that otherwise would be irrelevant, and enhanced deliberation within government. The busyness serves well, or fits nicely with, both public and theoretical expectations of American democracy. Busyness, and the watchfulness that goes with it, is also often that highly appropriate good pressure. It's so noisy in American politics that few organized interests can get overlooked or hide from scrutiny—a darned good thing.

Describing the multiplicity of techniques and the three functions of lobbying behind them are still of limited value in accurately presenting what it is that lobbyists do. Only a start has been made. So far, for this volume, lobbying remains too abstract, without much of a setting. To clarify the setting somewhat further, the next three chapters turn to the targets of lobbying. These, too, are each related to one another, and so tasks taken to reach them overlap one another. The emphasis in the next chapters is on who those targets are, how they're each best reached, and what impact reaching them has. Less attention is given to the types of organized interests and what each does best or usually. Chapter Four starts with the public and its attitudes, moods, and opinions. There is a kind of generic process at work even if some lobbies do one thing while others do another.

4

Targeting the Public

It may seem obvious to some that public policymakers are the one and only target of lobbying, that everything lobbyists do aims only at reaching and at influencing those in government. There's a certain logic to that interpretation. Who else makes laws? Regulates? Yet there's a fallacy there as well. How are decisions made, or left unmade? Why? American politics is incredibly complex, with one target being used to influence others. And it's so very democratic, open. Political access points where interests can complain are numerous. If one access point fails to grant entry, another one always exists and its doors might be persuaded to open. This and the next two chapters emphasize the complexity of that political process and the resulting proliferation of what are interrelated lobbying targets. Remember, lobbying is advocacy by organized interests to influence public policy. Even members of Congress and radio commentators sometimes operate as lobbyists.

The existence of such a great many lobbying techniques, as seen in Chapter Three, certainly hints that policymakers are not the only targets. The public, media sources, and other interests all feature prominently. All can be used by organized interests to make a case. As one lobbyist said: "Go first to those who'll most likely listen. Others will follow if you play the right cards." In fact, a combination of all three are often targeted in a single, and often not elaborate, lobbying or public affairs venture.

Aren't other targets only secondary ones? Aren't lobbyists just using them to reach policymakers? The answer is both yes and no. Of course, mobilizing the general public aims at getting, for example, those on a specific congressional committee to respond. That's the yes side of the answer. The no side has a far less linear, two-stage interpretation. After all, linearity isn't a good way to understand lobbying. Lobbying, as noted earlier, isn't actually sequenced. A member of Congress once stated well why the other targets are often the primary ones: "You can frequently tell what the exact content of a yet unintroduced bill will be just by looking at a story in the news. If it's dramatically persuasive, Congress will bend over backwards. The same is true of the public's mood. The electorate can create so much local sentiment that you get a national tide of opinion. When that happens, decisions are already made."

That member was saying that freedom of choice for policymakers is often long lost. Legislators aren't free agents. Nor are bureaucrats. They're often not a secondary target either, but only a yet-to-be-pushed reactive button. Under those circumstances, lobbyists don't even need to target policymakers with their information. Public officials, after all, can read their own papers, polls, and constituent letters. There's little or no need for deliberation. The spate of news stories about decaying national parks is a good example. In 1996 and 1997, much of the media profiled that problem and the public read and watched. Congress tried mightily to find funds to fix them, dollars that were earlier labeled as unavailable.

The targets emphasized in this chapter are that public and, as part of a tandem operation, the mass media. The importance of both are described in detail on affecting short-term issues and in fostering long-term conditions of the political environment. Public responses are seen as determined by the importance of social values, often as these are set in myth, as well as by consideration of policy needs. Despite the fabulous success of the inane Tickle Me Elmo doll in 1996, no one can sell just any idea. The public needs to be already inclined or provided an education, especially on issues like popular parks, to which citizens will respond.

The focus of this chapter is on how and why organized interests advertise, or propagandize. It's also about the responses elicited by political messages from organized interests. It's truly important that interests often treat citizens and those who reach them as *the* main lobbying targets, ones that often force policymaking acquiescence rather than bring increased capital city deliberation. As much as anything else in politics, that targeting gets the all-important attention of those in office. The deliberation, or scrutiny, given those issues by the policy process has already occurred, long before such issues are actively considered by public officials. That limiting effect on the discretion of policymakers matters greatly for the direction later taken by public policy.

Not Just Mobilizing the Joiners

Targeting the public is *not* what interest groups do merely to retain their joiners. As was emphasized in Chapter One, interest groups do routinely contact their own members. And much of the reason is because those joiners themselves expect their interests to lobby and involve them.

These dues payers, and often even patrons, expect to be at least nominally active in interest politics: being invited to meetings, requested to write letters to public officials, and urged to personally contact policymakers when circumstances allow. Getting invited, requested, and urged to become politically active on behalf of their organized interests is mobilization. Regular folks think of it as being prodded, or kicked in the butt to elicit a response. Numerous studies describe it.[1] A recent survey of joiners finds that a very significant amount of the personal issue engagement of people comes through affiliation with groups.[2]

Mobilization, though, can hardly be restricted to just actual and prospective joiners. Lobbying is most effective when an interest's issues are generally popular, or at least acceptable to large populations of people. Members are rarely thought of as sufficient targets. Also, since many interests aren't groups and are therefore without joiners, such organizations can't rely on affiliates to demonstrate the popularity or acceptability of what they want from government. The public needs to do it instead.

As a consequence, targeting the public takes on a broad range of pending political issues. It goes on in two ways: The general public can be targeted, as for example when defense contractors advertise the need for a strong and technologically superior national defense network. The message is: Get those letters pouring in! Alternatively, selected parts of the general public are targeted. The American Medical Association (AMA), for instance, aims to influence primarily the well-educated, professional, most probable private health care consumer. It does no good for the AMA to expect an attentive and mobilized public from among people who fear physicians, practice no prevention measures, and don't go to the clinic or hospital even when their legs or ears fall off. Those people won't write to policymakers either, and the AMA would hardly benefit politically if they did send out what are likely to be unusual letters to Congress.

The public, however, can't be mobilized with any efficiency simply through direct lobbying contacts with individual citizens, especially one at a time. And more especially, mobilization can't be accomplished merely by explaining interest issues to each target within the public. Interests are too small in their organization; the public is too large, too hard to reach.

How then does mobilization take place? And under what circumstances? Both questions are addressed in the following pages. But before getting to them, one point needs to be made about targeting the public: Organized interests have always utilized the most up-to-date communications techniques and technologies available to them for their political business.[3] That has always meant a prime reliance on, and even a targeting of, each era's dominant mass media. Interests could never have gotten their public messages across without a cooperative media and captivating messages, as well as people who were inclined to both listen and follow. It seems that there's always been an understandable linkage between interests, the media, and popularly held beliefs and values.

But Isn't the Public a New Target?

New? No. But it certainly is a well-transformed target. Public relations has long gone hand-in-hand with America's interest politics, and not merely as an adjunct in reaching policymakers.[4] The adjunct business is only part of the tale. Development and settlement interests of the nineteenth century didn't restrict themselves to pressuring presidents such as Harrison and Cleveland. As emerging political interests with new ideas, these financial capitalists also sold the idea of the frontier to the populace, which was far from an easy feat.[5] Imagine being persuaded to leave the civilization of the eastern United States in favor of a wild and isolated West, characterized by lousy weather, often barely habitable climes, and various unfriendly, if not dangerous, inhabitants. It makes more sense for people to do that if one factors in American beliefs in "manifest destiny," or the predestined capture of the whole continent, and in the importance of furthering agrarianism and property ownership. That's what railroads and other business interests played on—that and adventure.

Of course the railroads' mantra wasn't "Come West, lose your life." Rather, rail and other interests used flyers, posters, stump speakers, and news stories to glamorize the West. Like Hill and Knowlton in the 1980s, they made the news. The West was sold, not just as a right and a challenge, but also as a mythic land of promise and a break from the limited personal opportunities of the East. People could own their own land there, and farm in pastoral splendor! Or so the story went. Particularly effective were the dime-store novelists, the *Geraldo* and *Jenny Jones* TV shows of their day. Some novelists were solicited to write for the masses. Others, with less noble talents, were merely given financial inducements—like a stagecoach ticket—to cover the popular themes of beauty and independence in the West. Also, of course, to emphasize the heroic figures.

Why? Certainly for reasons far broader than building a supportive public opinion. As industrialists and financiers understood, there were to be no railroads, telegraphs, extractive industries, and profits in the West unless people came first.[6] Lots of them were needed, the more the better. Development was useless without laborers, service economies, and, most importantly, customers. That was where settlement policy entered into development. For the same reason, the same interests encouraged and recruited for increased U.S. immigration. And getting new Americans West required that spin, built as it was on their existing hopes and wants.

At least as important to development and settlement interests was the meaning of a popular climate of public support in Washington. Enthusiastic voters moving West were certainly persuasive to public policymakers, especially since these folks and most Americans believed in the Jeffersonian ideal of farm and property ownership and its link to democracy.[7] Owning land supposedly made one a more ardent and care-giving citizen. There was a widespread understanding that public support for development was deep and abiding among average Americans who both glamorized yet still thought critically about the West. Public support for western expansion and development was more than just a temporary knee-jerk response to western glamour. It was deep and consequential. Therefore, policymakers, in turn, passed laws encouraging and often funding the developers, certain that their efforts would be socially and popularly rewarded as nation-building. In brief, policymakers did things for regular Americans as well as for Wall Streeters.

The Homestead Act gave away parcels of land to regular settlers and was but one example of these nation-building laws. Homesteading not only got people West, it also got them land adjacent to that given to the railroads. The value of railroad land increased and much of it was sold to these settlers. Not by accident, the Homestead Act and the Transcontinental Railroad Act were both passed in the same year, 1862. So were plans to provide agricultural and technical education to those going to these rural areas.

Settling the West was hardly the first act of lobbying the U.S. public, nor was it the most outwardly dramatic and well-publicized. One of the earliest lobbyists to both drum up public support and play the contact game was Mathew Carey, a wealthy and zealous advocate for federal commerce and industrial policy in the early 1800s.[8] He was like an early version of Microsoft's Bill Gates, who in the mid- and late 1990s preached around the country about the need for a new political order. Carey, like Gates, was his own lobbyist. And both realized that only the citizenry could persuade Congress. So Carey preached, wrote newspaper stories, and visited other manufacturers. And he entrepreneured interest groups. But Carey lacked the good fortune—and established myths—of the later development lobbyists who sold settlement policy.

Those interests were able to generate extensive public support only because the generalized Jeffersonian notion that linked farming, land ownership, independence, democracy, and stewardship had already captured American thought. Carey, in fact, was attacking that set of values in favor of economic diversity. People wanted to believe in the West and new opportunities, not in working in a factory. So they ardently supported development and settlement policy. For their part, policymakers wanted to support not just the developers but a diffuse public interest as well.[9] They found that chance. Too bad for Carey that he didn't better fit the existing mainstream values of an agrarian, as opposed to an industrial, nation.

The dramatic clout of citizens as part of the lobbying process came nearly a hundred years later, taking more of an issue-based tact than previously. Things became more free from myth, but not entirely. The 1920s were benchmark years for evolving lobbying. Not only did the Farm Bureau demonstrate its grassroots agrarian strength during that decade, so did others. And some won even greater free advertising and more widespread public support. These were peoples' lobbies. The well-publicized prohibitionist Anti-Saloon League communicated routinely with a half-million targeted citizen foes of alcohol.[10] Most were somewhat opinionated, became quite active, mobilized others, and really perplexed members of Congress. They were loose cannons taking pot shots at the ship of state, not just farmers and workers facing practical and understandable financial problems. Prohibition passed, of course.

Such techniques took on a pattern. During that decade communications technology grew and business interests moved from sponsoring dime-store novelists to providing "boilerplate" for busy editors who needed easy-to-format stories to fill their newspapers.[11] Not unlike Hill and Knowlton and western development interests, these businesses just kept sending out lots of already typeset stories, making their own well-spun and self-serving news. Papers printed it because doing so was easy. The reach of such interests was deep into society, even on not yet widely understood issues such as the need for tariff protection. People picked up ideas easily from their newspapers.

Certainly the public was having its range of issues extended dramatically, and even their beliefs challenged, by organized interests in the 1920s. More policy options were being considered than ever before. The simple days of laissez-faire government, already assaulted by the adoption of numerous development and settlement policies, were quickly drawing to an end. Collaboration by organized interests with public opinion began to kill laissez-faire dominance. The Granges had only started things rolling in the 1870s. But laissez-faire dominance was broken only when it became as easy for policymakers to know the content of issue-based opinions as it was to understand America's relatively small number of more deeply held social myths. Interests of the 1920s mastered more than just fitting with Jeffersonian ideals, beliefs in agrarian populism, and other deeply revered and existent virtues of sweeping public sentiment. At least substantial parts of that public were getting informed, not just having their myths tickled. As John Mueller concluded after examining twentieth-century poll data and public policy, don't ever underestimate "the breadth and depth both of the public debate and of the ability of the public to assess what was going on."[12] Lobbying and targeting the public have long been prominent reasons for the public making these assessments.

Public Targets in a Modern Era

If both today's public and the public of the 1920s could comprehend and process issue information, where then is their transformation as lobbying targets? Haven't they always been given maximum prominence? How has lobbying the public changed over seventy years? Much of that change was taking place in the 1920s, particularly as playing with myths gave way to issue education by organized interests. But far from all of the changes were made in that decade.

Modern interest politics is resplendent with examples of using the emergent electronic media, with its proliferating specialized and targeted print sources and previously unimaginable communications and analysis techniques and technologies, to win public access. Interests commonly use computer Web sites today. Simply put, there are better means today for reaching citizens, more specialized magazines and news outlets to use in doing so, and a far more sophisticated knowledge of how to get and hold public attention. Organized interests today are just more capable and their staffs more skilled. The constant evolution of lobbying tools and talents has made the biggest difference in public response since the 1920s.

A few examples best illustrate this. Let's start with the surge of environmental awareness and, subsequently, policy regulation.[13] The environment, and most certainly ecology, were near alien concepts as late as the 1950s. The aliens who used such phrases were not from Mars or Jupiter, but a few academic intellectuals and a rather motley collection of back-to-the-earth cultural isolates. They themselves didn't much reflect mainstream values, but there was a related set of organized interests that very well-fit existing social myths and deeply held public beliefs.

These were conservation groups, and they were linked closely with both Theodore Roosevelt's protect-the-wilderness theme and Jefferson's ideal of stewardship over both property and what lived there. For reasons of basic member interests—hiking, traveling, bird watching, shooting, hunting, fishing, and trapping—conservation groups wanted to protect what they used.[14] The Audubon Society, the National Wildlife Federation, the Sierra Club, and countless local sportsperson groups were the most visible of this lobby. State departments of natural resources grew to be their natural allies. These were policymakers with clients.

Support for conservation and use of the outdoors grew considerably after 1930. Even the United Auto Workers (UAW), through its president, Walter Ruether, aided the cause.[15] Almost none of the rhetoric of restoring environmental order, protecting whole ecosystems, and restricting human use was initially evident. Conservationists just wanted more game and more pristine wildernesses in which to play. Like most Americans, Ruether just wanted to be able to be in lovely places, for him the UAW's northern Black Lake retreat.

Nonetheless, it became apparent eventually to conservation activists that natural resources remained in decline despite public policy efforts to reverse those trends. Government couldn't just keep planting more fish if its planted ones only gagged and died. That realization prompted greater appreciation by conservation interests of those previously isolated scientific ecofreaks and their rather odd reports about broadening attention to whole natural systems and entire environments—not just to species or parks. While conservation interests subsequently and faithfully took on that broadening agenda, all in pursuit of self-serving wants, policymakers did not, especially not the elected ones. When first confronted, they saw too much conflict and competition with other social and economic goals in this new environmentalism. Businesses would be hurt; jobs would be lost; costs of compliance would be excessive. Releasing a few fish or gamebirds was inexpensive—and therefore good—but limiting river or air pollution in industrial regions was not—so therefore bad. Few public officials then embraced, or even gave the least credibility to, the switch from conservation wants to environmentalism.[16] At least for several years.

These groups, mostly one at a time, redefined their targets and moved to long-term strategies of creating public education and awareness. But where to start? An ecological emphasis based on a previously unrecognized science was hardly of any more concern to most citizens than it had been to policymakers. Few would watch rather boring reports on TV or read them in the paper. Children, through their elementary school teachers, were targeted instead. Teachers were better educated than the general public, and they, at that level, usually taught some basic science. They also needed materials, especially inexpensive and even free ones. The former conservation groups distributed nicely prepared environmental materials for use in classes, most notably the National Wildlife Federation's *Ranger Rick* magazine. It was sort of a comic book combined with a newsletter.

These organizations also reached out to help teachers with their own continuing education, both in professional association seminars and at the collegiate levels. Issues that could involve children were developed as projects. Films were made. Dramatic footage of destruction was incorporated as technology increased that capacity. Curricula were designed as models for teachers. Computer-generated lists were maintained. Requests for information were encouraged and quickly processed. Data were collected. Opinion polls were taken—of teachers, children, parents, and the public. Using electronic networks, local activists were asked to help the schools, and to report back on progress. Group employees and sometimes hired consultants attended and presented materials at educational meetings. The media was encouraged to cover and report environmental projects from local schools, not just from that nebulous and faceless world of science.

In a steady progression, issue education moved from the elementary school level to secondary schools, to parents, to colleges and universities, and then to the general public. A critical part of this mainstreaming was popularizing a few new and easily understood words such as "ecology" but otherwise speaking out on behalf of such old values as songbirds, the wilderness, bears, and healthy air and water. That ancient value of responsible stewardship was also resurrected, with its mythic and also biblical connotations. As the progression continued, there were a great number of very relevant ideas that the public could conjure up as reasons to support environmentalism.[17] Voters could even very easily talk politics about this once incomprehensible stuff.

The result was that the policymakers and environmental opponents found considerable difficulty in keeping escalating environmental wants off the public agenda. Policymakers responded, of course. A new social myth of environmental responsiveness was developing. With each new and initially small step, environmental protection was obtained successfully from municipal and state service facilities, then from industries, and eventually from the protected agricultural sector. All that policy change became possible only because the priorities of the public had been transformed from simply liking the outdoors to, very idealistically, saving the planet.[18] Quite obviously, this environmental strategy was a huge and sophisticated advance in the lobbying techniques pioneered by the Farm Bureau, the Anti-Saloon League, and the early providers of boilerplate. Not a new concept, of course, but certainly a technology-based transformation applied by a coalition of emerging organized interests along with a few much older ones.

Stories of the rise in political access of the God-fearing religious right, institutional reformists who promise to stop political corruption, and anti-tax activists all have their own unique variations.[19] But there are similarities among them. What they and environmental groups each have in common is tapping into, through modern technologies, what large percentages of the public can easily comprehend, become familiar with, relate to, respect, and see as appropriate policy responses. People *have* to favor morality, clean government, and lower taxes. They, in general, will see these as good issues.

That's why several interests that are otherwise lacking in mainstream popularity still manage to appeal to the public by using very indirect ideals or some of those old myths. Tobacco interests in the 1990s couch their opposition to regulation in terms of people's freedom of choice. They don't praise cancer sticks. Homeless advocates never say, "Hug a derelict." Rather, they emphasize that large numbers of children also are suffering, an intolerable example of man's inhumanity to man. Gay and lesbian groups are hardly publicly popular, so they appeal to the broader public, not principally for understanding but for nothing more than a reaffirmation of basic human rights. Rights! Americans know all about those, especially since the civil rights battles of the 1960s.

Where else is there commonality among these different movements, especially in terms of likely policy impact? From Christians to tobacco, all six of these interests kept or won substantial public access. They each found ongoing listeners within the public, people who followed the issues based not necessarily upon the obvious, but upon the easily marketable, the acceptable. Emphasizing the acceptable but not the unpopular was the spin that all of these interests shared. They also reached that public marketplace in ways impossible in the 1920s. Christian fundamentalists used TV along with the press (so has the government reformist group Common Cause). The Christian Coalition would have gone nowhere without television. Preachers had their own cable networks. And where but on television do most Americans even listen, at least a little, to the political demands of gays and lesbians, of people who sell tobacco, of homeless folks, and of rather socially abnormal tax rebels? The Internet, e-mail communications, and mass, but select mailings are used as well. It's so easy to just sit home and take in messages. As a result, this new electronic wizardry is a real growth industry in lobbying.

Combined with old and familiar messages, new technologies have then continued to make the public even better and more accessible targets of interests. Interests can far better pull strings and push buttons today than they could in the 1920s. The idea of such lobbying is simple: Make the public understand the interest and its fit with what Americans value and cherish. If lobbies win such support, then the public matters politically in its own right, in largely irreversible fashion. Certainly policymakers pay attention. The idea goes on; never let some ideas and issues just die of neglect.

The Media: Interest Partner or Follower?

Quite apparently the media plays some significant role in the evolving transformation of the public as targets of lobbying, but how much? Why? Also, is that media role changing? In a very useful analysis of one newspaper, the *Toledo Blade*, Reo Christenson helped sort through those answers years ago.[20] The newspaper reflected six characteristics: a penchant for making advocacy judgments, a desire to lead, a willingness to follow the general public mood, a sense of appropriate timing in getting attention, a competitive advantage over other information sources on those issues with which the paper dealt, and credibility on the issues it reported. As a consequence, the *Toledo Blade* was well worth targeting by organized interests. The United Auto Workers liked to promote its problems with employers in the paper, and the coverage was extensive. Today's mass media shares all of these characteristics in varying degrees, and it sometimes gives extensive coverage over several weeks' time.

A few other scholars of journalism add particularly significant findings that also are important in understanding organized interests and their lobbying of media targets. First of all, political reporters are perfectly willing to get and secure information from whatever sources they can find, from press releases to off-the-record comments by anonymous political insiders.[21] Burdensome deadlines and limited budgets account for the need to use those sources.[22] So does the desire to report appealing stories for their audiences. Not surprisingly, a widespread view exists both among the public and the media that a certain level of political bias invariably enters the news.[23]

Nobody really cares much about that bias, at least in general terms. Credibility still exists. News also is presented in a highly orchestrated manner by reporters, but even more so by those they cover.[24] The sources, that is. When Citibank lobbied for newspaper coverage, the *Wall Street Journal* didn't turn to a debtors' group for another perspective on bankruptcy laws. Biases only increase as a result, in large part because those who are covered understand that reporters can be misled.[25] As investigative reporting—or the propensity of journalists to attack those they cover—has grown in stature and application, reporters have become far more willing to make attention-grabbing charges on the basis of less than hard evidence.[26] More bias enters and more easily.

More than bias matters, however. Those who study press relationships find routinely that reporters develop frequently revisited sources among public officials.[27] Because of the issue concerns of both, it's also obvious that reporters feel an obligation to cover organized interests.[28] There may be a story, maybe there should be a story. When two or more interests are in conflict, generally all get at least some chance at presenting their views. That provides more story, except when coverage of some oddballs doesn't seem warranted, as with debtors' groups. With media responsibility directed at exposing interests and others that might prove to be the bad guys, public-interest-style groups and politically disadvantaged interests certainly get more favorable and frequent coverage than do business interests.[29] They do, that is, if they seem to evoke sympathy. Citizen group stories seem inherently more appealing than, for example, electric company executives' complaints. These citizen group stories are more likely to be listened to or read than business complaints. Businesses then are less likely than other interests to cultivate the media. Nonetheless, a great many business interests do it when the need comes up, such as with tobacco. Resources still get directed to where they matter most, not always to favorable places.

All these findings only provide indirect evidence that reporters must work well with lobbyists and other interest staff. Surprisingly, no one has ever systematically studied those relationships. But the relationships do indeed exist, both short- and long-term. Successful Washington lobbyists like to say that over 50 percent of the stories they see in the media each day have their origins with organized interests. While that number is highly debatable, the extensive use of such media targeting is not.[30] During debates over health care reforms, literally dozens of medical, insurance, and labor groups took different complaints to the media and won lots of often conflicting stories.

Other examples illustrate these points. No single interest wins more attention than the Center for Science in the Public Interest (CSPI), predominantly a nutrition lobby. In the early to mid-1990s, it had a high profile on TV and in newspapers. CSPI wins its greatest coverage by blatantly attacking foods, which at first glance seems quite silly and unappealing. People like food after all. But no, the Center lays out quite elaborate campaigns to challenge such things as Olestra as a fat substitute in snack foods, genetically altered tomatoes, and wide varieties of restaurant foods. Unhealthful ingredients are displayed, and possible side effects are discussed; high fat and nasty cholesterol content are revealed. And, of course, strokes and heart attacks get attention.

Why does CSPI get such great coverage? For several reasons. The Center claims, in an overly exaggerated way, to be about cutting-edge science. Credibility as such is instantaneous. Great visuals are possible in covering the Center: obese people lined up at McDonalds, dripping, gooey cheeseburgers from Bennigans, and Chinese cooks loading up their woks with bubbling cooking oils. All of those things are appealing because of the timing of this coverage in a health-conscious era. People want to know about their own or their neighbors' sins. Spreading guilt also is nice, especially when the warnings are seen by reporters as both helping media consumers as well as turning viewer heads attentively. This feeds journalistic ambitions about doing investigation, going on the attack.

The Center also carefully solicits reporters, especially those at *CBS News*. Advantages of solicitation abound. Friendly people get good coverage if they have newsworthy ideas. Plus when one source, such as CBS, reports a good story, others follow the contagion. Center materials also are easy both to understand and to use. It's science without scientific mumbo jumbo. Science is good, but reading its results, of course, is bad, or at least too difficult. Reporters' time is thus conserved by Center staff. Deadline pressures are minimized. Budget costs are low. Moreover, individual reports can be, without harm, pushed back to future newscasts and editions on particularly busy news days. Finally, reporters have formed warm relationships with the Center's director, Michael Jacobsen. Jacobsen keeps coming back, offering great visual clips, protecting the public, being helpful, and he looks so darned healthy posing in the park in his jogging suit. In consequence, few have ever checked on either the quality of the Center's science or whether the public really follows these reports. Everything is simply accepted and well-received.

What policy goals does the Center maintain? Greater authority for the Food and Drug Administration and its increased political freedom from Congress, plus reformed nutritional standards. Increased regulation of what people can buy from private sources is also a goal. Extensive scrutiny of any new food products is desired, especially those that are "unnaturally produced through biotechnology." Protection of natural foods ranks high. Those goals are good for a start. They give the Center lots of different complaints, but all come from a common focus on food purity. This gives CSPI a media and public identity as well as some variety.

The Center for Science in the Public Interest is hardly unique in its approach. The tobacco industry behaved very similarly for decades. Phillip Morris was everywhere in the media and in the public eye: promoting its products, the economic value of its sales, the company's contribution to farming, its help to university research, and certainly the allure of smoking. The company cultivated the media, won friends, supplied stories, and was rewarded with more than one newsperson puffing away reflectively while on camera. Several of these old friends persist, assisting tobacco interests in getting time and space to tell their side in medical conflicts and to spin the stories of smokers' rights, non-smoking uses of the leaves in science, and the economic value of international sales. More than most businesses, the tobacco industry never avoided working with and targeting the media. Its interests either had no fear, or on the other hand, the fear was too great to inspire reluctance.

Other examples can be found across the spectrum of organized interests. The American Agriculture Movement premised its populist protests of 1977 on the likelihood of winning sympathetic media coverage. The American Association of Retired Persons, on becoming aware of any political threats to Social Security or Medicare benefits, always goes first to the press, not into official offices to play the contact game. As one of its lobbyists chuckled: "And the bastards always fall all over themselves to get us on the air. I'd really like sometime to preempt *Monday Night Football*. Just a dream, I guess."

One interesting example shows how this works, with great effectiveness, on emerging and sensitive political issues. In fact, things can't really be more sensitive than when insurance companies and farm interest groups want to wage war on those ever-popular and beautiful herds of wild deer. After all, efforts by state officials to increase and protect deer populations have been extensive, costly, and well-publicized. They were all part of the conservation movement, in fact. Deer herds were sold very persuasively to the general public as fun to watch, economically and biologically important to hunt in carefully managed but limited numbers, and symptomatic of a healthy and harmonious environment. Can there be a reversal of opinions? Or is this a terminally bad issue? How did economic interests move to reduce state deer herds with all this against them?

The answer was simple. Farm and insurance industries sought first to redefine the issues, and in so doing neutralize hostile reactions. Laid out was a carefully articulated policy goal: reduction of deer herds in selected areas where the animals exceeded ideal populations. Only some states with high populations were targeted. Then, with equal care, the economic and personal damages of the presence of too many deer were emphasized. Automobile accidents and repair costs were soaring, it was reported, and insurance costs were increasing substantially as a result. Human lives were being lost in more and more driving accidents. All that awful propaganda was presented, very directly, as news. Farm financial losses were shown as staggering. Some farmers told how they loved the deer but had such high losses that future of the family, and maybe even that of the farm itself, was threatened. Almost anyone could relate to these problems.

Neither insurance nor farm interests argued that deer shouldn't be plentiful, that hunting opportunities should be lost. This neutralized the image of sportspersons as likely foes, at least for a while—or at least long enough to win a competitive head start and, therefore, an advantage politically. Nor did these interests argue that homeowners suffered too, as deer rummaged through their yards and plantings. That argument had only resulted some years earlier in intense and escalatingly hostile conflicts between land developers and conservation interests. The appearance of selfishness had to be avoided. Keep up the spin on the public interest—accidents and economic loss, not suburbanites' gardens.

State legislatures were avoided initially, as were state departments of natural resources. And neither farmers nor insurers took out advertisements, which could have been seen as too self-serving. Advocates of smaller herds took their news right to the media, with an emphasis on television and high status outlets. Nightly news shows featured bloody accidents and downtrodden—rarely angry—farmers, maybe with some of them crying. Great visuals as well.

Similar, but always regional footage, was shown in states across nearly the entire continent. In Michigan, even before local reporters were targeted statewide, the state's most listened to radio station editorialized on several prime time broadcasts against the deer. And Michigan's only statewide newspaper headlined the problem. Both media were cultivated by organized interests to do so. The same went on in other states. When influential citizens were already talking about the problems, only then were local and regional media targeted. Even in prime hunting locations, coverage was abundant, one-sided, and well-spun.

Does targeting the media, though, truly pay off? Or is it only a last ditch struggle of desperate interests? Evidence shows that it certainly pays, and not just for the unfortunate few. Perhaps, in fact, the least fortunate can use the media to least advantage. Debtor advocates certainly didn't win sympathy at the *Wall Street Journal*. By highlighting the possibilities of change, as Doris Graber explains, the media creates believability.[31] If the message is clearly understandable, that is. For the first time for much of the public, it brings forward alternatives. Best of all, it brings alternatives to which people can relate if they actually think over other policy options. As the public realizes the need for options, deer herds get reduced, the Food and Drug Administration finds an hospitable environment for food safety regulation, and protesting farmers win costly policy concessions even in a budget-strapped, inflation-fearing era.

Targeting the media also works for those organized interests that wish to maintain policy advantages, the things that people already get and like. Politicians are extraordinarily reluctant to mess around with retirement benefits of the elderly. For years, tobacco was almost beyond policy reproach. Only when health problems became largely undeniable in the face of science and known by nearly everyone did public officials forcefully attack tobacco use. The tobacco industry's competitive advantage was lost at that point. For the use of both interests, the media was formidable. And neither senior citizens nor tobacco companies are truly disadvantaged. Nor are farmers, insurance companies, or many of the other interests that routinely target the media for their lobbying.

Is this then a change since the 1920s? Of course it is. It's one of the most evolutionary aspects of lobbying. Lobbying the media is far different in its evolution than has been simply targeting the public. The technical innovations and more sophisticated techniques explain a greater change in media than public relationships with organized interests. A lot has transpired since boilerplate was in vogue. Therefore, from the perspective of interests, the power—

and the chief target—is often that of the media rather than the public. In this view, the public only rides along.

In particular, a kind of odd mix has emerged in using the media. It's straight-forward reporting of what interests want, blended with an often visual and sometimes just rhetorical display of symbols. It's more than just tapping into social myths, though. It's creating new myths, like the less than legendary myth of the Barbie-Doll-as-American-woman. With all its popular imagery, modern advertising gets used in order to demonstrate, variously, how very healthy milk must be, how deadly deer accidents are, and how horrible life is for very old and low-income Social Security recipients. It's propaganda, and the media has to be persuaded by lobbyists to use it in ways that arouse public imagination.[32] But it works. Only with its use will the public or policymakers be affected, taking on or reinforcing values to protect milk, drivers, and the elderly.

This transforming emphasis on targeting the media has solidified the importance of TV, radio, magazines, and newspapers for most types of interests—either those playing offense or defense in policy making.[33] This goes for both old interests and new, passing something or trying to kill a proposal, starting an idea or keeping one alive. Targeting the media is not just a last-ditch political strategy. Without the modern media, the public could still be reached, but not in ways to which people have become so accustomed and responsive. People can be reached through things they find unfamiliar.

Does This Really Fit?

Is targeting the media such a cynical, even ugly task that it hardly fits what's best or important for the public, those who truly need political information? And isn't the historically evident tendency to reach the public by alluding to the myths citizens hold, their beliefs, and the things they just plain like and fear even more of that cynical manipulation? Aren't both only interest politics at its worst? No, no, and no.

Far more than merely cynical manipulation is at work. This isn't just lying by use of a well-designed spin. Murray Edelman's classic analysis shows what else goes on.[34] The spin is there, of course, but wait a moment and think about it. As Edelman explains, most people need a political controversy, a head-turning experience, or they won't act. More basically, they won't even pay attention. They simply lay back on old predispositions. Symbols have to be constructed by someone. If they're not, American politics fails to evoke new interests among people. It then loses its democratic aspirations; lethargy sets in. Symbols range from basic American myths to a particularly attention-grabbing TV presentation by someone like Right-to-Die advocate Jack Kevorkian.

When the media reports a compelling story people pay attention, even if the story's planted by the religious right or by cigarette manufacturers. At least more people care about having those messages than they otherwise would. And their attentions are issue directed, focusing not just on the problem but also on what can be done about it. In the process, politics and government take on more of the appearance that U.S. constitutional founders once hoped for.

The same thing happens when interests bring up old myths or socially favored products. Heads turn. People think twice about things. Issues become hot potatoes, things to juggle, at least in public minds. People reflect on what it is that they like or hold in disdain, and they think about why they feel that way. Charles Elder and Roger Cobb summarized this phenomenon especially well: The use of symbols is necessary in creating stakeholders on public business.[35] Stakeholders are those who see that an issue matters personally to them. The more complex and less easily understood the political world, the more important are the symbols, and the less likely are self-aware stakeholders to emerge without them. One can realistically ask: Where would feminist political goals be if it wasn't, first, for *Ms.* magazine and, second, for sympathetic mass media reporting? The answer is: less advanced than they now are.

Today's political world is certainly complex, and easy to ignore because of it. The public needs all the stakeholder awareness that can be generated. However, doesn't the public just follow meekly? Is there any independence of thought? Countless examples show lots of independence. Not everyone went West, or wanted to, or even agreed with those who did. Lots of people didn't want western settlement. Options were considered after the appeals to manifest destiny and agrarianism were held out. Likewise, anti-abortion rhetoric inspired pro-abortion arguments, and the problem as well as the degree to which any ban should be extended both came to be hotly contested. Not everyone, of course, follows diet standards of the Center for Science in the Public Interest, nor do they want to. Nor do they believe Center messages. Watch the crowds still line up at McDonalds, Bennigans, or the neighborhood Chinese restaurant.

What's long taken place in American politics has been a broad-scale creation and adoption of otherwise neglected and ignored issues. Much of it results from organized interests. Mathew Carey's industrial policy eventually came about, years and years later. Intentions to settle the West overpowered laissez-faire tendencies. The politics of ethics and morality of the 1990s, both religious and secular, added a wide range of demands and controversies to the public agenda. Federal lobbying reform even passed as a consequence, despite the reluctance of public officials to pass it. Sure, maybe some citizens were manipulated on these and countless other issues. Perhaps some people reacted without thinking. But more importantly, new stakeholders indeed moved forward new issues, and laws and regulations were passed in response. Old ones were thrown out as well, and some proposed ones were killed.

None of this could have happened if politics had been treated as a debate society, housed only in auditoria reserved for such symbol-free forums. Almost nobody would have been there. And certainly those in attendance would not have looked much like mainstream America.

So yes, lobbying the public and the media as a means of outreach to citizens really does fit—and has long fit—well with what Americans value and expect. It's been found that publics do behave differently in politics when they don't get their news, their information.[36] And such lobbying fits what American politics, as democratic and open, supposedly requires as well. Such targeting fits, not by standards of the loftiest philosophical ideals, but rather by reaching people through what they like. It works for both interests and society by being entertaining, by informing, by reducing problems to manageable ideas, by being easy to consume, and by not requiring much in the way of response. Even agreement with the ideas isn't a prerequisite to thinking about issues in new ways.

Summary and Highlights

One of the frequent journalistic critiques of lobbying is that it's an elite process, a one-on-one, man-against-man contact game. But that process is neither quite so macho—yes, women also lobby and become policymakers—nor anywhere near so elitist. Regular people enter the picture. It could hardly be otherwise in a politically open, democratic government, with its representative structure and numerous points of policymaker access each sharing power. The notion of lobbying as a closed process was debunked in Chapter Three. In extending that analysis, this chapter looked at the specific importance of the public and of the media as it actively reaches people.

Both the public and the media become meaningful and frequent targets of lobbying, in accordance with the way U.S. governing institutions were designed. Probably because of that uniquely American institutional structure, interest politics since nearly its onset has emphasized influencing the general public. The intent has been to create a favorable popular sentiment that largely captures, in turn, the choices of public officials. Don't, as one U.S. senator explained, "screw around with what people believe. You won't win. You *will* lose." People's beliefs are bad issues to attack and attacks tend to be avoided, as will be seen later in this text.

Mathew Carey recognized that unavoidable element of American politics, and therefore of interest politics. So did railroad and finance executives when they wished to develop the West through public policy intervention. Even tobacco interests have long understood playing to popular themes, not just creating consumers in a vacuum. Interest representatives have always looked for popular myths, ideas, ideals, and products that can, in turn, be used to latch onto and market their issues. They've succeeded so often because their messages were entertaining, informative, easy to comprehend, and very much expected in a politically engaged society. Moreover, the messages of organized interests have long been delivered through familiar media, from bombastic stump speakers such as William Jennings Bryan to ads for tantalizing and healthy beef recipes sold through prime-time TV commercials.

Playing with myths—of agrarianism, of stewardship, of manifest destiny, of human rights, of the glamorous—characterized the

earliest attempts to lobby the public in our nation. Myths are stories of a society's "sacred history," part true and part reduced to
simplified symbols. [37] "You'll be fiercely independent in the West"
was the mythic way to say, "Things are harsh out there. If you
can't take care of yourself exceptionally well, you'll just die. Starve,
be shot, whatever." The first statement was true; the second was far
more accurate. Myths such as these were the only things socially
shared, and so they linked a very diverse population that otherwise
had little means for communicating information. Of course, organized interests were limited in both what they could get across and
how they could do it. No one can sell just anything, and it's even
harder for lobbies to sell ideas when broad and skeptical public
scrutiny comes into play. Thus, interests tinkered effectively with
myths.

However, as communications techniques and technologies
were refined, more direct issue appeals were favored by interests.
Appeals were made that stood more on their own merits, or the
familiarity with which they were received by citizens. Myths mattered less when society had improved means of sharing ideas,
common values, and its basic identity. This ideological transition
was only possible, though, because of an evolving and highly
cooperative media. Newspapers, TV, and the like—or at least their
reporters—wanted to lead as well as be read and heard. As a consequence, they became targets of lobbying, not new ones but certainly more primary ones.

That evolution from manipulating myths to just playing with
the immediately popular was accompanied, it seems, by one significant change. People had always possessed some degree of personal
interest in actually judging what it was that organized interests
wanted: "What's in it for me? Is it really for me?" But with changes
in reaching the public, there was much more of that scrutiny to be
found. A well-lobbied modern media opened up issue options and
policy ideas that the public never would have considered on its
own. Citizens might well have liked to think of those things, as
apparently they still do. But, in real life, they depended on someone else to formulate definitions of problems and possible
responses to them, or just to think things up. That's why by the
late 1980s, most business lobbies tried at least sometimes to reach
the public first. It's also why large multiclient lobbying firms

devoted lots of money and manpower to public relations. Boiler-plate had been replaced by boiler rooms, or office communications centers with lots of electronic and communications equipment.

The politics of the 1990s certainly shows that type of interest involvement increasingly at work, as well as such lobbying at its greatest efficiency. In some ways, as the 1920s were, the 1990s have been a benchmark decade, especially for smaller and emerging interests—not just for the rich guys, the old organizations. Using the media, popular sentiment, and carefully planned messages, even once sacred cows have been successfully attacked, slaughtered, turned into bad issues. Megan's Law is the best example. Seven-year-old Megan Kanka was killed in 1994 by a paroled child sex offender who, unbeknownst to residents, moved into her neighborhood. A massive media campaign ensued, led mostly by a small local following that grew. With lots of national coverage, tears, public anguish, and resulting public outrage, Congress passed a law requiring community notification when criminals with child sex convictions relocated. When the public responded, it was clear that the protection of children was more popular and more deserving in the public's eyes than that of time-honored civil liberties.

Interests wanting the death penalty gained increased national support in the same way two years later, much to the shock of their opponents who cried, "Unfair, unfair." Polly Klass, age twelve, became a national symbol when kidnapped and brutally killed. The family grieved; the media covered it; death penalty advocates showed up; and before long, Polly became the image of the need for legal change. Campaigning politicians of various parties invoked her name, over and over and over.

Even automobile air bag regulations were changed that year in the same way. It happened almost overnight, when over fifty child death cases were graphically reported to and by the media. An advocacy group had emerged, worked the media, and lobbied public officials after winning attention. Federal laws favoring air bags, once felt cast in stone, were quickly altered. Debates over what else to do to protect kids from air bags went on seemingly forever. Public officials, including President Bill Clinton, fell all over themselves in order to react to these new public sentiments. As Americans have seen for almost twenty-five decades, a newly alarmed or aware public means considerably more than any old, but now tired and irrelevant yet once sacrosanct value. It does, that is, if it's lobbied appropriately through the technologies of the time.

While none of this may be appealing to many Americans, and while several of these public policy changes or proposals may be disliked by many of them, one thing remains clear about targeting citizens: It really does fit well both the expectations of the general public and, in some twisted way, basic precepts of American government. It fits especially since that public can't be sold just any old idea.

5

Targeting Policymakers

The targeting of public officials by lobbyists has been written about so frequently—and often so well—that it almost seems like there's nothing else to say. Besides, Chapter Three explained what it involves. Alan Rosenthal produced the best analysis ever of how lobbying, as it's centered around the contact game, takes place.[1] The analysis is both thorough and sequenced in such a way that readers can trace a clear progression in the pathway to winning influence. According to Rosenthal, lobbyists determine their interests, learn the rules in which they do business, stick with those rules in building political relationships, play the political game of winning friends by being friends, generate broader political support for their goals, and, finally, explicitly make their cases.[2] It's a little bit artificially tidy and linear, but Rosenthal states accurately most all that there is to it.

Two other wonderful accounts of going after policymaker targets stand out and add to Rosenthal's work. By looking at specific cases, Jeffrey Birnbaum demonstrated how deals are made through a systematic expansion of issues, interests, contacts, and public officials.[3] In a nutshell, lobbyists use those they know to meet policy players whom they previously didn't know. Then they swap support. James Deakin artfully summarized what lobbyists do as their bottom line and why they succeed. In the broadest descriptive sense, lobbyists are only "out to make life easier" for office holders.[4] Deakin then outlined how lobbyists have done just that.

So a considerable amount is known about lobbyists and their relations with public officials. There exists a well-ritualized process, a strategic and expansive avenue of success, and a specific route to winning favor while traversing that avenue. For example, always stop at the corner candy store. More accurately, always check with the committee chairs. And so on.

What's left to say? Well, as a start, one can move beyond discussing what lobbyists do and look more clearly at the extent that it matters for public policy. And, also, the importance of the contact game should be played down a bit in favor of those many other interrelated lobbying tasks and techniques, to emphasize more why the contact game doesn't work by itself. By moving beyond an inventory of what lobbyists do to directly target policymakers, scholarly inquiry can move both backward and forward: backward in the sense that the evolution of the lobbying process over time can be used to shed light on long-term policy effects; forward in theory in that analysis can help judge whether interaction between lobbyists and policymakers—as Rosenthal, Birnbaum, and Deakin seem to imply—is indeed the central and most vital feature of the lobbying process. Or is there, as earlier chapters of this book have emphasized, more than that at the heart of policy success? Don't lobbyists need to cover all their potential targets?

This chapter revisits much of the theory of organized interests. It's a kind of academic heresy, questioning lots of scholarly convention. But it also agrees with and makes substantial use of several interesting works. Attention first is on the evolution of political relationships between lobbyists and policymakers: Why and how did they come about? Then attention turns to shifts in those relationships, particularly in response to the changing institutional structures of American government. If lobbyists have been so important, why do they constantly need to keep adjusting their strategies? Is politics only like competitive sports, where a player initially fools the rest of the league, the league soon catches up to the player, and then the player learns new skills in order to stay in business? Yes, it is, in a way.

What this chapter finally emphasizes is the profound difficulty—as well as the general necessity—of organized interests keeping life easy for public officials. It also emphasizes that making things easy can't *always* be done, particularly at certain times and under some political conditions. Nor do interests *always* want official life to be all that comfortable. For these reasons, the relationships between lobbyists and their official targets are mired in considerable paradox: friendly but hostile, generally honest but resplendent with suspicion, always open but circumspect, centered on the few but conspicuously attentive to numerous players. Each irony gets attention here. Targeting policymakers is, it seems, far more than lobbyists joyfully building cozy political relationships, especially if they want to win rather than merely play the game.

The only thing that has long tied these relationships together is the need to figure out what should be done policywise. As one very smart but irreverent veteran lobbyist put it, "Those bastards who hold office and fill up staff jobs wouldn't know their penises if we didn't point them out. Probably all the better, eh? The level of awareness and understanding in national government is deplorable. Without lobbyists, these jerks don't know what to do or why to do it!" Overstated probably, but once again as revealing an assessment as those of Rosenthal, Birnbaum, and Deakin. As will be seen, you can't always inform people by being nice, by having only a friendly chat.

Institutionalizing the Contact Game

Emphasizing policymakers' need for information is nothing new for interest theory.[5] Indeed, it's nearly the most common point raised in all those scholarly volumes. Yet, even as a common point, it needs some brief revisiting because of what it implies as truth.

The first thing to recall is that lobbyists—who like to call themselves collectively the third house of Congress or of state legislatures—haven't been so greatly popular or revered, not even by their policymaker targets. Public officials have just used advocates, not loved them. Maybe American government would find it necessary to invent lobbyists and organized interests if they didn't already exist. But don't count on public officials voting overwhelmingly for a revival of the third house if it were suddenly to disappear. A congresswoman said it best: "There must be another way, can't there be?" Remember also what President Cleveland thought of the pressure: hardly that it was wonderful, or so essential. Easy to live with? The Wall Street lobby was never that.

Ambivalence tinged with resigned acceptance better characterizes public officials' attitudes about lobbyists. Taking the comfortable with the blows to the back of the head, it seems, is their resigned view. History teaches why. In 1808, when the term "lobbyist" was first being used in congressional records, these Washington representatives were listened to in large part because there was nothing else to do in the nation's isolated capital.[6] Also, of course, governing was fraught with difficulties over what should happen in public policy. The result was not that lobbyists should simply be protected by constitutional freedoms of assembly and speech.

Since those lobbyists were going to be there anyway, use them. With boredom aplenty, strangers *could* easily walk up to a U.S. senator in the hallway. Those who entertained were a particularly valued commodity. Got a party? How about an idea to go with it? Those were the dual legislative hopes of the early American era. The easy approaches made Washington life a bit more tolerable, if not itself easy. What developed in the eighteenth century and a bit later were much anticipated relationships between those stuck in Washington and those who went there to help them. What also happened, with lobbyists corralling their own favored policymakers, was that it became exceptionally difficult for a strong political party system to develop. Legislators and executives were played against one another, both within and between branches of government.[7] Another sports analogy suggests that those on the same partisan teams lacked cohesion and discipline. The coaches couldn't control the players and their entourages. So much for the good.

Now the bad. A fascinating counterpoint to Mathew Carey, Thurlow Weed was one of the first Washington lobbyists, and a New Yorker as well, who parlayed social networking into considerable policy influence.[8] The New York connection helped, with Weed at the center of the U.S. social world. While Philadelphian Carey saw influence emanating from lobbying the public and then organizing manufacturers, Weed first followed stump and media practices and, with his reputation established, simply reverted to making friends with policymakers, much more so than did Carey. Weed's career was finally made by cultivating industrial leaders, such as Cornelius Vanderbilt, and local political bosses, such as New York's William Marcy Tweed, and through their friendship putting public officials into their company and companionship. Weed also became a party operative, for which he's best known, managing the Whig Party's 1848 electoral campaign. Indeed he was an ultimate insider, but one who'd proved himself as well at the grassroots. Weed moved from railing against slavery in the South to becoming "the father of the lobby," the veritable and always present point man for arguing and pursuing methods of economic growth and development for the United States.[9] Where Carey only made a few inroads into industrial policies by spreading its gospel, the partisan Weed made things go much further, still managing to work both political parties of his day as they came and went.

Lobbyists from development and settlement interests, or the Wall Streeters, plus numerous other factions kept pre–Civil War sectional differences obvious and acute in Washington.[10] Theirs was not just a moral crusade, as public rhetoric so often emphasized. Mostly they advised on advancing national business needs. That was where Weed's linkage of slavery in the widely perceived-to-be-awful South merged with national business needs. Prime among lobbyist complaints were the anti-business sentiments of what they saw as a paternalistic and backward southeastern region, the section of the country that not incidentally ardently opposed western expansion. To get rid of the South was the solution, or to take those states over. When reorganization of the largely rural South after the war was necessary, development lobbyists and their allies in office led the change for harsh and repressive radical reconstruction. This was more of the getting-rid-of-the-bad-guys school of thought.

Development interests wanted and won southern destabilization, something that moderate public officials such as Abraham Lincoln had argued against. What historians often see as the sensible preferences of Lincoln gave way through contact-game lobbying to punitive treatment, or the "Great Barbecue of the South" as it was called by historian Kenneth Stampp.[11] The development and settlement lobby, which had already scored so big policywise in 1862, was a deciding factor. Thurlow Weed mattered as a big, big, big fixer.

How was the fix put through? Did information about the value of national economic growth carry the day? In part it did, of course, as networks of friends and cozy relationships developed, shared their ideas, and came to commonly hold the same values. Discussion *can* bring consensus, or at least agreement. And it did then. A Washington-based vision of the nation emerged and, in turn, was further sold to a willing and already inclined public. But it wasn't just entertainment, brandy, cigars, and fine dining that lobbyists used to make life easier for public officials of the day. That's what brings the ambivalence of public officials into the story.

Bribery, corruption, and simply buying votes became instrumental in making political relationships productive. Blackmail worked too. Nothing more than hard cash from organized business was need to make life easier for many public officials. Brandy was nice, but dollars in a congressman's pocket were far better. Mark Hanna, who succeeded Weed as "king of the lobbyists" from his Ohio law offices some years later, certainly informed policymakers of what best to do.[12] And he had clout because he, too, was a party operative. Who in office knew what business needed to win national economic growth? Not many. But Hanna succeeded even more by just paying off public officials, which wasn't all that difficult, since Congress was more party dependent and more sensitive to national controversies as a consequence. Lobbyists didn't have the same urgency to speak of what constituents wanted as they do today.

Hanna and his allies, nearly single-handedly, outlined what strategies government should follow in opening up natural resources and regions for business use. Both partisan leaders and congressional committee leaders were targeted. Then the lobbyists networked among private and public officials to sell those strategies. They indeed were brokers, or middlemen. And, simplistically explained, they made it all happen—at least in a supportive public environment where myths also mattered. The myths won the public, leaving policymakers to follow the good life without worry.

Development interests gained by lobbying the public and the media, but they actually won legislatively by being truly on the inside of Washington politics. Hanna was both an ardent Republican and an active "good government," that is, a civil service and anti-machine reformer. Yet even many of his best policymaking friends had doubts about whether corruption, as Hanna practiced it, was the proper way to run such a fine government. Many people had been abused. Moreover, many saw the abuses. Developers were so successful and so obvious that, by the middle of reconstruction and after years of corruption, Georgia state legislators took the symbolic but ineffectual action of banning lobbying. Georgians had just seen too much bribery; in fact, at one time, they'd seen it of all but one of their state legislators. And that corruption had been led by one of the state's own U.S. senators, acting as a paid lobbyist while also in office.[13]

Georgia notwithstanding, the contact game of lobbying, no matter how shabby it was, became firmly institutionalized in American politics by the 1870s. In the largest sense, it was part of the creation of a government in America that placed the nation-state at the center of change, as an active problem solver. At least lobbying was widely accepted, and certainly expected, if not exactly beloved behavior. At least on publicly popular concerns, personalized lobbying was a winner. Direct contacts by networking public officials converted public sentiment to government action. Some officials did not feel too guilty about living with lobbyists— what they were lobbying for was popular, after all. Other officials were just offended and, because of their resulting opposition to the insiders, suffered personal and political attacks that weren't all that easy to take. More than one of the opponents were written up in a well-lobbied press as dangerous radicals. Public reputations were destroyed. Lobbyists of the nineteenth century helped make American politics an often bitter battleground, one plagued with hostility and conflict. The third-house guys met legislators and made their threats known. And they conveyed a widespread impression that government and politics were quite sleazy. Many public officials believed it, and the belief prevails even to the present day.

The contact game grew not from what would be considered interest group politics. With the exception of the Granges and their extensive relationships with state legislators who pressured Congress, this wasn't group activity. What was being practiced so effectively by Weed, Hanna, and others who reigned for their own short times as kings of the lobbyists didn't make use of joiners, just of financial patrons. There were institutions, particularly lobbies but also parties. But it *was* interest politics, played with skill by what were seen in Chapter Two as those "other interests": railroads, banks, industrial manufacturers, commercial firms, and the law offices that represented them. All were playing politics because, after the economic collapses of the late 1850s, they needed subsidies in order to move western and southern development forward. Institutions could no longer muster the financial capital to do it on their own. There was then a kind of fuzzy merging of organized interests and parties during those years, which was not startling, since John Aldrich emphasized that American party politics periodically went through metamorphoses.[14] Parties often changed institutionally.

Despite Carey's early efforts to organize business interest groups, such associations gained little acceptance until almost the turn of the century. That was why other interests pioneered the contact game and worked so closely with parties. Groups later followed and refined the paths pioneered by the kings of the lobbyists. The National Association of Manufacturers (NAM) was not only one of the first interest groups that gained a following among firms as joiners, it also was a group that some members of Congress urged to form. Government was doing things that led to industrial policy, and policymakers needed assistance. NAM also became one of the best and most innovative interest groups when it came to winning policymaker friends. It was so good, in fact, that NAM was provided a private office in the U.S. Capitol and, enjoying such proximity to legislators, creatively put the head page of the House of Representatives on its payroll as well as the government payroll. The page became NAM's watchdog, its provider of intelligence and inside information.[15]

That doesn't mean that American interest groups weren't to be found with some frequency in the nineteenth century and even before. Not at all. There were lots of them, not just groups composed of institutions. Farmers were organized well, of course, through the Granges, becoming an organized interest as they attacked the railroads in favor of regulation. Labor groups were even more prolific than politically active farm groups. By the late 1820s and growing in number through 1840, workingmen's groups existed literally throughout industrial cities and regions. Labor organizing continuously increased after 1860, especially in manufacturing industries.[16]

Assorted abolitionist interest groups were also active, as were suffragettes and even utopians. Daniel Shays became an American political legend, famous for his organization of insurrectionist farm followers in the 1780s.[17] Whiskey Rebellion leaders later entrepreneured a similarly strong yet less long-lasting farm interest group in Pennsylvania. Other farmers kept forming interest groups from then until the early 1900s, all organized around social protest.[18] As other interests in their own right, churches greatly aided these interest groups as they became the forerunners of today's American Agriculture Movement, Common Cause, Public Voice, and Consumer Federation of America. Why? These groups were seen widely as advocates of neglected issues of interest to all citizens, or even to outsiders, so some churches felt obligated to help. It was their social responsibility.

The unfortunate thing for all of these interest groups was that very few public officials wanted to grant personal access to their representatives. It was more of that ambivalence to lobbying. That was less true of the preindustrial artisan groups that found homes inside Boss Tweed's Tammany Hall social and partisan order, but they were an exception. Neither the Noble Order of the Knights of Labor nor the Socialist Labor Party found more than a few elected officials who would even talk things over with them. And those who did were malcontents themselves, elected from hotbed political districts, and far removed personally from the political mainstream or the inside of contact-game politics. Nobody within Congress talked to them, even if they were members. The executive branch was almost untouched by interest groups. Cleveland and other presidents certainly didn't want to talk to the rabble when they were already tired of listening to business elites—and overwhelmed by all of them.

As a consequence, the direct lobbying of public officials became part of the American nation-state under four unique conditions. Kenneth Crawford addressed each of them indirectly in 1939.[19] First, insider lobbying was business inspired, led by the need for policymakers to find ways to enhance national economic development. Government officials required the knowledge of financiers and industrialists. Second, the contact game had little to do with mass membership interest groups. It was based on other interests. As such, direct lobbying grew up as suspect, a perversion of sorts regarding democratic theory. This was true even as the public generally supported business goals of western expansion and punitive treatment of the South.

Third, as relationships between lobbyists and public officials became part of the nation-state, participants used them to discourage public and media scrutiny. The myths were enough; the public swallowed all that and were otherwise left out. Back-room politics and assorted images made perceptions of the contact game publicly unpopular. It truly was the sleazy thing to do. Understandably, people complained. Many public officials were likewise against it, particularly as they themselves were left out of considerable opportunities for governance and were often attacked and slandered by the insiders. Many also felt just plain used and unable to add to legitimate policy debates.

Fourth, and finally, the contact game was maintained as much by corruption and bribery as it was by social networking and providing legitimate information and ideas to policymakers. Under those four conditions, it is no wonder that the contact game became both irreversibly part of American politics and a frequently discredited way of making policy decisions, no matter what it contributed to American nation building. The lesson became culturally well-established that mothers shouldn't let their babies grow up to be lobbyists—even if they did make a lot of money and if things happened because of them.

Paying for This Colorful History

Lobbyists and other interest representatives have paid more of a price for the historical evolution of the contact game than just their mothers' dismay. Moreover, that other price has been a high one, affecting the difficulty of how they do their job. There's a prevailing expectation among policy players that someone from each interest must both know well and seek the comfort of those public officials with whom they most routinely meet. Of course, that's impossible, but still expected. Because of that expectation, lobbyists generally try hard to follow it, and interests buy—or more accurately, hire—those individuals who can do it. Beliefs structure behavior. "What I dislike most," noted the previously quoted irreverent woman lobbyist, "is that those assholes in office treat me like I'm some kind of servant. Be there when needed. But be quiet about it. Be quick. And don't expect anything in return for being there. It's as if I've a damned duty to the government." And, she could have added, only speak when asked to do so.

It's a small wonder that such an attitude exists. The legacy of American politics is that personalized lobbying became institutionalized and accepted as elite interests informed and entertained policymakers in out-of-the-way places. The lobbyist mentioned above understood the impact of history quite well: "Right! If Daniel Shays and a lot of other hotheads periodically would have hung a few federal officials from the trees, our jobs would now be much different. Better. We'd strike a little fear, not just shamelessly suck up."

So what? What's the gripe, where's the complaint? It's very simple. As was indicated in the chapter on lobbying techniques, interest representatives not only need to know policymakers, they also need to keep reminding those individuals that the group or institution is still active, involved, and playing the game. And public officials want to know that constituents back home agree with them. Without reinforcement, remember, interest influence is short-lived. What lobbyists gripe about is this constant and personally burdensome contact. They complain that contacts need to be made with far too many policymakers, and they need to be made with officials often irritated or bored with the presence of lobbyists. It's expected, but not felt to be necessary beyond just playing out the lobbying role. "If it wasn't expected," said a lobbyist, "I could win without it."

Things become often absurdly complex because of trying to play the contact game well. After Republicans came to control Congress in the 1990s, one multiclient lobbying and law firm began to feel left out. Verner, Liipfert, Bernhard, McPherson, and Hand had long been a firm linked to Democratic policymakers. What did they do about the need to play contact with Republicans? They hired Bob Dole, the former Senate Majority Leader and 1996 Republican candidate for president. Dole was to help develop lobbying strategy, smooth the way for less recognizable firm lobbyists to actually get into congressional offices, call a few members with his good Republican words, and recruit a few more clients to pay for it all. The Verner firm has developed a superstar complex of sorts, and Dole has recently joined with a few more high-profile former politicos. Former Democratic Senate Majority Leader George Mitchell already worked there, as did former Texas Republican Senator and Treasury Secretary Lloyd Bentsen. Also, a couple of former governors who had especially good access were already on staff. The firm now stands ready to shmooze and yuck it up with just about any policymaker, no matter how hard to reach.

Ernest Griffith identified some reasons for this costly condition—the one lobbyists see as their problem—at about the same time that Crawford was commenting on what he saw as insider lobbying.[20] Crawford's and Griffith's views meshed well. By the 1920s and into the 1930s, lobbyists made their contacts and sought their influence in what Griffith called "whirlpools of activity." These whirlpools of swirling routine contacts were composed of nothing more than the interactions of those who dealt most regularly, even daily, with specific types of public policy, such as trade or labor. According to the whirlpool view, these were the true insiders: the experts, the specialists, the ones who understood the technical aspects of what was covered in legislation and regulation. Defense, treasury issues, trade problems, banking, agriculture, and most major other policy areas produced their own whirlpools, as well as intense consultation between those inside them. The real insiders included members of Congress from the committees having jurisdiction, administrators who planned and analyzed, and— without a doubt—the lobbyists who sought to exercise influence over these individual players. Three points of a triangle, that's what it most reminded observers of in their analogy building.

In at first an academic sense, Griffith started a brushfire. A raft of political observers followed his lead.[21] Scholarly fire bugs set their matches ablaze attempting to understand these whirlpools for several decades. Commentators not only described numerous whirlpools, or subgovernments and iron triangles as they were more generally called, they also came to criticize them. At times nearly all of the ills of American politics were laid at their collective feet. Triangle theory was christened, and there was agreement on its few key features: The whirlpools or triangles brought together all the players who really mattered and were constantly ready and able to play. Dissenting public officials were excluded. And triangles did not bring into play the unorganized public; policy decisions were made through small group discussions, not in public forums. The end product produced, given the obvious interests and jobs of the players, exceptionally narrow public policies.[22] This was seen as constituency politics, that is, taking care of the prime constituents of the insiders. Wherever they were located.[23] Issues that were considered were for bankers, or the military, or road builders, or any other well-organized interest. Public policies, when passed, then rewarded farmers, or the military, or road builders, or whatever interest. Those unorganized to oppose these things lacked a political voice, they had no access.

Triangle theory, with its emphasis on the three points of key legislators, administrators, and lobbyists, went on to explain how this all worked. Again there was scholarly agreement on several matters—never solid evidence, but still agreement. Leaders of the executive branch and legislature exercised poor oversight.[24]

Partisanship, which was always kind of weak anyway, gave way to bipartisan cooperation as politics evolved. In a checks-and-balances-separation-of-powers process, centralization of government floundered. Too much government and too many policy areas explained the reasons why. There was just too much going on and too many players doing the going in, too many little isolated policy places for anyone to keep track of everything. Nobody could integrate it all. The public and media were overwhelmed by all this policy activity and so couldn't care less.[25] Neither could even understand the complexity of the process, so procedural scrutiny was out, gone. Finally, the post-Griffith theorists applied their *coup de grace*; reciprocity between triangles.[26] The various triangles prevailed because each traded off the others, leaving everyone else alone in return for being left alone themselves. Lobbyists worked to see to the triangles being left alone, which of course meant an endless set of lobbying tasks.[27] Public policy quite understandably grew topsy-turvy.[28] Policy bases expanded in leaps and bounds.

Or so the triangle story goes.[29] The point, though, is not whether the story is entirely accurate. Understandably there are truths and wisdom within it. Some anyway.[30] So much suggestive evidence exists. What's far more important than precise accuracy is that the central features of the triangle story, even without the preaching, produced for lobbyists a really tough and demanding job. It became conventional wisdom for people inside and outside of Washington. Beliefs about the game then came to structure strategy about how to play it. The emphasis was on playing triangle politics correctly, assuming that this would bring winning. That's where Crawford and Griffith merged in their separate analyses from the 1930s.

Crawford found what came to be called insider politics. Griffith and the triangle scholars showed how the insiders managed to manipulate successfully from that insider perch. Lobbyists, in turn and apart from theories of academics, found that they needed to cultivate and network *all* these key triangle players, or ingratiate themselves to lots of them. They were expected to do so, and they, in turn, expected to do it. But it was a much smaller number than to whom they feel obligated to lobby today. Norms of government determined who was empowered to do what, and norms were different then, more rigid. Lobbying in America took on a highly formatted style starting in the 1930s. It was guided by the ideal of constant interaction with all the regular players. Legislative committees and public agencies were blanketed with lobbyists, all paying homage to their very own public officials.

At the very least, the contact game was becoming extraordinarily cumbersome for those of the third house: "See all our pals routinely." That was a tough change. Because interest representatives did the politics for the triangles in some nebulous and variable ways, lobbyists also had to reach often beyond those regular players—even walk in and threaten any dissenters. Lobbyists knew that winning demanded more than just a few friendly chats and a good policy plan. After all, the critical innovations of the 1920s had been in mobilizing the grassroots.[31] Lobbyists had to cultivate political leaders as well as the rank-and-file public officials who made bills pass into law. And they targeted the public. But triangle scholars didn't pay much attention to all that, and even lobbyists still had a gut-level belief that triangles mattered most.

With the contact game institutionalized and accepted, and its perks expected, lobbying life became hard. "Always check in with all the jerks," said the aforementioned irreverent lobbyist, "or the boys will gripe and sit on their hands." Interest representatives had to be good to *so* many demanding people in order to merely have a chance to win. For decades, that was life in Washington and in a great many state capitals. To a great extent, for most interests, this near constant running remains much of their lobbying lives. But, basically, this was politics 1960s-style, where more organized interests were emerging but where the explosion hadn't yet been appreciated. There were just lots more people to see, more busyness going on. As a congressman explained in conjuring up that word again, "There's a *protocol* to politics. One must, absolutely must, follow it." See 'em all was the rule.

But playing the game correctly doesn't make every interested player a winner. Certainly the protocol of lobbying exists. It's indeed followed. But does it always pay off? No. Many winners and many losers follow protocol. One of Washington's most well-known trade lobbyists, or "advisors" as he prefers to be called, networked both the capital and the nation for decades. He gained intimacy with nearly all of his contemporaries in his policy area, from both private and public sectors.

It came to be a tenet of faith that trade questions in this lobbyist's field couldn't advance without his involvement. He even played poker routinely with the Speaker of the House of Representatives. Yes, he networked well. But he also hadn't made any policy inroads in many, many years. Nor, for years, had he had any creative thoughts. Nor was he able to continue to, as had Weed and Hanna so successfully, broker contacts among the unacquainted. He really didn't know those who represented interests critical of his friends. Nor did he know many of the recently emerging players in his policy area, the ones replacing his old cronies. Said one of his best friends, he's "just a very well-paid old bastard who knows all the good old boys and masters a great line of B.S. People are afraid not to hire him and nobody's tested what must be their frequent reluctance to give him bucks."

Dozens, probably hundreds, of other lobbyists play contact well but seldom win because they're not really much good at the actual complexities and strategies of doing what's needed as lobbying. Or they're not good in picking good issues, as will be seen later in the text. They believe too much in triangle theory as it trickled down from scholars, or they're just lazy. The American Farm Bureau Federation, Dow Chemical U.S.A., General Motors Corporation, the Independent Bankers Association of America, and the National Manufacturers Association have all in recent years employed high-profile lobbyists who networked their friends well. But, as a congresswoman remarked of all of them, "nobody paid these guys attention on policy questions. Even their pals didn't ask them for advice." As in other professions, these good players who can't win are seen as showhorses, or "pony boys." But they're not seen as workhorses, the ones who do more than rely on old networks and on keeping their personal contact games going.

What are the implications of there being so many showhorses? There are several, all of which increase the price for successful lobbyists of actually winning.[32] More and more public officials question the usefulness of interest representatives and what they can be expected to offer. One legislator complained that "there isn't enough time in the day to see all those lobbyists." So he didn't. More interests playing in a more crowded, or very dense, world of lobbyists means that personal relationships have become less important. So members of Congress mostly see those who have good information, or at least fanciful charts and tables. To make matters worse for individual lobbyists, legislators get plenty of that kind of information from numerous public and private sources.[33] Policy experts in universities and government policy analysts are examples of these sources.

More frequent challenging of lobbyists and less acceptance of them also goes on. Access and attention are ever harder to gain, which is quite understandable. Some of the oldest groups in Washington, such as the National Farmers Union, can no longer see but a few members of Congress. The Teamsters Union has had similar problems, mostly because of charges of corruption. Unfortunately for lobbyists, the impression grows that even politically prominent interests can be ignored: that the very information they offer can be found elsewhere, or at least enough of it can. This breaks much of the protocol that networking lobbyists once found both so useful and so tedious. Nobody wants to go to lunch anymore, even if they could under changing rules about gifts. It's no longer such a leisurely politics. Of course, the more successful interests try harder to develop more complex lobbying strategies. But not everyone can hire a Bob Dole. As Gary Mucciaroni noted, interests have had a reversal of fortune. Perhaps it's just more public officials catching up with lobbyists and questioning whether it matters if they win or not.[34] Many legislators think having clients of the committee may not be such a great deal.

None of this should be surprising. Lobbying has been made difficult for some time by the ambivalence held by public officials. Policymakers know that third housers aren't so friendly to those with whom they disagree. History shows lots of merit in their skepticism. Congressional investigations of lobbying relationships popped up several times after 1850. Press reports of corruption were rampant. By the 1930s, Congress began the endless task of tinkering—or trying to tinker—with the regulation of lobbyists.[35] Those actions continued seemingly forever.[36] Even as lobbying reform passed in 1995 as the Lobbying Disclosure Act, many policymakers still judged regulation as inadequate.[37] Those with money continue to get pestered to death by policymakers who want their spare change. Grassroots lobbying isn't even covered.

What, though, is the exact price that lobbyists and their interests have paid for the legacy and emergence of the contact game? Basically, it's threefold. First, lobbyists have had to work primarily at the whim of public officials: See everyone, follow their protocol, play networking, give priority attention to legislative committees, solve the political problems of those in office. And, as noted earlier, that's all impossible. Some policymakers are offended, or at least irritated, as a result of perceived slights.

Second, interest representatives have found their work made much harder by those among them who just show off. The happy networkers who offer little or nothing hurt the image of all lobbyists. And they most certainly crowd the halls and, still too often, legislator schedules. Showhorses, as well as too many endless and often unproductive meetings with lobbyists, have created great skepticism among office holders. So successful lobbyists need to work even more diligently in additional ways to prove that they matter, that they can help or be a threat. They need to revert more and more to the expanding array of lobbying tasks and techniques.

Finally, lobbyists live and work under a perpetual cloud of public distrust. And policymakers both share those suspicions and more frequently exploit them. What public official hasn't decried the special interests? And who among them hasn't cooperated with such interests? It's hard to find that person. Investigations matter little. The public finds them boring. But nasty press reports, if linked to even hints of scandal, can wreak havoc with any interest and its issues, at least in the short term. That cloud means mostly that lobbyists just have to do more than they otherwise would, both in solidifying their relationships and in promoting the images of their interests.

The nineteenth-century kings of lobbying did, as a consequence, leave their mark. They turned lobbying into what's seen, first of all, as a burdensome insider game, always suspect on several counts, and an awfully difficult one to play well. On at least some dimensions, playing the insider game is quite simply harder than it ought to be.

And the Price Goes On

The regulation of lobbying has never been terribly stringent given constitutional freedoms of speech, assembly, and the right to petition government. Regulation does have some consequences, though, particularly in removing the worst vestiges of Weed and Hanna–style insider Washington relationships. Lobbyists in national politics must register if they contact public officials, report whom they work for and what they spend, and limit the gifts and entertainment they give to very small amounts. Lunches are

included, or more accurately excluded, unless at the local Booger
Burger drive-through. PACs are also controlled under federal campaign finance regulations. The 1995 lobbying act modified the regulations passed in 1946. As Common Cause noted, the intent in
1995 was "to change the way that money and lobbyists have inter-
acted with members of Congress," to "make a change in the way a
lot of Washington works."[38]

State regulations of lobbying vary from place to place but are
similarly intended and generally tend to impose the same type of
limits. At both the national and state levels, reforms have always
been met with organized interests adapting their strategies and
emphasizing other tasks. Washingtonians quickly concluded in
1995 that the just enacted reforms would mean more grassroots
lobbying, more money from organized interests going to parties
for sponsoring political functions, and more fund raisers and other
campaign contributions. These were just different ways of pursuing less personal relationships and making public life easier. Prog-
nosticators were correct. Whereas the one-time kings of lobbying
of the nineteenth century would have been blunted by such
rules—that is, if they were rigidly enforced—modern lobbyists are
much more mildly disadvantaged. Some even like it: "There's just
less pressure from [policymakers] that I, as a pressure kind of guy,
have to put up with." This change leaves the most creative and
innovative lobbyists free to lobby more targets, such as the public,
from more directions.

Even as it continues to the present, regulation of lobbying
quite clearly imposes a very low price on lobbyists and on lobbying workloads. But it hurts a little. Expensive capital city restau-
rants are hurt far worse, and so are local entertainment industries.
The worst thing for lobbyists are probably public charges that
these people still need attentive watching. Yet that belief is widespread, so it's small peanuts and nothing new.

Other emergent phenomena, though, do impose costs on
insider lobbying that are more than small ones. These include two
closely linked trends: first, the systematic expansion of participants in what many still see as those once closed iron triangles,
and second, more conflict in the basic values among an always
expanding array of organized interests. These two, it seems, led to
a third and parallel trend: organized interests targeting ever more
policymaker targets.

By the late 1970s the literature on American interests had taken yet another course. This new course seemed more pleasing to those researchers who generally prized broader policy review— for the better good of the public. Hugh Heclo pointed to these things first. [39] Small, cozy relationships, triangle-style, were out.

What Heclo found when he sought out those few important legislators, bureaucrats, and lobbyists were far more meaningful policy players. Policymaking involves informal "shared-knowledge" issue networks. [40] And knowledge comes from many sources. The same kind of participants are present, from the same institutions. Unlike triangles, though, issue networks include indeterminate numbers of players who freely come and go as their expressed interests make it necessary or appropriate. For example, environmental groups suddenly got involved in 1997 in federal transportation bill negotiations. It used to be that contractors and the states just pressured for new highway projects. Now environmentalists were networking to add bike paths and pollution controls to that bill. Another surprise to many policymakers was when conservative Christian groups showed up in trade policy hearings. Usually businesses had the main say there. But Christian advocates won over many legislators by noting that the Chinese were anti-family in their public policies. Therefore, they claimed, China should not keep its Most Favored Nation trade status.

Also, as post-Heclo scholars found, more policy conflict characterizes network relationships than the triangle story suggests. It only makes sense that with more players and an open politics, disagreeable policy activists would enter the shared-knowledge network. They're not necessarily welcomed there, but, especially for dissenting organized interests, they've found for themselves rules and tasks that have forced networks to be inclusive: "You wouldn't have believed it. One of the environmental lobbyists walked in past the staff, and demanded to be included in a meeting. He was seated. I feared not doing it." That was a congressman's quote. The same happened when China trade debates included scuffling between economically conservative businesses and socially conservative Christians. One particularly nice analogy to the networks has been drawn: The little triangles had become "sloppy large hexagons." [41] To Heclo, they were like ever transforming clouds. Clouds changing due to the wind is an analogy that occurs frequently. Soon after the networking conflict began between conservative interests on China trade policy, another new player waded in. Liberal human rights groups supported the right-wing Christians, which was really a strange twist of currents.

Changes in political relationships may well have encouraged newly organized interests to enter politics. There's now room for a pro-family lobby, and lots of supporters for one. On the other side, maybe it's just been that new interests coming to government capitals made politics open up. Since politics is naturally reactive, it probably was a little bit of both.[42] Regardless of cause and effect, what's obvious is that the 1960s and 1970s brought an explosion of organized interests.[43] Possibly 40 percent of today's interests organized between 1960 and 1980.[44] At least a third did so. The 1980s were no less entrepreneurial. The elections of President Ronald Reagan led to a host of conservative interests becoming active and appreciated. And those elections also reinvigorated and galvanized liberal interests that saw serious political threats by having conservatives operating government. After all, lots of interest groups form because of what governments are doing.

It's not that all of these interests were brand new after 1960. What also happened was that established social groups and once quite marginal interest groups became far more politically active. Old organizations such as the Sierra Club turned their relatively staid political behavior into near crusades. They joined the lobbying fray quite ardently. What else could they have done? A succession of events had energized, stimulated, and even irritated American political processes. It was all much like poison ivy. The civil rights movement, Vietnam War protests, the women's movement, environmentalism, and assorted smaller causes all erupted. Citizens got itchy. As self-perceived outsiders in an insiders' world, lobbyists who won their political spurs in social causes didn't accept the old politics.[45] They responded to that citizen itch and attacked public officials on behalf of supporters.

These advocates wanted to shake things up, disrupt the easiness, make changes, rock cozy political relationships, join the game—yet alter it. They also wanted to elect like-minded people to office. They thus tried hard to embarrass, where possible, the old guys. Weed and Hanna had done the same, so this was a throwback to interest politics. Of course, the old guys fought back, in ways that Weed's and Hanna's enemies could not. As a consequence, the universe of organized interests became far bigger than it had been in the 1950s. It was also considerably more intense, and full of different styles of players. An interest group veteran of three decades in Washington sadly shook his head thinking about it: "Suddenly lobbying ranks were full of hotheads, contentious individuals, anti-economics, and people who showed no respect." He was right. One had to be among lobbyists in the 1960s to appreciate how different things were by the 1990s. Every player had their list of good guys and really bad guys. And now they all wanted to stick it to the bad whenever they could.

The third trend was becoming obvious during this transitional period, one that lots of people saw producing what was popularized as a "new politics."[46] Lobbyists were no longer gravitating to the same old players in order to win. Not only were they making life hard—not easy—for public officials by protesting, lobbying an investigative media, arousing the grassroots, arguing for procedural reform in government, and attacking "monied interests;" they were also litigating, or at least frequently threatening law suits when they couldn't win through the contact game or by going to the public. The efforts and successes of civil rights groups in the courts were literally worshiped by most of the new-style "public interest" lobbyists.[47] Where possible, imitation followed admiration. And the imitation soon extended to established business interests, who saw a task that worked. Logging and milling interests, for example, beat up on the U.S. Forest Service in court in the 1990s. Everybody was getting ready at least to lobby in all directions, with all the targets as parts of interrelated strategies.

What happened was that organized interests, in an ever troubled—and therefore more difficult—political environment, looked for policy making friends and targets wherever they could find them. Triangles became relics except in the narrowest issues, at least to the extent they ever existed.[48] What issue was so remote that only a few committee members and a handful of administrators cared about it? Firms like Verner, Liipfert and Patton, Boggs, and Blow saw the writing on the wall and got ready, or newly organized, to do any sort of lobbying.

Insider politics became a symbolic opponent, the general target of everyone's attack for its closed ways, no matter how artificial the insider-outsider distinction had become. Interests fought to gain recognition and inclusion, often bitterly. Political institutions also were changing to address more openness.[49] The White House gave greater authority to its specific policy area liaisons. And these liaisons gained more responsibility to make and to block deals. Congress enhanced both leadership and rank-and-file influence. Overlapping jurisdictions were assigned both to two or more congressional committees and to multiple federal agencies. As a result, several committees in the House of Representatives could hold hearings on a trade bill, and two or three agencies might implement related features of soil and water policy. A dissenting legislator could find a hearing someplace, not just face discrediting, as he would in the old days. Leadership in both branches followed all the action and tried to coordinate everybody. Additional points of public access for private interests were thus obtained. More people to lobby was the result, as well as simply more lobbyists. "Find the target that best gets you into the game, someone who really likes you or your issues," was one lobbyist's advice. "The committees by themselves just can't keep you from exercising influence any longer."

Of course, as did the old, this new politics depends heavily on committee and agency review and policy preparation. Influence still gravitates primarily to those who actually write the laws. It's just that the writing happens in more places. Moreover, this hadn't been a revolution in institutions of the nation-state—not by any means—just evolutionary changes in procedures. So lobbying had now become an odd blend of following many of the precepts of triangle theory while still playing a farther ranging, more open, and frequently more contentious game. The above lobbyist went on, "You've got to give the committees their due. But, if chairs don't cooperate, run right over them. Try to crush 'em. Even they know you can."

Archer-Daniels-Midland (ADM) provides a good illustration of this rough and tumble politics in the firm's attempt to gain government support for new uses of food and fiber products. ADM targeted the White House intensely, a federal agency set up for the program within a cabinet-level office, Senate and House leaders, several legislative committees, individual members of Congress who had ADM plants in their states and districts, and the National Corn Growers lobby.

What new price have lobbyists paid for more interests, more targets, and more networking? More work. Organized interests all need to deal with a dramatically expanded policy making environment. Learning what to do is harder. Doing it takes more time, more contacts, and more discussion, as well as more money. New lobbying disclosure records show that. In the first half of 1996, General Motors (GM) directly lobbied federal officials on seventy issues. GM's thirty-six corporate lobbyists spent nearly $7 million, while its numerous contract, multiclient representatives earned almost $300,000.

But that's not the entire price of always emergent policy-making clouds. A secondary result of this expansiveness brings more casual, less routine, and more sporadically maintained political relationships. The contact game, or personalized lobbying, has evolved a great deal. Contact isn't so freely arranged. Access is not so freely given. All the targeted players are just much busier, too busy for that nonsense. Trust, then, isn't so easily given or won. Public officials can't trust those lobbyists who can't be personally tested.[50] And the reverse is true as well. Because of less trust, lobbyists are more cautious and more circumspect in what they say and to whom they say it. A General Motors lobbyist no longer goes over to old friend Representative John Dingell's office and spells out all the firm's strategy on an issue. The Michigan Democrat may well be too close to other lobbies on that one. So trust is limited and total candidness avoided, even with those held near and dear.

So what? While lobbyists still primarily inform public officials, they're far less direct about how they're spreading observations than were interests from those mythic triangles. They fail to share much of what they might once have openly admitted. A trade association executive summarized: "You can't let *anyone* know how you're managing your issue, what you're planning to do. Lie if you must. I know that's a big change from the old days. Things here aren't nearly as pleasant or as much fun as previously."

Changes in Governing, Changes in Interests

Quite obviously, public officials have benefitted from associating with lobbyists, at least generally. Even though they haven't always liked and respected the third housers, they've gotten things from them. (Egos often got in the way of real friendships, anyway.) Information has always been important, both in deciding policy directions and in understanding pending political events: "The currency for influence is research."[51] Lobbyists, though, once added an even more pleasant dimension to political interaction, with elaborate dinners, hookers, brandy, and big cigars. Over time, lobbyists cultivated relationships with policymakers, took them inside high-level social whirls, accompanied them into the less public and less glamorous back rooms of politics, made political life more comfortable, and enhanced personal and political self-images. Being made comfortable by lobbyists didn't necessarily mean, however, that lawmakers felt comfortable *with* them—or comfortable with *themselves* having to spend time with the sleazy bigshots. And, in different ways, lobbyists still will do this sort of thing if it works. So comfort levels will vary as a result. By their attentions, lobbyists have made public officials feel ambiguously more important yet a little tawdry. In an historical sense, organized interests have been good friends to mainstream policymakers. And, since the mainstream runs the show, organized interests have achieved, despite some ambivalence, a great fit within the policy process.

Yet that statement about a good fit remains but a generality. This chapter has emphasized the degree to which lobbying, as a contact game, has changed over time. Today's lobbying of public officials isn't starkly new, it's an extension of that old need to provide policy information. So it's probably more accurate to say that direct lobbying has been a good fit in its several evolving forms. Quite clearly, Thurlow Weed and Mark Hanna couldn't have prospered by bringing their nineteenth-century behavior into the early twenty-first century. Lots of players would have been locked away in federal prisons. Nor would an advocate such as Ralph Nader have done well—probably not even survived—in Hanna's time. There wasn't much room for boat rockers and those who vigorously attacked corporate wants. They were painted as real nasty types, or oddballs, by opponents and the press. Character assassination was big in those days, bigger than even today. But again there's evolution in the lobby. "Enemies of the people" was a bad label to win. In contrast, Nader, as an enemy, became a mid–twentieth century political icon, a hero of sorts to many.

Nothing then shows the lasting importance of directly lobbying policymaker targets more than its adaptability. As Elaine Swift has shown so well, political institutions of the nation-state have always changed greatly.[52] There also have been cultural changes in what defines appropriate political behavior.[53] The bossism encouraged by Weed and practiced by Tweed lacks any real place in modern American government.[54] But new political influentials have replaced them. In their own individual ways, the states also have changed.[55] Active state policy development, or bigger policy bases, has happened in every instance.

The U.S. Congress has shown the most obvious transformations, and it has remained the main arena for American interest politics. The strong leadership of both House and Senate in the early twentieth century gave way to committee dominance in legislative affairs, more so than there had been in the nineteenth century.[56] In the 1970s, committee powers were reformed, and both the leadership and rank and file gained new influence.[57] Through it all, however, lobbyists just kept trucking along, working hard to make contacts and become friendly with whatever congressional members or types mattered most at the moment. That practice indeed marks resiliency. Lobbying on the inside always seemed to fit public life, even if it eventually required a modified tweaking in its definition.

Being inside fit as long as the contact game was sufficiently adaptive both to nation-state and state development and to social changes. Adaptiveness seems to best explain the shift to what appeared as iron triangles after the demise of strong congressional leadership and the kings of the lobbyists. Adaptiveness also explains why, in a more open and democratic Congress of the mid-1970s, impressions of triangle politics obviously gave way to broader policy networks. Public-style or social cause interests were better able to find allies in an even more open politics. And they often found those allies by engaging in lobbying tasks, techniques, and tactics that were once quite frowned upon, or by doing such tasks once seen as only the appropriate works of the inappropriately hopeless: the Knights of Labor or suffragettes.

An evolution in governing institutions, therefore, fostered an evolution in the targeting and contacting of public officials. In biblical terminology, a lot of begatting went on. The committees were still there, as were agencies. So? Lobby them in the old ways. Kick them if needed, though. Jolt them. Don't be too supportive. Don't make political life too comfortable, not always cozy, not always easy. Rouse the public and electoral constituents back home. Help the media attack the insiders—reverse the press tactics of the one-time lobbyist kings. Sure, go to court. Stage protests. Even picket and litigate as a well-established business corporation, such as Mitsubishi, or as a university trade association. Encourage campus protests from, not against, the university president's office. What an odd twist on an old theme!

Under such changing targeting, less cooperative issue networks were at least clearly visible, or maybe they were just developing. Certainly they were becoming more commonplace. The result was that the old outside approaches to lobbying policymakers were appended inseparably to the still desirable insider aspects of interest politics, forever merged. Lobbying became more complex in general, involving more of a balance of the historically embedded things that interests have long done. And it was extending the range of those things as well. Much more of what was once unconventional lobbying now goes on, for many more issues and policies. And nearly everyone does it, from American businesses to those who challenge them: environmentalists, consumers, labor, liberal congressional enterprises, and numerous others.

Such attractions have kept the fit of the ever changing contact game constant. Targeting of public officials remains necessary and grudgingly appreciated, even if it's harder to do. While lobbyists now may be more frequently annoying, and while they don't supply policymakers with as many personal goodies as in the past, they still manage to penetrate the process. As John Heinz and his colleagues found, that's why doing more things is better for lobbying success than doing fewer things.[58] That's why lobbying now brings forth even more of an all-directional, do-it-all strategy. Or, at least, lobbying is now much more a readiness to do more targeting in more ways for nearly everybody.

Why do lobbyists still get in to see policymakers? Without lobbyists, there's a shortage of influence peddlers to react to and listen to, and that's still needed. It quickens legislative inertia. As Michael Hayes concluded of their shared environment, there remains a great basis for exchange between lobbyists and public officials—even as more of both types of not so friendly players now matter to the public policy process.[59]

Summary and Highlights

Deals aren't closed until they're closed. And, in politics, they may be reopened next year.[60] Or tomorrow. Negotiations, then, are essentially endless. That's why the contact game goes on, and why direct lobbying has such importance.

Yet the emphasis of this chapter has been to discredit much of the importance of, and even the concept of, "insider" lobbying as a continually exclusive and workable strategy. Three reasons have been discussed. First, seen in this and the previous chapter, successful targeting of the public and targeting policymakers go together. They represent different tasks, but they're intertwined. Lobbying as a contact game gained its prominence in the nineteenth century, largely from the efforts of a raft of development and settlement interests. Those interests never neglected the public, however—nor could they have. Rather, development and settlement interests played on publicly held myths about western expansion and agrarian values. Under favorable conditions, lobbyists just planned and closed the deals that gained their own interests' government subsidies.

Things have never varied much from that combined sort of targeting. Sure, a minor change in patent laws may be made apart from public or constituent concerns, but that's so seldom. Relatively unexciting issues *do* go through the public and its support filter: new auto air-bag regulations, Megan's Law, imports of automatic weapons, bankruptcy laws, Health Maintenance Organizations, farm commodity subsidies. While these are not major public policies of widespread social import, nor the most important object of politics, parts of the public elevate each of them to that status. For them, these things are important as interests, even if few elections are won or lost on them. So these issues need to be lobbied accordingly. Only then, after lobbying success, can deals be made.

"Insider" lobbying—at least as it's usually presented—has been discredited from a second perspective. While the contact game has gone on, and gone on to the benefit of organized interests, it's probably seldom been made up of only easy and cozy relationships. Far from it. There's always been more to direct lobbying and what's called "insider politics" than the simple flow of information and research. Corruption carried much of the day, dealwise, in the nineteenth century. Dissenting public officials were not just ignored by the insiders, they were retaliated against, attacked.

In the twentieth century, any cozy triangle-style relationships were but a fleeting fancy, maybe a fluke of analysis. The targeting of policymakers gave way during a period of institutional change to conflict, openness, and extensive participation. Things were as nasty as they were cozy. The point is simple: Public policies didn't pass or change just because public officials were provided an easy time. By itself, the direct contact game doesn't explain all that much about what resulted from government, its newly passed policies.

The presumed primacy of the contact game also needs reassessment because it fails to square with a third observation. Much of the interaction on that so-called inside of politics is but an unproductive show, a silly waltz before the heavy metal band comes on stage. A protocol of playing out the rituals of lobbying and its public postures takes place, and that protocol provides policymakers with some comfort and ease. It's a familiar tradition, like an old childhood blanket. Accordingly, and historically, officials expect it, like it—usually. But, as lobbyists themselves indicate, successes could be won without that dance, at least in modern politics.

Scholars may well have been misled by this protocol. They've taken it as an indicator of closed, insider relations—of triangles. Rather than see it as analogous to comity and its conflict-muting effects in Congress, lobbying protocol has been taken to be a vehicle for stifling dissent through institutional roadblocks. That view certainly further elevates the status and importance of direct lobbying, but much too far to have ever been entirely accurate on the major issues of any day.

Thus this chapter does have something else to say about the contact game and the targeting of policymakers. Even so, and for some of the same reasons, Heinz Eulau suggested it first.[61] Eulau called lobbying a wasted profession. That seems hardly likely. Individuals other than professional lobbyists waste their time at it. Plus the many tasks and techniques of lobbying combine to produce much more than wasted effort. The accurate thing to conclude is that much personalized political networking is indeed wasted time, even as it's sold as so important.[62] A preoccupation with only contacting policymakers obscures perhaps most of what, from an interest perspective, produces public policy.

6

Targeting Other Interests

Lobbying lobbyists? Certainly. Lobbyists are one of the primary targets of advocacy. They have been since American politic's time began. While the idea may seem silly on the surface, it makes a great deal of sense. As cooperation among interests goes up, politics is easier. Conversely, as conflict goes up, politics is far more difficult. Maybe it's more fun, since it's a bigger challenge, but certainly harder. And interests are in politics to *win*, not merely to have fun. There indeed are plenty of wastrel lobbyists, but those who hire the freeloaders don't know that. Interests aren't hiring lobbyists, or otherwise sending them to the capital city, for the fun of it all.

So, since interest politics is serious business, it makes sense that things stay both as easy and as winnable as possible—which is really difficult in a political world crowded with interests.[1] There's even competition in Washington for parking space. The heavy competition is why lobbyists lobby other lobbyists. Doing so is an integral part of the strategy of minimizing conflict and, therefore, lowering the political risk of losing.

Unfortunately, interaction among interests, which is a nifty way to refer to lobbyists lobbying lobbyists, isn't well studied. Lobbyists talk of it all the time, though. Yet academics who study organized interests seem focused on only one type of interest interaction, on the single task of assembling policy coalitions. Coalition building, or the joining of ad hoc alliances so interests can work in unison, has gained nearly all the attention even though there are other tasks involved in interaction among interests. Academics seem fascinated by interests joining together and, presumably, giving up part of their own goals for some common good.

This chapter goes beyond that, while still, of course, discussing the importance and limitations of the many tasks involving coalition politics. Essentially the following pages look at four common forms and numerous techniques of lobbying target interests. The first set of tasks is the most simple, that of hiring some interest supporters—buying them or renting them, through a contract. With the preponderance of different types of interests, cooperation of this sort abounds. With the scarcity that lobbyists face in generating such useful resources as time and energy, there are extra incentives to hire help. But it's not easy to buy people, especially those who carefully manage their own interests. Respected lobbyists are extraordinarily reluctant to enter into contracts or agreements with those they find suspect or otherwise lacking in stature.

Hiring interest supporters gives way to that second, more costly lobbying that leads to the actual forming and joining of coalitions. Those that an interest joins with logically demand some degree of sharing, cooperation, common purpose, and often control. Or they try to. On the whole, then, it's better for one interest to buy a few bodies who can play for the team. Coalition politics is touchy business, very much on a difficult par with building policymaker relationships. As a consequence, coalitions are full of complexity and variability. Levels of interest involvement vary, as does participant commitment, their reasons for joining, and even their precise policy and issue wants. More than anything else, organized interests don't join coalitions in order to weaken their own group or institution.

That simple fact of lobbying life gives rise to a third set of those tasks that find lobbyists lobbying each other. These might be called a kind of sneaky mini-coalition politics, for a great amount of multi-interest lobbying involves forming new interest groups, managing trade and other associations, and financing and mobilizing groups that have recently been less active. Another mini-coalition format is cooperative support on large projects, such as oil exploration in eastern Russia, by which each participating interest gets a piece of the action. Like coalition politics, all this brings greater cooperation, a common sense of lobbying identity, more resources to bear on policy decisions, and the simple strength of numbers. Yet such projects are also no panacea. They don't offer solutions to the inclination of each interest to—first and foremost—think of itself, and even abandon the others.

Finally, there's a fourth form taken by these inter-interest tasks. Lobbyists often just badger, threaten, coerce, and generally make pleas for cooperation—or at least neutrality—from other interests. That covers two points made earlier in the text: First, lobbying isn't just about cozy relationships. Second, interest representatives often don't *want* to work with others. They just want to clear the battleground of unnecessary players, to have a less cluttered policy area. That's turf protection.

What will be emphasized in this chapter, regardless of the type or level of cooperation, is easy to understand. Interests in today's large universe of lobbying organizations can't go it alone in politics, no matter how much their representatives might like to do so. Some common alliances, or at least agreements, are most often necessary. If needed agreements can't be made, an interest and its issues get lost in the crowd. They get seen as far beyond the mainstream. Lobbying and the targeting of lobbyists becomes a central feature of public policymaking for that reason alone. Given the problems of getting and keeping cooperation, targeting other interests often doesn't work. But trying to do so is almost always important, as is trying everything else, or lobbying in all directions.

Buying Help

Scores of impressive organized interests would have little advocacy work to do if there weren't others to hire them. That's mostly true of multiclient lobbying firms, the contract lobbyists that were noted in Chapter Two. Just like commercial and financial institutions once hired Thurlow Weed, Mark Hanna, and the other kings of lobbying, these organizations are for hire today. But it's also true that individual congressional enterprises get purchased, organized as they are to efficiently pursue issues for their legislators' own interests. This happens most in national politics, where congressional offices are well-staffed. To a lesser extent, interest groups and important institutional interests get bought as well, as do personalities-as-interests, such as TV evangelists and radio gurus.

Why, though, is buying help so difficult? Why does it require lobbying? Contact lobbyists *need* clients. Members of Congress *need* issues in order to both advertise at home and build careers in Washington. Other interests occasionally *need* an infusion of resources, especially ideas. Also, they periodically need an infusion of supporters. Very few of these interests, however, work with just anyone on any issue. There must be something in it for cooperation to take place. Something very specific has to be there, beyond mere cash or publicity. That's where the lobbying of lobbyists comes into interest politics.

An illustration of the problem of lobbying these people shows this best. While in Congress for fourteen terms, Guy VanderJagt made lots of friends.[2] Most of the friendships were won as he chaired the National Republican Congressional Committee (NRCC). Through the congressman's hard work and countrywide personal appearances from 1975 until 1992, NRCC raised considerable money and support for GOP candidates. Many Republican legislators, in fact, credit VanderJagt with providing the impetus for their party eventually winning control of the House of Representatives in 1994. Despite losing his 1992 primary election, and even though many conservatives didn't like his moderate politics, VanderJagt still won plenty of goodwill in Congress.

As a result of those friends, the former NRCC chair was well-positioned in 1994 for the Republican victory. He had joined a modestly successful multiclient firm, but after that important election, possible clients came from everywhere: "Out of his ears." In the first half of 1996, lobbying disclosure reports showed him with thirty-two different clients. Most were prominent and highly respected, such as the Motion Picture Association of America, Ford Motor Company, and General Mills. Lesser interests without such stature were turned away, as were interests with really difficult problems to resolve or ones in need of highly preferential policy treatment. The newly successful legislator-turned-lobbyist admitted that he found it too difficult to ask old colleagues for favors.

What the VanderJagt example indicates is clear: An interest must first lobby VanderJagt's firm with care in order to actually buy him. And to do so means completing several informational tasks. As one successful purchaser said: "It was 'Tell me about the group? Explain what you want. Why do you want it? Have you offended anybody by wanting it? Who are your friends? What will they do for you?'" In other words, VanderJagt thoroughly auditions his possible clients, at least as long as Republicans keep congressional control. It's probably something he learned in Congress, since congressional enterprise staff ask similar questions before being rented, or agreeing to spearhead for another organized interest.

So buying the right people isn't easy.[3] There are lots of choices, both for renters and for the rented.[4] Even finding out which is the right interest to hire is hard. Lobbyists look for just the right congressional enterprise, radio talk show, or interest group to help them out. Senator Conrad Burns was picked up by lobbyists from high-technology producers that wanted easier exports of encryption software for scrambling computer messages. The Montana Republican was chosen because he had long worked on two related issues: broadcasting rights and protection of small phone companies. Plus, he was especially adept at mastering the issues of this changing technology.

The rental or hiring process has a certain distinct logic, at least according to the claims of lobbyists. So does evaluating whether or not a regularly retained multiclient lobbyist is good for a specific issue, or whether hiring someone else would be better. There's a checklist of sorts: Who needs something? Who's available? On what issues do they each have credibility? What strengths does each available organization have? Where do hired interests need to go, or whom do they lobby? What's the price? How do you pay it? Is the cost for the purchase worthwhile? Can everyone just walk away from this alliance once the cooperative lobbying is done? Will reputations be tainted by the association, or will they be enhanced? Will future needs of the hiring interest be affected? Is a third-party broker needed to make the hire and manage the agreement? All these questions and the answers that must be determined constitute added tasks that hiring interests generally undertake. Without a doubt, the ensuing hires are viewed as instrumental participants in a venture of a single interest. They aren't partnerships, although the price may entail a future payoff, including additional cooperation.[5]

How does the hiring work? New examples can be found daily, but a good one is from the 1980s. When the Farm Credit Council needed to pass a quite controversial reform of the agricultural credit system, Jaenke and Associates was hired to manage the bill.[6]

First, Ed Jaenke brought multiple participants together from the hiring interest and from those in its business. The idea was to come up with a plan. With that completed, Jaenke rented those *he* needed: a gifted and knowledgeable bill drafter with farm credit experience, a banking expert, a respected Democrat to work one side of the Congress, an equally revered Republican to work the other, a White House confidant, and someone else who knew all the right agency officials and problems. Because price wasn't a consideration, Jaenke got whom he wanted. With everything covered, the bill passed largely as planned. The opposition was outgunned. No matter how important the policy problem was, the win would have been impossible without the rentals.

A bigger rental success was Toshiba Corporation's 1988 effort. A Japanese firm, Toshiba had irritated U.S. officials by selling sensitive high-technology military-use equipment to the former Soviet Union. When rigorous import penalties were imposed on the company, it rather frantically hired help—tons of it. (In comparison, Jaenke looks like a piker.) David P. Houlihan of Mudge, Rose, Gutherie, Alexander, and Ferdon coordinated a complex lobbying strategy. "They did everything in the book—grassroots, insider-stuff, reporters—very sophisticated," recalled a member of Congress. It should have been. Houlihan's firm took in over $4 million in just over a year. Congressional estimates were of $9 million in total expenditures. Nobody had ever seen so much lobbying money fly around. What was the result? A compromise was reached and penalties were reduced. Toshiba saved millions, but not without the hired help.

Even public-interest-style organizations buy help. The National Resources Defense Council (NRDC) once employed two public relations firms in its effort to stop the chemical spraying of Alar on fruit. NRDC wanted to get the issue on national media programming and used east coast and west coast firms with such contacts to do it. Alar was soon profiled as scandalous on CBS's *60 Minutes* and, after public controversy, pulled from use earlier than the Environmental Protection Agency had already dictated.

The federal tax reform bill of 1986, welfare reform in 1995, and lesser bills to regulate oil tanker safety features and truck safety all passed as well because of the essential participation of hired help, including some enterprises in Congress. Big and small measures, then, both often involve hiring. For example, the insurance trade association the American Council of Life Insurance hired lob-byists from three multiclient firms just to work out limits on puni-tive damage awards against defendants. That seems like a minor matter, except that millions of dollars are at issue in corporate earnings. A lobbyist summed things up nicely: "Even health care reform and social security changes could pass if the right people were hired by one side. Right now the hires offset one another. Too many sides." But a colleague ridiculed that view: "There ain't enough money in the whole town to finance those deals. Like the Farm Bill of 1995, those await dumb luck."

Shopping in Congress isn't quite as costly as hiring Ed Jaenke. "Rent is cheap," explained one lobbyist. Conrad Burns only sought greater influence in a factionalized Senate. He had regular oppo-nents in some key colleagues. All that Florida Republican Repre-sentative E. Clay Shaw wanted was publicity in the home district. And campaign assistance was nice, too. So he willingly introduced a conservative welfare reform bill in 1993. Members of Congress do this sort of thing all the time from their offices, especially if they—like Shaw—can be effective stalking horses for a bill that might eventually pass. Lots of attention comes then.

Of course, that's the intended strategy: Don't buy someone and her office staff off with actual dollars, simply make political life easier for them. These are great trades. For years, Minnesota Senator Rudy Boschwitz advocated "decoupling" plans, to remove the amount of produced farm commodities from federal determi-nations of farm price supports. His very Republican firms in the home state, most notably Cargill, fed him the ideas and materials. And they gave him electoral support, which kept his enthusiasm high. Eventually decoupling passed in a slightly modified form. Like welfare reform, skeptics abounded as to its unlikely prospects. Without enterprise rentals such as those of Shaw and Boschwitz, however, Congress would have lacked awareness and familiarity with either of these reform plans or their goals. Winning some pre-liminary understanding years earlier was central to finally passing both measures.

Far more frequently, though, congressional enterprises work for individual or personality interests, especially constituents, in order to incorporate narrow issues into large bills.[7] For instance, members like to help local firms obtain federal purchases and con-tracts. Why do they do it? Electoral support is one reason. Quieting negative noise in the home state or district is another. Building popularity is a third. Or, they sometimes do it just because somebody asked. They think that maybe some favorable publicity will result in such instances. Hanna and Weed would have undoubtedly been surprised at how relatively inexpensive members of Congress have become over time. There's not much need to even feed them any longer.

Not all enterprises are likely targets for interests that are seeking policy wins. Having the member on the appropriate committee is most desirable, as was the case with Burns as committee chair. The member's electoral safety is often a bigger concern. What matters far more is respect for the member among colleagues. Those who must eventually pass the bill want an idea that comes from someone they trust. Ideology, or at least perceived ideology, has surprising importance: "I want tenacious advocacy from the congressional member who carries our proposal." So interests shop for the truly committed when an entire bill is at stake. Again Burns is the example. As a lobbyist said: "He's a freedom freak." Since an enterprise can't really be held accountable by the interest that rents them, truly believing is assumed to bring commitment. It's a modified trial by fire.

Things are often done in far less strategic ways when it comes to hiring help from among existing institutions and groups. Shopping for these "big-time" players is more hit and miss, yet still carefully thought-through when likely targets and scenarios are discovered. Desirable results most often occur when large or prominent interests find an offer that can't be turned down. In the 1950s and 1960s, the American Farm Bureau Federation (AFBF) added all sorts of nonfarm conservative issues to its lobbying agenda merely because banking and manufacturing interests asked.

But there was a well-acknowledged payoff. The political climate for AFBF was one of intense competition with the National Farmers Union (NFU) at the time. The Farm Bureau needed all the help it could get to ward off NFU's policy wants, which included AFBF's highly despised federal controls on farm production. Business interests tipped the balance against the Farmers Union. NFU supported farm issues that most businesses didn't even understand. It was a nice trade. Both Farm Bureau and business interests won, even after Democratic President John F. Kennedy was elected in 1960 with NFU support.[8]

The most fascinating examples of big-interest rentals come up when such organizations need to solidify, recover, or repay goodwill. In the 1990s, General Motors (GM) found African-American congressional enterprises unexpectedly renting the company. At least the two sets of interests had a rental understanding. Otherwise members of the congressional black caucus in general, and Michigan Democratic Representative John Conyers in particular, indicated that their cooperation on GM's many pressing policy issues would be very cautious and restrained. GM really needed help on federal gas mileage requirements.

In thinking things over, GM both raised money and worked on two African-American bills. The two bills are incredibly narrow in purpose. The first aims to build a Black Patriots Foundation memorial on the National Mall. The second is to mint a commerative federal coin for African-American Revolutionary War veterans. Not only did GM help, but the company contributed $1.5 million to the memorial and, in 1996, sent twenty firm and contract lobbyists to Congress in order to pass the legislation. Without GM, both projects were hopeless.

What's the point? It's simple: A great amount of help can be found among interests when some very basic exchanges are made. Buyers are needed who themselves want help. There must be interests for rent, even if they wouldn't initially be expected to be for rent. (Or even if they don't expect themselves to be.) Yet most organized interests of all types are prepared to be hired if the need to cooperate arises. Interests cooperate when they get help for giving help. A prominent national radio commentator who vocally resisted policy reforms in his area of expertise was once neutralized by being brought to and allowed to moderate a retreat for members of Congress. The discussion of issues by prominent players and merely the honor of being there led to a change in his behavior and articulated views. He wasn't given a fee, but he could brag about having been there. One congressional enterprise that had been especially bothered by the radio personality planned and arranged the rental. An unsurprised lobbyist noted: "Golly, you might have to go to bat for a whole variety of players in this business. And not really know it. Dragged into their games, I guess."

Moreover, there's more to this hiring process than just a systematic expansion of interests. There's also victory, which lobbyists really like. When gained by artful free agent purchases and the strategic acquisition of a bigger lobbying arsenal, lobbyists still find satisfaction even if they needed assistance to win. Anyone would rather do it alone, but lobbyists do learn to love their hired friends.

Forging Coalitions

Other lobbying of lobbyists is different from mere rentals. Coalitions are literally forged: subjected to intense heat in very closed quarters with the intention of breaking down individual properties.[9] That epitomizes a real political hothouse. More literally, though, coalitions are the classic form of cooperation among organized interests, and they are built in negotiated sessions. At these sessions, representatives from different groups and institutions argue whether the attendees are in agreement or disagreement over particular public policies. Even more accurately, they argue over whether they need to be more in agreement. That's why coalitions, by nature, are shaky, or inherently unstable.[10] Individual interests of the organization come before the combined interest of a partnership. That's why each organization is present.

But what is a coalition of interests, other than another one of those transitory political shapes and forms? In the most basic sense, coalitions of organized interests exist when several diverse groups or institutions rather informally agree to work together on a specific public policy problem. Often coalitions include adversaries of one another, and they tend to be short-term, or ad hoc. For example, the benefits of passing a commonly accepted bill are seen as a way to satisfy the numerous issues desired by different interests. So they combine things in one package.

There's even a bit more to coalitions. An extensive public policymaking environment, where there exist both more targets and more interests doing the targeting, provides sound reasons for cooperation.[11] That's true even among very different types of interests, such as a business firm and a consumer group.[12] Cooperation, though, matters to different organized interests in variable and more or less intense ways. As a result, some lobbyists become core players in a coalition.[13] Those from other organizations are hangers-on, there only to watch and to gain information.[14] Maybe they just want to meet serious players. Maybe they hope to get their name on a list of people who want something popular. Even some entire coalitions are used more for spreading information than for generating action on public policy.

On some of the most difficult policy decisions—those that require the hardest and most unpredictable lobbying—greater seriousness may transform the coalition. Increasingly severe competition forces more compromise.[15] As Marie Hojnacki demonstrated, interests under highly competitive conditions must worry more about the hoped-for collective policy result. The bill passing or the regulation being rescinded takes precedent over each participating interests' own more narrow issue concerns.[16] After all, these interests all have some generalized concern with the outcome. As an environmental lobbyist once said, "We had to get a Clean Air Act passed. I worked hard for that, even though my issues were basically ignored."

Because interests come together to share resources, make use of a wider range of policy contacts, gain economies of scale, and win political credibility, the most disadvantaged interests may use coalitions the most. And they seem to have the greatest concerns for the coalition itself.[17] After all, the coalition expands the scope of the conflict to advertise an interest's claim when the group can't do that on its own because it's too short of resources. But, it seems, nearly all interests join at least sometimes, over and over. That explains why coalitions themselves are generally similar yet not quite all alike.[18] They use the same approach, but many different and variously committed players keep coalitions from being always the same. It also explains why, all things being equal, lobbyists would rather buy help than win over partners—if they could buy help that worked. Coalitions work to solve problems that hired help can't negotiate alone.

What's going on? Let's look historically. It could be tempting to think of interest coalitions as relatively new, as late twentieth-century discoveries made important only because of more players in modern politics. There's really not much that's new, though. Again, it's just more evolutionary changes in interest politics. Colonial-era planter interests in the southern United States were quite varied and had their own regional concerns and economies. The cotton South, for example, was not the same as the tobacco South. Nonetheless, when it came to the politics of building a new nation, plantation interests met and spent time together because they feared domination, or simply being left out, by industrial and commercial interests.[19] Virginians supported Carolinians, just as Ford often supports General Motors. The southern coalition successfully defended slavery for a great many years. Mathew Carey was another early coalition builder, working to build a manufacturing alliance of firms for his desired industrial policy.

Then, too, those all too prominent development interests also built at least one very solid coalition. When bills were to be passed and policymakers won over, lobby kings didn't do it alone. The hired help brought roomfuls of people together, without further purchases. Thurlow Weed even forged interest alliances between immensely wealthy Republican financiers and urban political machines, the real Yankee Democrats of that era. Most commonly, however, coalitions were made of railroaders who repeatedly helped bankers, who in turn helped timbermen, who in turn helped mine operators, and on and on. As was seen in the previous chapters, the West wasn't settled policywise one interest at a time. Rather, it was through coalition politics, along with a few other tasks.[20] King lobbyists were kings not because they ruled but because they brokered cooperation among disparate interests. And only after being successful among those interests and policymakers were they kings.

Some see this nineteenth-century politics as one of elite domination, or merely preferred positioning, rather than coalition building.[21] But the two aren't necessarily mutually exclusive. The terminology of coalitions, however, awaited modern discovery. The idea behind a theory of elites was that big businesses were monolithic. In reality, businesses simply agreed to mutual support. They made use of their diversity to engender a monolith. Railroaders, thus, got their railroads. Banks safely made money. Timber from the Great Lakes won a market in the West, and had transportation to it. Minerals and farm products gained a ride back East. All of these interests won more together than any could have won separately. Doing so entailed cooperation around lots of successful bills and several White House decisions. Unlike with rentals, these interests agreed to stay together for a far longer term in order to stifle dissent and exchange support. They earned, though perhaps unfairly, their preferred position. It wasn't a gift, nor a conspiracy.

It wasn't, at least, unless one considers the whole of American politics the land of great conspiracy. But that would be silly. Business conspired? Fortune 500 companies conspired? Farmers conspired? Labor conspired? Environmentalists conspired? Consumer interests conspired? The elderly conspired? African Americans conspired? Daylight savings time advocates conspired? Somebody believes each of these examples to be plots. But nobody believes that they all were, except maybe the Posse Comitatus and other interests of general paranoia. All the above so-called conspiracies, however, do show something else: a clear pattern of coalition building that persists over time. In other words, all involved interests lobbying other interests in order to win—not renting them, but joining them.

At the height of the civil rights movement, that kind of lobbying led such venerable organizations as the National Association for the Advancement of Colored People (NAACP) to lobby upstart new groups. The Congress on Racial Equality and the Student Non-Violent Coordinating Committee threatened NAACP goals by assuming strategies that were too confrontational in lobbying the public. Coalition politics soothed many differences, and fights were less apparent within the movement than they were between the movement and the rest of society. The movement was stronger as a consequence.

Later, when feminist goals were splintered and new groups were forming, various women's groups coalesced to discuss differences, emphasize commonalities, and construct a comparable women's movement.[22] Quite obviously, just as it had been for western development interests, cooperation paid off for African Americans as a racial minority and for women and their gender. These were collective victories, gained by several partner interests. But coalition politics never obliterated differences between the NAACP and Congress of Racial Equality (CORE), or between the often radical National Organization for Women (NOW) and the National Consumers' League. For that matter, politics healed no rifts between NOW and the even less mainstream interest group, Seattle Radical Women.

During all this movement activity, coalition politics was still being practiced by economic interests. Causes weren't the only ones working at alliances. Coalition politics was going on, though, with a bit more elaborate and more structured organization than in the previous century. A wide variety of manufacturers formed the Sugar Users Group. It had obvious interests. Like tobacco and cotton planters in the eighteenth century, the de facto—or emergent—leaders of sugar using firms and associations met and planned a cooperative strategy. The same types of agreement making went on in both instances. Fortune 500 companies organized the Business Roundtable as another generally permanent and semi-structured coalition in 1972. The Roundtable allowed public declaration of the policy wants of big American businesses in very general terms, but left the lobbying to individual firms. Participants, however, were still rather constrained by Roundtable agreements and, especially, the press releases and declarations that went with them. It's hard to make policy demands inconsistent with public agreements, or to lobby both sides on an issue.

The Business Roundtable actually mimicked a somewhat earlier coalition, the National Conference of Commodity Organizations (NCCO). Organized in 1957, NCCO partners feared that open public disputes between different farm crop interest groups would both further undermine and then create an impasse in making farm policy.[23] Without organizing its own trade association, the Conference articulated how important each crop was to American agriculture overall. Then participants hammered out agreements based on available budget dollars. Essentially, they set the levels of federal price support to be given to each crop. Once again, big business and large-scale farmers both generally prospered, as the respective coalitions went on to lobby policymakers for corporate and commodity subsidies. Not every interest within the coalitions won the same amounts of largess, but all interests won.

Studies of numerous types of American interests make it clear how significant coalition politics has become. Congressional enterprises—those personal member offices or small businesses—have joined together to form the Mushroom Caucus, to protect growers. And they're coalesced around the Rural Health Care Caucus to expand medical services to their own rural districts. Groups face greater difficulties. As Henry Pratt observed, the elderly in America are represented by a far more diverse set of interest groups than in other countries.[24] And they fight with each other. Farmers and agribusiness interests reflect the same diversity.[25] Fights, again, are common. Consumer interests are also diverse, even though these tend to be patronage-supported organizations rather than mass membership groups.[26]

As a consequence, coalitions have repeatedly become responsible, if not always successful, forums for cooperation in each of the four policy areas: targeting a single piece of legislation, encouraging each participating interest to find or incorporate something it wants in the proposed bill, asking all allies to stick to the agreement, and minimizing the problems of different organized interests with different voices. In fact, under those conditions, the large number and variety of organized interests in each policy area become somewhat of an advantage. There's lots of group activity, plenty of mobilization of supporters and members, clearly distinct types of constituents affected, usually different regions working together for a minimization of ideology and rhetoric, and still an amazing degree of general consensus and political noise. It's hard not to enact something favorable when so much support exists. Policymakers, as one said, "are cowed. Coalitions, especially big ones, create an importance and urgency when there's otherwise chaos and a sense of reluctance to act." Lobbyists who lobby lobbyists are the ones responsible for bringing forward that importance, for making things seem so urgent.

Environmental groups demonstrate this best.[27] They keep coming together even as environmental issues have entered the political mainstream and, as seen earlier, gained a respected position in politics. But no single organization claims to be *the* number one spokesperson for saving the planet. In preparation for the 1995 debates on renewing federal agricultural policies, forty or so environmental interests cooperatively planned their agenda and strategies. To avoid the distractions of Washington, the coalition met in De Kalb, Illinois. Politically, De Kalb is exactly nowhere. But De Kalb is where agriculture *is* what people do. Environmental interests needed and used that setting to focus on the problems of degradation in crop production and processing, which very few of these organizations consider in general terms, or in any integrated or wholistic way. Environmental interests tend to be organized around far more specific concerns that are affected by more than just agriculture: river water quality, soil contamination and abuse, wetlands and marshes, songbird protection, duck hunting, fisheries, air pollution, chemical contamination, and a plethora of other concerns.

Lots of lobbying of other lobbyists must go on for environmental advocates even to gain a common focus when the topic is agriculture. Farming? Agrarianism? What's that? Why's it bad? Aren't farmers the sons of toil, the reliable stewards? In 1993, in De Kalb, some still wondered: "Why the hell are we here? Let's get ready for the next Clean Air Act instead." Lobbying among interests had to correct that impression first, and lots of visual imagery was used to do it. So, they went to De Kalb.

Environmental interests, or enviros, are so good at politics because they keep more or less duplicating the De Kalb example nearly every time a piece of legislation comes up that has important environmental consequences. As a result, they truly frighten likely opponents: on the Clean Air Act, on Clean Water, on pesticide policy, on timber policy, on scenic rivers legislation, on nuclear waste disposal, on funding national parks, and on countless others. As one Chrysler lobbyist said, "Those guys are always there. Like Tonto for the Lone Ranger." And, because the opponents know that the enviros are there with a well-earned and well-coordinated place in interest politics, other interests plan for them. Potential opponents usually try to modify their own public policy wants to incorporate things pleasing to the enviros. This modification solidifies further cooperation on environmental policies, often bringing bigger and more adversarial coalitions. Yet it also ironically encourages enviro interests to escalate their demands.

What can be seen, as well, by looking at the enviros is just how numerous the tasks of coalition building have become. Coalition builders, as do renters, ask and answer several questions: Who's out there with similar goals? Who knows them? Does anyone listen to them? Are they each reliable players, willing to keep their word and not grandstand too much? How can their involvement be ensured? What do they represent? On what issues can they contribute? Can their issues be worked into coalition goals? What's winnable with these interests involved? What'll happen if someone's left out? Finally, coalition building demands lots of interaction, putting up with those few silly players who join the alliance merely for fun or to suit their own egos, and riding herd to prevent interests from joining the other side. "Who's going to lead?" is a related question.

Under those conditions, quite obviously, coalitions tend to be inclusive as opposed to exclusive acts of multiple interests joining together. More, that is, not fewer. If the organizers can get them, congressional enterprises may be invited to join. In theory, interests want to keep coalitions just small enough for them to win.[28] That saves resources. It also saves sharing the rewards and the glory of public policy wins. In reality, there's a problem, though: Nobody knows just what's a small enough number of partners needed to win. And anyone left out may whine so much that the coalition's credibility is lost. Plus, participants in the coalition should get much more information from more contacts with more joiners, not with less. So invitations to coalesce go far and wide to those who pass the itemized checklist of questions.

More than any reason, that explains why coalitions bring groups and institutions together whose representatives dislike each other, both personally and ideologically. When political needs came up, the American Association of Retired Persons (AARP) worked tentatively even with the Gray Panthers. These are very different groups. AARP was started by an insurance firm. The Panthers were led by a true radical. And their respective representatives hated each other. The more traditional National Wildlife Federation and the Sierra Club sometimes sit and plan with protest- and demonstration-minded groups like Greenpeace and the even more radical group Earth First!

Uncertainty, or merely a lack of perfect information, also explains why coalition builders think more broadly than exclusively. Coalitions frequently are made by going beyond interests with an obviously shared concern—such as the elderly or labor. Charcoal manufacturers, quick-stop party store chains, lawn and garden retailers, and amusement parks joined the quite typical Daylight Savings Time Coalition.[29] All benefitted in sales from extended sunshine at the end of the day. Again, the idea of the alliance was to show *all* the support possible.

Sometimes coalitions of this breadth emerge when more seemingly logical coalitions break down. When it became clear that environmental interests would lose on most of their goals in the 1985 farm bill, a small number of environmental interests abandoned the enviro coalition. They then joined another coalition of prominent farm commodity and agribusiness interests to reincorporate some of the environmental provisions into the legislation. Congressional leaders insisted on the cooperation, a condition that underscores yet another two tasks of coalition building.

Joiners need to determine who it is that's really putting the coalition together and why they're doing it. Is it an advocate, and if so, why? Joiners also need to find out what will happen if they don't play. When, for example, revenue sharing was finally passed in the 1960s, it was because of a coalition of true mutual ill will. That coalition consisted of several local government interest groups and several others representing state government.[30] Both sets of players had for years crafted competing policy proposals. That, however, just led to congressional inertia. Policymakers finally said, in effect: get together and come up with a compromise, or nobody gets the goodies. With millions of dollars at stake, a coalition plan was hastily arranged, but only after lots of lobbying and negotiation. After Congress intervened, neither the negotiation nor the agreement was surprising.

But, as so often happens, these local and state officials weren't interests that *wanted* to work together, and revenue sharing as passed wasn't a plan either preferred. That's why, despite all the work involved and their importance, interest coalitions are so shaky and unstable. After their agreement, both state and local interests went back to trying to change things to their own advantage. Endless tinkering with policy formulas ensued. An astute Scottish observer of American politics, D. W. Brogan, observed rather incredulously in the early 1950s that organized interests here have to *use*, not actually *change*, the system.[31] Sometimes who uses whom cuts several ways in coalition politics. But lobbyists know that a small win is still a win, and it's better than a complete loss.

Other Lobbying of Interests

Yet coalitions still lack personal appeal for lobbyists, and not just because they need to share or divide up the spoils of policy outcomes. Lobbyists certainly understand that they have to coalesce, but they don't have to like the need to do it. It's an affront to one's sense of efficacy: "I like to do it alone." As a long-time coalition builder explained, "You do something like that to bring order out of the chaos, not because you know it will work."[32] So, with the prospects of success—or winning—risky, and because of the inherent difficulty of managing coalitions, many interests try to head off the chaos before seeking to coalesce with others. Heading off chaos helps ensure that an interest can as much as possible work alone, or with a hired hand.

There are numerous techniques for staying independent, lots of ways of securing cooperation. Most revolve around "taking out political opponents."[33] The means cover a wide range of tasks, limited only by the creativeness of the players. Essentially, however, there are five main ways to lobby lobbyists, take out likely players, and keep levels of policy making chaos low: keeping contact, organizing a new interest, developing internal consensus in a group that several interests jointly support, coming up with joint non-lobbying projects, and quite simply, attacking potential players so that they stay away from what the initiating interest wants. All just build comfortable relationships, that is to say, more or less cozy.

None of this is too terribly hard, but it consumes time and money. Alan Rosenthal described how Texas trial lawyers did it.[34] The attorney group maintained routine contact and friendly relationships with those that most *might* like to limit either the right to litigate or the amount of damages that can be awarded in a case. The lawyers held a joint annual retreat with physicians, did volunteer work with the American Association of Retired Professionals and other senior citizen groups, and made an informal peace pact with automobile dealers. The Washington Discussion Group (WDG), where top lobbyists entertain public officials, facilitates in similar ways the idea of diverse interests getting to know and understand each other. A few friendships even come from WDG.

As the Texas attorneys demonstrate, maintaining contact and making pals aren't, though, the primary objectives. Interest representatives discuss each other's business, the prospects of mutual agreement, and reasons for exchanging support. They also bargain over the issues that each will avoid, or the other party's issues. When it works, which it often does, participating interests learn to avoid conflict. Lobbyists certainly like doing it: "It's so much easier than coalition work, and it mostly serves the same purpose of winning agreement." This also improves the odds of winning on public policies. For years, most agribusiness firms disliked government support of farming and resulting limits on crop production. But most didn't complain about it. These businesses had other issues; farm interest groups had theirs; each stuck to their own; and agricultural policy never broke out in open warfare.

Such contact work pays off, to an extent. While Social Security reform was under way in Congress in 1983, various interests were informally sharing information and negotiating among themselves on a daily basis. But that didn't keep the chaos down or make other lobbying of lobbyists unnecessary. With 200 organized interests active on reform, a dozen or so different coalitions emerged and at least 200 multiclient firms were hired. Approximately one-quarter of the contract firms employed prominent, big-time players.[35] "I remember," said one of them, "I felt like starting an autograph book." Chaos wasn't managed, though, it rampaged on. Too much was going on for it to subside.

Given the impediments to agreements, organized interests have looked for other ways to minimize the chaos, or maintain friendly relations and win agreements. An immensely popular practice among businesses is to form a new interest group. To some extent, the Business Roundtable was built on that idea. But not quite. It has little life of its own, whereas new groups do.

When puzzling policy problems appear or government embarks on a new policy approach, affected interests often see many others that share the same bewildering situation. In order to stay with their own issues, continue to do their own regular work, and just to cover all the ground that the new problems pose, affected advocates prefer to let somebody else take care of the added responsibilities—someone of their choosing, if possible. The organizations, or oftentimes their members, start the new interest group, hire staff, and pay dues. The new kids specialize in the emergent issue, become expert and informed, provide selective member services, and generally handle issues that the joiners agree upon. As with other interest groups, though, the joiners set policy. New groups are started like this routinely, but they are obviously not as common as coalitions since they cost so much to form.

As the twentieth century comes to a close, most of the new problems, issues, and interests are concerned with various and sundry aspects of technology. Electric automobiles, biotechnology in medicine, biotechnology in agriculture, computer software, video movie rentals, and online computer networks have all generated new interest groups. Intellectual property rights, or the patent protection of individual ideas, brought about a dizzying array of new lobbying organizations. First, interests that conceived of new products were formed—representing chemicals, plastics, and technologies to improve other products. Then came technology associations. Computers, programs, communications, and the like all gained new advocacy groups. Finally the entertainment and cultural industries came, trying to protect films, books, and other things that can be reproduced cheaply and easily.

All those interest groups descended on the federal government. As it later became obvious that foreign production was a problem, they complained to U.S. public officials and also lobbied internationally. For instance, the more than 1,300-member International Intellectual Property Alliance moved to have trade sanctions imposed on three countries that the group saw as the worst violators and offenders: Russia, Greece, and Paraguay. All of this was heady stuff for the interests that had sponsored the new groups: "Wow, foreign policy!" A relatively new member of Congress also thought it heady: "Aw, jeez, man. I hope they can work it out among themselves. Jeez!" Otherwise, there would be too many hassles for him.

Forming new interest groups by established interests is time-honored politics, but also certainly a major reason why the number of lobbies has grown so since 1960.[36] The policy disturbances created by citizen advocacy, or public-interest-style, groups led to new issues, new challenges, and a resulting usefulness for new interests and other forums for planning for cooperative action.[37] The Tobacco Institute provides the highest profile example. Founded in 1958 by the largest U.S. cigarette manufacturers, the Institute is *always* in the news. Red dresses are prominent, which are nearly all that the Tobacco Institute's main spokeswoman seems to wear. They're like a symbol of power, which tobacco interests need desperately. Previously the different corporations just lobbied the old-boy networks of congresspersons from home. It was easy in the 1950s, however. Tobacco politics thereafter took on new complexity as health critiques began to grow both in number and in the severity of their charges.[38] The old tobacco companies needed updated representation: professional images, knowledge about bureaucracy and administration, ability to argue the fine points of scientific research, and a common ground from which executives could explore and reach agreements on strategic lobbying options. The emergent Institute did all that, as well as building further on old-boy politics wherever possible.

The Tobacco Institute is hardly an anomaly. As shown in Chapter Two, business firms play this game all the time. It's a routine of institutional interest politics. Food politics is a fantasy land of such unique, often rather odd, interests created years ago in the face of new threats.[39] Each large agribusiness manufacturer boasts several products and, accordingly, finds representation in several trade associations that organize the many different resulting industries. Archer-Daniels-Midland belongs to several groups, ranging from commercial fish raising to ethanol production to refining products from corn. Of all those trade associations, the Corn Refiners Association (CRA) has taken on the greatest importance. For years, only seven corporations, each with intense rivalries and innate political instincts, dominated this huge industry. The inclination, of course, was always to "screw the other guy in both business and politics." This, of course, led too often to chaos, and political losses. CRA helped ease tensions between firms at least a little bit.

The U.S. Feedgrains Council brings farmers, grain traders, and shippers together on newly developed international issues, and it has done even better than CRA. Council work has at least obliterated the business view that all farmers are stupid, as well as the farm view that all businesspeople are crooks. That certainly makes compromise and shared politics easier. Nasty words between the two forces are rarely heard in today's politics as a result.

The importance of such specialized, multifirm affiliation isn't the result of continuous interaction, however. For the most part, the associations simply watchdog politics, attack minor problems, and go about providing selectively received member services. They hold many conferences. Sponsoring members leave them pretty much alone under routine conditions. Yet when major issues of the association come up, things change into a flurry of member involvement. The old interests, inside the new groups, take on new life around their own policies. Efforts to negotiate on a mutually desirable response among members are, at those times, assumed to be warranted. Lobbyists from each supportive interest show up. Arguments to put aside firm rivalries are frequent. And new resources, usually to hire still more help, are often allocated. Such associations are, in other words, a kind of ongoing repository in which lobbyists can lobby each other intensely whenever needs arise. Because of at least casual long-term member ties, periodic revivals of these groups as major policy players are a whole lot easier and quicker than starting a new group or feeling out unfamiliar coalition partners. Going from the routine to the intense is easier and quicker than establishing cooperation all over again. That's important, because timing matters so greatly in public policymaking.

The weaknesses of both coalitions and new or revived groups are essentially the same. If members can't agree, they lobby on their own and that old chaos reigns. As Richard Cohen so nicely demonstrated, the politics of what eventually became the 1990 Clean Air Act kept getting more and more chaotic.[40] Policymakers had tried for a decade to write it as a replacement for the first Clean Air Act. Agreements couldn't be reached. Coalitions were splintered. Trade associations were split. Opposing organized interests were bitter and in no mood to join with adversaries. And congressional committees, as Cohen said, just "crumbled." Nothing happened for years.

The legislation was written and passed in a very weakened interest group setting. And it only happened when congressional leadership insisted on a policy result quickly. To that end, leaders organized their own coalition of other interests to make something happen. The coalition was made up of and propelled by a broad assortment of congressional enterprises, all working with their key interests back home. All of these homefolks feared something in the bill and wanted those troublesome items contained. What resulted was a hodgepodge of constituent wants rather than a well-detailed and logical environmental plan. Yet, as a staff member of the Speaker of the House roared, "By God, it *was* a result, a product!"

In a sense, this second Clean Air Act was little more than a common project. It was a big puzzle that members of Congress pieced together only because they agreed to do it. The project, rather than really clean air, was the immediate goal. It was the instrument for cooperation in an otherwise chaotic situation. Because advocates understand the frailty of coalitions and collective associations, organized interests rely on such projects frequently because of the enforced binds they create. Cooperating players have to get the project done because commitments and promises have been made.

Projects work, then, also for interests outside of the Congress. Archer-Daniels-Midland (ADM) joined that cooperative, multi-interest federal project to develop new products from farm commodities and their by-products. Why? Because committed cooperation was the best way possible to maintain farm and small industry support of the federal New Uses initiative, a project that ADM found to be worthwhile. Those once marginal other agricultural supporters were made full-blown partners in the project, just to keep them committed.

Another splendid project united the highly competitive U.S. sporting goods industry, a set of interests always trying to win an economic edge over their competitors. Firms such as Nike and Puma were once felt to be willing to underbid their mothers if needed for new product economies. They were all very competitive. So none of them were crazy about eliminating child labor in the foreign production of their goods. Child labor was cheap, especially in the Far East. They also knew that somebody would violate any association agreements if they were mere suggestions or guidelines. However, as international child rights advocates gained the media spotlight, the sporting goods companies felt compelled to act. They committed themselves not to an abstract goal but to an actual multifirm public campaign to fight against soccer balls made by kids. The project set effective limits on firms that gained market advantages by using child labor. Pleased that chaos was being managed, members of Congress praised the action and backed off in sponsoring child labor restrictions. Congress was preempted, and members were happy about it.

The scope of projects committing multiple interests can be huge. It seems that anything can be done to obtain something that interests see as mutually advantageous and worthwhile, but impossible to do on any one organization's own. And what can be bigger and more impossible than the prospect of five American, Japanese, and European petroleum-related companies leasing Russian mineral and oil rights, negotiating terms of agreements and markets, securing U.S. government support, getting investors, and convincing the Russians to adequately stabilize both their economy and society? Perhaps only getting a highly competitive oil and service corporation policy coalition could be more daunting and cumbersome. Nonetheless, a small number of international and domestic companies worked on and arranged such a project in the mid-1990s.

The lobbyists and other executives who did it found themselves with an awesome set of tasks required to make the project work. Since much of the project was beyond what company executives do, and obviously within the whirl of government, several Washington and foreign representatives were given expanded duties and found a new need to trust one another. Paula Freer of USX subsidiary Marathon Oil lobbied the U.S. Congress, the White House, American diplomats, the Alaskan governor, Russian bureaucrats and legislators, the Russian public, and various entrepreneurs and investors. She dragged Russians to America, helped establish food programs in Russia for the elderly, battled congressional restrictions, flew to the far reaches of eastern Russia to review facilities and took a U.S. Senate delegation there as well, worked with diverse international corporations, and generally stressed herself into a frenzy. But the project advanced well through 1997, stymied mostly by Russian crime and economic insolvency. Nobody, though, had thought that a collection of cross-industry firms could even stay together long enough to accomplish any of it. The common project was usefully binding, across even international boundaries. As a result, the firms worked together nicely in their lobbying as well.

There are, then, considerable variations on lobbying other interests, or on what both scholars and lobbyists too imprecisely call coalition building. Most of the variations don't involve real coalition politics at all, but refinements and innovations on informal interest arrangements. If lobbyists can afford or merely identify the alternatives, they seem to prefer these agreements, at least when circumstances warrant. They're simply less confining than a coalition: "You retain your freedom. Yeah, freedom." The hired help, the new group, the common project, and the old standby association are all forms of interaction among interests that can be rallied around as strategies. All can be seen as improvements of a sort over forever shaky but still very commonly used coalitions, steps forward in better lobbying of lobbyists. All are things lobbyists would rather use to clear the clutter.

At least in terms of cooperative civility, there also are tactics that are steps backward, of course. This brings up another whole set of lobbying tasks. Not shockingly, lobbyists can be lobbied by personal threats and intimidation. Threaten them with losses, damaged regulations, bills that will lose in the future, loss of credibility, new contracts, future job prospects—all work. While that doesn't lead to consensus, negotiated agreement, or a lessening of hostility between organizations, it goes on. And chaos can be muted this way to a great extent, at the expense of fear. As a high-profile contract lobbyist mused, "If I can scare the hell out of someone, he or she eases off and looks for something else to do. It's as good as getting a partner, a very silent one." Silent indeed. What lobbyists who threaten others want is, as true of all lobbying of lobbyists, to be left alone. Lobbyists want to be given more of an open, unrestricted playing field, to keep their issues their own, on their own turf. And to do it they're willing to let others do the same.

More threatening goes on than many realize, at least in subtle and indirect fashion. At least lobbyists say it does. The proof can't be found in a database, but examples are plentiful. When American Civil Liberties Union (ACLU) lobbyists resisted campaign finance restrictions on a major reform bill in Congress, old liberal allies were angry. Their threat was simple: If ACLU didn't come up with a proposal, rather than just say no to it all, the group would be dropped from all negotiations on the bill. Indications of the threatening tendencies of lobbyists lobbying lobbyists also can be seen in public policy results more generally. Several scholars have noted that numerous—often most—issues and bills are uncontested.[41] Others have found that interests often avoid bills and regulatory decisions that seem germane to them or to their members.[42] And it has been found that lobbyists seldom try to overextend their interests, or promote more than they can manage.[43]

At least in many cases, the reasons can be seen in the informal contacts made in the large universe of organized interests. Many produce friendly results; others do not. The subtle threats made as lobbyists position themselves aren't friendly. When lobbyists rub elbows, though, they do learn things from one another— some good, some bad. Environmentalists, for example, learned not to challenge farm interests until they had first won on easier issues. In the same way, the NAACP learned that the focus of the civil rights movement had to be on issues of political and personal participation, not on economics. They preached that lesson, in turn, to peer groups. Likewise, contract lobbyists learn *not* to work for certain firms, and to try to work for others. Those too disadvantaged to win are to be avoided.

In essence, there exists a social networking in any community of lobbyists. Within the networks, or through the grapevine, interest representatives teach each other who can win what, what should be avoided, and how to build careers. Those who make internal policy within interest organizations teach the same things. However, the intent of networking is not just to develop friendly agreements. There's a tremendous amount of positioning that goes on, bluffs if you will. Puffing up at the expense of someone who has little courage for a tussle often wins a lot.

So, a great deal of lobbying of lobbyists is much like lobbying policymakers. Information is spread with a spin. Cards are held close to the gambler's chest so that other players can't see. Ideas are planted. Fears are instilled. This process involves several tasks that have often been identified with lobbying but that haven't been seen as instrumental or strategic actions: hanging around, going to all the proper events, shooting the bull, telling stories, winning collegial respect, and helping others sort out their options. Lobbyists aren't social workers or journalists. In public at least, they never stop lobbying. In the immortal words of lobbyist Jack White of Patton, Boggs, and Blow, they just keep working the crowds until they have to say FIDO: "Fuck it, drive on." Then they end their day.

The Resiliency of Interest Politics

Scholars and lobbyists both describe interest politics as made up of communities, where people are familiar with one another. Andrew McFarland calls them little villages.[44] Each policy area in each government is its own village setting. People in villages adapt, quite obviously, to one another. It's plausible, then, that lobbying of lobbyists rather sensibly—and without becoming a logistical nightmare—brings about an odd mix of cooperation, coercion, and agreement. And it quite plausibly brings both honesty and subterfuge.

The general adaptability of interests over time was evident in the last chapter. Interests reacted by playing variations of the contact game as governing institutions changed. In other words, make contacts, but now with different folks, other lobbyists. Moreover, it's well understood that interests adapt to one another, being together in those little villages. Rosenthal explained that compromise became ever more the order of the day as more interests organized and as more policymakers showed greater concern with issues than with old-boy friendships.[45] Virginia Gray and David Lowery demonstrated even greater interest adaptability.[46] By looking at the various environmental settings in which lobbyists do business, they found that both the number and the diversity of interests varied substantially. In large part, it was the different locations that mattered most. The more policymakers in a place, the more organized interests, too.

So it's no surprise that, as more interests form, more lobbyists rub elbows with one another *and* try to influence each other's behavior. They must do so in order to win their public policy goals. As a result, organized interests hire more help, enter more coalitions, form more working relationships, and continually try to keep other lobbyists out of their way. Sometimes when other things fail, they even enter into government-sponsored negotiated settlements with one another.[47] Reg-neging it's called, or negotiating regulation or rule-making. Public officials act as referees, or try to. It's almost a cliche, then: Lobbyists are lobbying other lobbyists with greater frequency.

All this affects the policy making process. One noticeable change shows Congress passing fewer bills but more big—or omnibus—ones.[48] States are doing the same in many legislatures. Omnibus bills deal with bunches of related, or sort of related, issues all at one time, in bits and pieces, additively and cumulatively. As such, omnibus bills are a great deal for mutual lobbying agreements.[49] It's one item for the Teamsters, another for the United Auto Workers, and something else for the National Education Association, all in a labor bill. Pretty soon a big package keeps nearly every active interest happy, one piece at a time.

Only the scope of lobbying other interests is new. Interests for nearly two centuries have hired other interests—remember Thurlow Weed. And they've played coalition politics—remember industrialists and financiers developing the West. Both were done then, as now, on matters of great national importance. Another thing that's not new is cooperative success. When lobbyists lobby other interests, public policy decisions frequently get made—far from always, yet often. And only because chaos is minimized.

Minimizing chaos brings up another vital point. Interests have fit well their environments through alliances and opposition. They've made the continuity of politics possible, not dragged the process into oblivion. Sure it's harder to make public policy today and for many reasons, more interests being only one of them. But organized interests do their part to contribute to an active government. Plenty of lobbyists want bills passed and regulations made. They get them, as they always did.

What's significant about the current fit is easily observed. As more and more interests burden the process, substantial policy reform that truly changes who gets what is increasingly tough.[50] It's next to impossible. Brogan the Scotsman implied that. But it's not impossible because of overt conflict among interests or just because there exist too many lobbyists. Rather, it's because the size of the total lobby makes it harder to be familiar with the many players. Too many have moved out to the village outskirts. Too many have even changed villages, both permanently and temporarily—that is, they've moved on to less traditional issues and even new policy areas. The old sense of community is lost. Lost, also, is a lot of political trust. Even policy analysts are suspect today as just from another lobby.[51] So lobbyists work harder than ever to lobby other interests, win solid and credible supporters, and keep what relationships they can.

Where does this get public policymaking? Simple. Lots of old issues, old policy provisions, and old issue benefits are preserved. Farmers keep getting government money, even as programs are altered. To placate organized interests who want change, such as mandated nutritional standards for foods, agreements are reached that give them some. Most of this goes on by working more things into cumbersome omnibus legislation, things that challenger groups want and things that don't terribly bother established lobbies.

Agreements between interests let most players win a little, through the accommodation of other lobbies. If they can't agree among themselves, organizations hire help that can build agreements. When tobacco firms couldn't agree on how to negotiate a federal settlement on liability for their products in 1997, they hired former Senator George Mitchell to do it for them. Organized interests fit so well the dimensions of American politics—both traditional and modern—that they keep the games going, even under the most challenging conditions.[52] They keep the primacy of process alive. After all, process is the essence of the environment for all of them. While many would see that as an unfortunate situation, interests certainly fit an America that values its diversity more than it does a single plan for anything or everything. Accommodating diversity—as long as it is not too extremist—is easier to agree upon than a common good, and lobbyists can easily do the former.

Summary and Highlights

This chapter emphasizes that the majority of organized interests can't lobby successfully on their own most of the time. They lack the organizational resources and maybe just the prominence to do so. In particular, they can't just run over and destroy everyone else who's out there pushing. They're just like staff from the White House, unorganized segments of society, and firms that wish to restrain free trade: They cooperate, at more or less formal levels and in different ways. Confronted with various circumstances, then, organized interests do what it takes to win. They forage for help.[53] Or, more accurately, they lobby for help and accept help to win, and maybe even survive as organizations. Winning on some occasions demands hiring help. That's why there's plenty of it out there. On other occasions, starting new organizations or revitalizing old ones works well, as do common projects. Ties that, like marriage, bind at least for a while matter. Interests forming interest groups or other unique cooperative arrangements is one reason the number of groups continuously increases.

On other occasions, and for still other organizations, there are two polar opposite variations of agreement among interests. Coalitions *can* be ways that interests give up on themselves for a greater good, only to help society. Threats *can* keep other interests quiet, if a lobbyist just grabs, shakes, and punches another one. Of course, both of these extremes are rarely, rarely practiced—and they couldn't be frequent. How could supporters or opponents let others slide by that way? Yet interests, indeed, do cooperate in coalitions to promote their own issues. And there's a subtle kind of intimidation, or teaching about whose turf is whose, that goes on in all of the lobbyists' little villages.

What should be obvious are the following points. Lobbying other lobbyists isn't easy. They can and will say no. Also, though, and despite self-interest, lobbyists face a stronger tendency to cooperate than to fight things out with all possible opponents. That's one reason why they fit the political process so well. Acknowledging that tendency, and its widespread application, doesn't obscure yet a third point: Agreements, when reached, offer no panacea. They don't always bind, certainly not over time. Participants do bail out on one another. Frequently they simply just lose out on what policy goals they want.

Nobody wins all the time in American politics. That's why a larger lesson has so far been this book's major object. To wit. Since no interest wins all the time, rarely do good lobbyists and knowledgeable interests do only one thing or follow a single set of tasks, such as the contact game. They target all directions if needed. Since successful lobbyists must win attention, peddle their information, and reinforce their own usefulness in the eyes of public officials, their business is a complex one. And they work at it harder than many think. Easy conclusions about what matters most should be avoided. After all, even those often vilified development interests of the nineteenth century paid attention to public opinion, buying off public officials, explaining policy consequences, hiring help, and building coalitions. Most of that still goes on, for similar reasons of uncertainty, for fear of losing. As one retired lobbyist said, "I was never sure exactly what would bring victory. My group advocated before anyone who might count: the public, reporters, all sorts of officials, and all the groups I could recall. It was a hell of a job."

That then removes a few of the abstractions and provides some specific settings for understanding what interests generally do. That was the intent of the last three chapters. Yet is that enough to cover and consider? Does doing it all really count for everything? Is winning at public policy about good techniques, or about something else? What happens to interests that do very little within the political process? Is anyone in such a favored position? Are there good issues and bad ones when it comes to winning? These questions are the concerns of the next two chapters. Nearly everyone gets represented in America by someone, more or less. Let's now turn to *why* more representation is of far greater consequence for an interest than is doing less. And let's consider also why it matters for successful public policymaking.

7

Getting What Interests Want: The Winners

The cumulative effects of advocacy, or lobbying, produce American public policy. Lobbyist do what's needed, which is increasingly lots of things. No doubt. Other things, of course, enhance those cumulative effects. There's no doubt about that, either. But when organized interests employ numerous tasks, win access, provide information, reinforce their presence, keep their issues alive, and lobby multiple targets, it makes for more likely success. But they succeed also because they have good issues.

Issues seem to be a second key to understanding successful lobbying, or a second set of factors, because marketable and manageable issues make an interest successful. While well-organized interests can, in theory, do a great deal to translate clunker issues into sound ones, sound interests will usually leave the clunkers alone. In all likelihood, they can't be won. Lobbyists, and legislators too, tend to think of issues as either good or bad, either easy or hard to represent. In thinking about issues this way, they don't mean that the issues produce public policies that are appropriate, fair, and deserving. Nor do they mean the contrary. Good and bad only mean whether these issues are likely or not to pass.

As the next two chapters will make clear, what seems to be the highly subjective quality of an issue and the otherwise quite observable depth of the lobbying effort reinforce one another. There's mutual reinforcement at work. Issues that can't win don't make for solidly organized interests. Lousy representation, or an inadequate lobbying strategy, similarly can stall an issue that is otherwise respectable and winnable. A better organized interest often later comes along and sells that issue. But that hardly ever happens with a bad issue. So, to answer the questions at the end of Chapter Six, there's indeed more to successful lobbying than just doing lots of things well. Harold Wolman and Fred Teitelbaum rather obliquely hinted at these other things in quite an offhanded way.[1] They said that an interest's influence should be judged on the bulk of public policy that gives it benefits. That's very sensible, since lobbying is about winning rather than about waiting forty years for a single big score.

What else is there that matters? Well, Kansas Republican Senator Pat Roberts once said in describing a just enacted bill: "I think all the stars had to be right in the policy heavens."[2] That also makes some sense. And it's true, because the overall conditions of the political universe, or environment, make some issues good ones on which to lobby and others near impossible, or really bad ones.

How can one issue be good and another bad? On the surface, that's a totally subjective and value-laden distinction, and maybe even an offensive one. Good-versus-bad no doubt conjures up images of popular and unpopular issues. That's unfortunate, because it's not the distinction here. The distinction, in reality, isn't nearly as subjective as it seems.

The distinction between good and bad issues lies with who defines their substantive content, and why those players define issues the way they do. It's a matter of lobbied issues being placed in the broader context of public policy. Substance is nothing more—or less—than exactly what gets placed into law. What do laws and rules promote? What do they allow? And disallow? As much as governing organizations, those things *are* the public institutions of American policymaking.

Why's that important? It matters for three related and expansive reasons. First, when institutions are put in place, restrictive determinations of what can and can't be done follow, by definition. Also what follows is a determination of what dollars are spent on whom. Second, when new policy proposals are initiated, they must be filtered. The filters are the public officials who guard legal gates, who keep some things out and let others through. Third, none of these gatekeepers like to take away what members of the public gain, or value, in public policies. That's where the popularity feature *does* enter as part of the equation, but the tendency is more general than specific only to good issues. People just like, or find good, whatever it is that they've become accustomed to getting from government.

Here's the logic. If something fits what's been done before, that issue is easy to integrate into existing institutions. "Modify a policy," say the legal gatekeepers. If something hasn't been done before, and doesn't mess up those public policies that do exist, it's easily added as new policy. Gatekeepers find them OK. Both types make for good issues.

Now here are the bad issues. If something hasn't been done, and if it *does* threaten to mess with existing directions and funding of public policy, what happens? Generally nothing. It becomes a dead issue. Gatekeepers are dismayed by the lobbied issue. They fail to like it. They resist, unless changing social and economic conditions are so severe that a crisis determines the need for immediate policy action. Remember, crises have been hinted at earlier in this text as an important factor in policy making, infrequent but important. Crises present advocates with risky but still marginal issues. Gatekeepers are uncertain about them, confused as to their consequences. Nobody knows how the stars in the political heavens are realigning, just that they are. The only constant in crisis resolution is avoiding truly radical departures.

The result is easy to see. Public policy proposals are the issues that lobbyists initiate. And these issues won't very easily go far, or win, unless they're compatible with existing policy and its direction. That means that there's a base of existing public policies that original interests, if they really want to win, are ill-advised to threaten. That policy base of Wolman and Teitelbaum matters greatly, as much as does mounting a comprehensive lobbying strategy when it's needed.[3] Kenneth Shepsle said it well: There's a broadly encompassing policy equilibrium in American politics.[4]

Interests that fit or look like they fit the equilibrium have good issues. Those that don't fit it have bad ones. That's why good and bad have little to do with subjective popularity, just the overall ease of making decisions in government. Saying that certainly adds an expanded dimension to this analysis of interests. It makes it even more clear why the fit of organized interests is so important to explain, why the changing of fits matter. If they want success, lobbies can't pick up just any issue that their representatives or supporters might like, at any time of their own choosing. They can advocate anything at all, but they'll plod along like Don Quixote if they do. They'll be jousting with windmills, which are all too stationary to budge.

This chapter will look at who wins within such an institutional setting. Because politics isn't *that* perfectly predictable, it looks at who tends actually to win. Chapter Eight will turn to bad issues and loser interests. From these two contrasting perspectives, each chapter will emphasize, first of all, the difficulties faced by groups and other organized interests that want to be successful players, and that do or don't become successes. Second, the chapters will cover the responses and the problems of the gatekeepers as involved public policymakers. Both chapters will cover things that public officials like to face and things they don't like to encounter. Third, attention will be given to why either existing institutions, given their structure, are so compatible (this chapter) or so constraining (the next chapter).

Which Are Those Fortunate Interests?

A better question is: Which interests have good issues? There are lots of them. It makes little sense here to do an exhaustive inventory. A few examples, though, are useful, especially since a series of lessons emerge around them. Take the individual American states. They teach two important points: one about the idea of privileged positioning, the other about making such positioning pay off by asking for the right things. The Farm Bureau has good issues in Iowa, as long as it sticks to things such as agricultural research and marketing. But the Iowa Farm Bureau cannot change banking laws. Tourist interests and their issues are solid in Hawaii, Florida, and Minnesota. They win as long as they want state assistance for tourist promotion, as opposed to large fees assessed on vacationers or bans on commerce and industry. Both the United Auto Workers and General Motors have good issues in Michigan, if they stick to jobs and profits. Those issues become losers these days if either lobby wages a political war on the other. That's bad issue selection. Once that was a good choice, however, before political and economic conditions changed in Michigan and moved more to consensus politics.

For each of the above interests, issues, and state governments, there's an inherent logic in what makes for a good or a bad public policy proposal.[5] Strong interests fit their own state in quite obvious ways.[6] That's what Jeffrey Berry was getting at when he revisited Charles Lindblom's idea of the privileged or preferred positioning of American business.[7] Positioning has to do with more than tangible resources that assist lobbying. Berry noted that business won preference because it's also seen widely as critical to national economic well-being. That gives it a great fit. Those with such privileged status are interests that officials and the public in a particular state can easily rally around. Iowa prospers from farmers, and especially the meat industry. Michigan prospers from automobile sales. The other states benefit from loads of travelers. A second point, however, is that none of these interests in these particular states can demand just anything and still be successful. In all likelihood, they wouldn't try such an approach. So, at the most simple level, good issues can be seen as good for government, as well as good for those who want things from government.

Winnable issues such as these also build on what the states already do. However, all of those interests in each of those states mount extensive public affairs efforts. Public appeals, direct lobbying of policymakers, and agreements with related interests are all in play. Why? Those who want winnable things get good support, organizationally and politically. And then they easily find supporters to protect what they've won. That's a third lesson from the American states: Good issues bring forth solid lobbies because these issues so easily find supporters.

History expands on each of those lessons. Let's return again to farm interest groups, specifically the American Farm Bureau Federation and the Grange. Farming was such a dominant feature of American society in an agrarian nation that its interest politics was central to a broader and more general understanding. This wasn't minor politics. Indeed the lobbies of agriculture may well be as numerous as that of any policy area even today.

As discussed earlier, the Farm Bureau received considerable credit for passing farm price supports in the 1930s, as the first Agricultural Adjustment Act.[8] Yet David Hamilton failed to wholeheartedly agree with that claim.[9] As he pointed out, economists inside government had a great deal to do with both formulating and advancing those subsidies. Other scholars saw things as Hamilton did with his emphasis on the importance of public officials. They've cited the capacity, or carrying load, of the national government as the factor most responsible for those policies.[10]

Government was organized to do that policy. It's really quite a silly disagreement. Apart from their contrasting emphases, both sides see things pretty much alike. Who moved whom is the dividing question, as if one force *must* be the cause of the other.

Why were both points of view correct? Forget the line of players, or the idea of linearity in lobbying. Certainly the Farm Bureau mounted a superb public affairs effort.[11] It was pioneering. But the Farm Bureau also was advantaged by the institutions of national government. Decades of federal service to farmers were in play. A huge policy base of education, research, and extension existed. Plenty of laws and considerable financial investments had been made. In turn, these were administered by a wide range of technical experts whose jobs were to advance farmer interests and keep these people in production.[12]

In a crisis situation, as with the agricultural depression of the 1920s and 1930s, there was a relatively easy and painless way to realign the policy heavens: Just give farmers federal checks. The government already helped often. Now it had only to do a little more. At any rate, that was the logic of public policy experts who were part of the process. Jess Gilbert and Carolyn Howe had a marvelous insight.[13] Since both private interests and public officials were so active on the issue, it was probably the unspecified interaction of the two that produced public policy. Social forces didn't do it alone. Nor did economists from within the American nation-state. It was the two reinforcing one another. So another lesson emerges: Sound lobbies work well with public policymakers when the issues generally satisfy both. That's when good issues emerge.

But farm interest group success demonstrates even a bit more than when good issues emerge. Like the Farm Bureau and winning farm subsidies, the Grange won successful railroad regulation some five decades earlier. Both the Grange and Farm Bureau were advantaged by a growing plethora of government programs working to advance agrarian and western development. The two groups also experienced similar difficulties. Policy transformations were required, which are always touchy, but neither interest faced a reversal of existing public policy. Direct subsidies in the 1930s were a relatively new way to meet policy goals. So was regulating business, the railroads, in the 1870s.

Nonetheless, both organized interests and public officials could argue the very same thing on those two occasions, even separated as they were by five decades. State legislators, for the Granges, and federal economists, for the Farm Bureau, howled a common refrain. They pointed to all that was done earlier to achieve agrarian development. They wanted something concrete done because the previous policy base wasn't put there to bring about farm failure. Failure at that juncture, they concluded, would waste all those earlier federal and state actions. Ouch! Most especially, they maintained, they didn't want to break trust with those whom government helped into these difficult straits. If they did, they'd be sorry: Politics would only intensify. Lesson five: Mutually satisfactory issues for private and public forces matter when real, identifiable people are the beneficiaries, especially if those people have long-term policy standing. Those who sustain interest groups and who are in a personal way the direct constituencies of government are really of special consequence in making an issue a good one.

There are then five lessons: privileged positioning, reasonable demands, the resulting emergence of issue-dependent solid lobbies, satisfactory policy goals for both private and public sectors, and the identification of specific constituencies. Each can be seen a bit more clearly in reexamining a few other interests that have been examined in earlier chapters. Revisiting them helps illuminate earlier discussions, making it clear that more than good lobbying is at work.

Recall business interests first: firms, trade associations, coalitions, and cooperative projects. A grand political response by business developed in the late 1970s, when labor interests tried to quickly and quietly pass a relatively modest extension of the National Labor Relations Act. It was to be the Labor Law Reform Act. Labor interests were in a preferred position. It was their bill, their public policy, and it wasn't harsh or radical, just an attempt to secure a few more union rights.[14] Unions were privileged also to have loads of pro-labor Democrats in office. And they had lots of Democratic voters to keep these officeholders happy.

But labor's quick start did its organized union interests no good in the long haul. The issue was a bad one when battled by a formidable lobby. This period of time was not good for the general economy, for most large U.S. corporations, and for small businesses in general. The federal budget was in disarray. Labor union strength was often seen as a reason for this. So, when businesses heard of a new labor act, they mobilized quickly and well—even after the House of Representatives had passed the bill.

The Business Roundtable was especially significant, solidifying a consensus of Fortune 500 companies against reform.[15] More important were small businesses. The grassroots from main streets came alive, calling it deathblow legislation. An end to jobs, small companies, and local economic stability at home was the message. Congress was blasted with it. Given the times, all the opposition, and the resulting worries of members of Congress and the administration, Democrats backed off. Labor lost too many of its policy-making supporters, and with them its early position.[16] It became a dead proposal then. No one of consequence would further back the bill, agreeing that it was too risky to let it win. Policy experts wrote dire warnings. So much for the permanence of privileged and preferred position.

As a single institutional entity, business could not keep the winning streak alive for long. Coalitions, as seen, are, after all, ad hoc. Even when their Republican allies came to Washington with President Ronald Reagan in 1981, business unity was fragmented. The pro-business Economic Recovery Tax Act was the first one up: tax levels down, federal spending cut. It was a general plan, simple and popular. Business interests couldn't, however, agree to it. Nor could conservative, reform-oriented members of Congress from various parts of the country. Some opponents were midwestern Republicans; others were moderate southern Democrats; still others were supply-side Republicans from the West.[17] All they shared was disagreement. It was clear that the public wanted changes in economic policy and that a majority of public officials supported those changes too. But not all of the public officials wanted the same thing.

The Reagan administration was perplexed. It *needed* legislation. So, diverse organized business interests, along with their no less diverse supportive public officials, agreed to a very cobbled up and complicated bill.[18] Much came out of the chaos and into the legislation. Some budget cuts were made, as well as some considerable budget increases, especially for defense. Numerous tax cuts for specific businesses were added. Tax breaks for other regional interests were also added. And a big increase in the federal budget deficit occurred. There were far more tax cuts than program cuts in the final legislation.

Why had this seemingly prominent business consensus fallen apart when its very own president was just elected? That's easy to explain. In looking at the existing base of American public policies, including tax policy, business lobbyists couldn't lobby lobbyists enough to stick to Reagan's plan. Consensus was impossible. Why even try to work together? They believed a bill had to pass, no doubts. Reagan would do it. Cooperation, then, wasn't in their interests. And the public didn't know or care about specifics.

Regular citizens were all wrapped up in the election of the great communicator, Reagan. They trusted him. And he talked on, reassuringly. But his administration had a bad issue: major reform, big changes. The good issues of merely tinkering with the old policy base were commandeered by assorted and competitive business interests and various allies in office, in bits and pieces. All the winning players were happy that they fit into mainstream politics. That quite obviously was a position that Washington outsider President Reagan did *not* have. He wanted to take too much away, strip away too many beneficiaries. Under those conditions, businesses could win more for themselves without sticking together and agreeing on a simple bill. So they splintered, in ways that they had not in the 1970s with their consensual good issue of just plain defeating greedy old labor.

Well-organized social causes evidence good issues as well. As discussed at length in earlier chapters, environmental interests faced difficult lobbying circumstances. Most policy making players, both private and public, saw enviros as some kind of odd and unintelligible, religious-type figures. Maybe they were, in today's words, a cult. Nonetheless, environmentalists had good issues, even though they advanced them slowly.

Let's inventory the advantages.[19] First, there was the ancient stewardship myth of taking care of the world. It was linked to agrarian values of the countryside, a good place to live. This, then, was a great myth for lobbyists to cling to. Second, there were respected conservation interests that had been active in politics since the early twentieth century. Plus, numerous policies were in place, with federal parks, forests, game and fish programs, and lots of institutionalization in law and public administration. Supporters were in place inside government. So this was a very recognizable public policy position. Third, the public ardently did things that used those programs. They also joined the interest groups that advanced and protected them, sportspersons clubs and such.

Fourth, conservation programs were indeed failing at their promises, and so they were subject to criticism. Poor fishing and park and forest degradation were two among several obvious problems. Fifth, conservation lobbyists came to be convinced that new public policy strategies were needed. Sixth, the environmentalists had ready proposals, with believable explanations, and their lobbyists spoke as an extension of early conservation rhetoric. Enviros also didn't initially threaten natural resource use or refuse to negotiate. Seventh, environmental interests were slowly able to convert public myths into more specific public perceptions, especially through teachers, school children, and education.

Eighth, environmentalists identified themselves as outsiders to win sympathy and to label any opponents powerful bad guys and conspirators. Really awful folks were seen as opposing environmentalist goals. Ninth, enviros proceeded slowly, not challenging and beating too many established interests at any one time. They waited until a generally favorable public opinion emerged before they opposed *all* the bad guys at once. Tenth, those public officials who had not been supportive initially just had to eventually fall in line. At least enough of them felt they had to do so.

Finally, there were many groups organized because there were many different aspects—and so lots of issues—to the environment, to saving the planet. That gave each of many different public officials things to do, causes to champion. And, of course, these interests played coalition and cooperative project politics superbly, working together on parks and dirty rivers across the country, as well as on legislation. As would be expected from people commonly concerned with the planet's very own survival, that work was their symbol. In summary, everything came together to make clean air, clean water, song birds, soil protection, and the like all good—no, great—issues. Lots of successes were won by superior lobbying, and lots more by the nature and evolution of those issues into good ones.

What, then, did environmental interests share? More than just plenty of lobbying. They had preferred or privileged position and correct demands: political correctness if you will. Support and rewards for a solid lobbying effort were there. Members, patrons, and media opportunities became plentiful. There was convergence between private interests and what satisfies some very significant public officials. And, of course, there were constituents who believed, who were intense, and who valued all these environmental goals. These, too, were people easily mobilized around an ultimate cause.

The astonishingly expansive Right to Life cause in the American states also gains from a good issue, at least as these groups have been able to define it. Opposition to abortion is easy. What's better than protecting, not the planet in the abstract, but real human life? Babies. Unborn ones, but still babies. They bring out one heck of an issue. Even the pro-abortion rhetoric of a "woman's right to choose" pales in comparison. Choose killing babies? Get real!

Why is their issue so solid? Because Right to Life mirrored, in large part, the concerns and circumstances of the environmental lobby. However, Right to Life grew up, or more accurately is still growing up, much faster. It's more scary to policymakers, since it wasn't difficult to amass a public, a following. Opponents too easily charge, or mischarge, that Right to Life simply misleads or even intimidates public officials, by being unfair. That, though, is lobbying's own worst defense. What's advocacy really about? Most certainly it's not about sponsoring a nice debate. It's about winning.

What took place over twenty-five years was more than just good—very cumulative, multi-faceted—lobbying. That's why a great many pro-choice Republican policymakers will *only* take a policy stand that's publicly Right to Life. They're afraid of being part of a bad issue.

Where's the growing advantage of opposition to abortion? How do its generally good issues compare with those of environmental interests? Let's go over the five lessons again. First, Right to Life holds the socially preferred position of having hundreds of thousands of very intense members of the public. And there exist many others who somewhat sympathize, more against than for abortions. As Lindblom argued, interests in privileged positions stand to gain lots and lots of resources.[20] They outstrip their opponents. For Right to Life, those resources include money, a superior grassroots organization, zealous leaders, successful intervention in electing supportive candidates, and an amazing level of successful coalition politics. Much of the accumulation of resources and coalition politics is centered on churches. Catholics regularly agree with, and work on projects with, old-line Baptists and a whole range of evangelical Christians, many from small independent churches. And these people no longer fight with one another as they might have done as kids. They work together with a fervor. Cohesion among them is high on what Right to Life demands. Supporters don't debate where the abortion line-in-the-sand should be. Just ban all abortions, they say, at least the activists.

Thus, the groups seem to ask for the right things. Policymakers then respond, give them access and listen. They pass their bills banning welfare-funded abortions, for example, even though the groups are represented by a lot of volunteer, non-professional lobbyists. Evidence of their right stuff, once again, rests with the steadily increasing potency of Right to Life lobbying over time. As one advocate said, "As we keep winning, more people join the cause. They are truly moved by our successes." Of course, those successes allow for professional staff to be added to most of these state interests.

Public policymakers brought to office by Right to Life toe the line because of who got them there. Supportive officials argue a simple position: "For years abortion was flat out illegal. Only the permissiveness of a few bad years let it get out of hand. Those permissive policies are not so bedded in law that good Christian officials can't yank them out." That legislator is, indeed, correct about policy history. There's no big, expansive policy base supporting either side on abortion, just a few things to tinker with, such as state payments. There's no extensive or severe institutionalization. Yet there is a growing number of legislators inside government to push the changes, to take the initiative. Right to Life is not unlike the Grange in the 1870s.

There is no established constituency of respected, recurring policy beneficiaries *for* abortion, either. Another Right to Lifer said it well: "Who really gets abortions over and over? Poor children. Often blacks. Like that old loudmouth [who acknowledged multiple abortions] Whoopi Goldberg, bragging about it." She's technically correct. Those are *not* the people who make strong opponents or arguments for good issues in the public's eyes. Moreover, the proponents of abortion tend to be in the policy game for the cause, not to gain personal policy benefits. Their middle-class intensity is, as a consequence, more limited than is that of zealous opponents. It seems increasingly the case that the advantage is to Right to Life. And it's more than just the cumulative effects of lobbying at work. As objectively as it can be judged by looking at the broader circumstances of politics, opponents just don't appear to have grabbed a good issue.

Gatekeeping Politics

Without question, politics *is* subject to surprising things. As James Q. Wilson testily replied to Lindblom's notion of privileged position for some interests, others can win.[21] They can beat those who've become socially preferred. He's surely correct, but neither Wilson nor those who root for surprises are backing trends. There aren't public policy surprises every day. And lobbying monsters with impressive arsenals and encompassing strategies of many tasks seldom lose to the quiet and meek. Unless, like the late Mother Teresa and world food-assistance interests, those meek also have good issues while the monster lobby folks have bad ones.

What many who root for the underdogs overlook is that, by those mostly objective criteria, there are lots of good issues out there, and interests that have them are bound to regularly confront one another. Some good issues will lose, but not a whole lot of them. Much more frequently, good issues get compromised with one another as public officials avoid saying no to any of them. Part of it is through coalitions. That's also the essence of gatekeeper politics, at least in a very representative form of government, where public officials have little in the way of binding ties to one another. Gatekeeping is only guarding the gates to political heaven so that the no-lobby people or the bad issue people don't get in and enjoy the assembled goodies.

What's going on with those officials who actually get to be gatekeepers?[22] With what will they cooperate? Which lobbyists are they willing to let win and why? Which issues? Why are the issues and interests discussed above so favored? There's slightly more to it than so far considered. An additional perspective exists on cumulatively effective lobbying and the development of good issues. That perspective starts with one important observation: The monster lobbies don't win because they're so well-liked, or cozy people to play with. Far from it. The evaluations lead again to public preferences, especially linked to policy beneficiaries.

Policymakers are quick to remind anyone who'll listen, and not broadcast or print it, that they put stamps of governing approval on many disliked lobbyists. That dislike comes mostly for reasons of personal lobbyist style. Some quick observations can be made. Corporate lobbyists from interests such as Ford and du Pont tend to be needlessly arrogant, or generally stuffy. Even among old colleagues, multiclient lobbyists are resented. Said one legislator of an old pal: "What I hate most are all those clients to which he's hardly committed. He's not a believer. But, yes, I work with him all the time and truly trust his judgment." Then there are environmentalists and Right to Lifers. In the words of a member of Congress, both "use bothersome grassroots volunteers, pushy tactics, and even the best reek of self-righteousness. I cringe when I see them coming. I get irritable." No, gatekeeping isn't about regularly saying no to those who public officials simply don't like. It's not about letting in only the doormats who routinely ingratiate themselves.

Gatekeeping is the assessment of all those things that make for good issues—not popular ones, but rather those objectively good ones. Public policymakers get informally trained, quite plainly, in judging the fit of issues and interests. Or maybe it's their well-attuned instincts. Gatekeepers are the ones who keep lobbyists thinking and picking strategically, or best defining the logic of issue selection and its content. They get lobbyists culling out, like spoiled oysters and clams, the issues that aren't good. That's how government uses its capacity, the talent of the state and nation-state.

Let's look at this pleasant but tedious work and three criteria that are part of it. A member of Congress observed the contrast. Pleasant: "I *get* to choose." Tedious: "I *have* to choose." Policymakers want issues that can be sold to the public in a diffuse way as serving a broad and appreciated social interest. Western development and settlement was that type of issue set. That's why clean air and water are good, as is protecting a bird or fuzzy animal. Protecting human life fits the same category. The issue that's most overwhelming, however, is safeguarding the public's economy. For citizens, all these are understandable as well as emotional issues, at least in general terms.

If issues don't serve that diffuse interest of much of the public, policymakers look at a second criterion. Will the public pay attention? If they do, are they likely to be irritated? Not generating much attention and not angering very many people make for good issues from a gatekeeper's view. Even if those issues are not generally cared about or even understood, they're still good. Protection from soil erosion, lowering levels of nitrates in groundwater, cutting capital gains taxes, banning abortions in the third trimester: All are boring as topics of popular conversation. They're too complex for the public to jump on. Yet all are hard for citizens to attack if they do pay any degree of attention to them. Without much scrutiny, these things get stamped as good issues.

None of that matters, though, unless a third criterion can be determined. Does the issue and resulting policy give something to a specific and designated beneficiary? And can agreements be worked out so that competing interests also are beneficiaries of sorts?[23] If an issue does both, gatekeepers love it. If not, they're skeptical, and for three reasons. First, such an issue shows a highly specific demand. Somebody in particular wants it. It's good to react to it then. Second, that particular somebody, whoever it is, gets seen as obviously well-organized into an active interest. After all, interests do organize around the issues that satisfy them. Policymakers assume that sound lobbies also know well what they want. Interests have learned what's of value, and how to exert some degree of control over public policy in order to obtain more of it.[24] Gatekeepers react accordingly.

Third, there's the clincher reason. If the resulting public policy goes badly when implemented, blame the lobbyists who wanted it. Those private representatives begged for it, pushed for it, and gained its advantages.[25] But don't blame the gatekeepers if there's failure. If things go so badly that the public is angered, there's a closely related and ready excuse. "What I always say," commented one legislator, "is that we had more cheating by greedy special interests. We wuz conned. That always gets people off my back."

These reasons explain why the Reagan Economic Recovery Tax Act was chock-full of good issues, even though it was economically self-defeating. Different business interests all wanted specific things; they were organized appropriately to get them; and these things each rewarded the specific claimant, the champions, the advocates. Moreover, the public wanted economic action. With all that covered, and with interests of all sorts to blame, members of Congress weren't too concerned whether or not recovery would actually result from the legislation. Even with public policy uncertainty, all those things that business wanted were still really fine issues, by gatekeeper standards. Observed one gatekeeper, "Yes, like I said a minute ago, it's not facts that guide policymaking on the Hill. Emotions do it."

This brings up the Ultimate Warrior of public policymaking in the late 1960s and early 1970s: urban programs for central cities, or for decaying areas of them. Gatekeepers instinctively rolled over to let these programs through. At the peak of President Lyndon Johnson's Great Society initiatives, with their war on poverty, cities were particularly visible and prominent.[26] In no small part it was because poor and unemployed African Americans, with full TV coverage, were rioting and burning the cities down.

With the targeting of poverty and social unrest, urban policy just sounded good for all of society. In addition, not too many Americans paid attention to the specifics of what was passed anyway. Heck, many didn't live in central cities. Why care? Finally, urban policy benefits were always handed to designated beneficiaries: specific city budgets, parks and recreation programs, housing construction, neighborhood project groups, and a raft of others.[27] As a result, all kinds of organized interests lined up to design and win from urban policy: mayors, city administrators, park directors, model cities operators, builders, advocacy groups for the poor, churches, racial factions. It looked like real pluralism. These were great issues, as the gatekeepers saw things. Urban policy had it all.

None of this should be too surprising, and the comments shouldn't be thought of as just the ravings of an unabashed cynic. Far from it. American politics *does* work. Public policymakers, as gatekeepers, define good issues this way only because of the nature of those governments in which they do *their* work. Representatives are *supposed to* react to constituents. The public is to be followed, even parts of it. Analysts and experts aren't to be in actual charge of policy decisions. Those who assemble, speak, and petition are to *be* sovereign, at least sovereign enough to set the policy agenda. The United States is a series of open, democratic, republican governments where gatekeepers, as public representatives, appropriately read shifting public wills. There's nothing wrong with that.[28] It's not a perfect process by any means, but it's not wrong that it works in conjunction with basic rules of government.

As the practice of American interest politics has been carried out over time within those rules, some things have become clear about interest politics and public policymaking. The public *isn't* expected to be too involved in policymaking. Citizens don't by themselves determine the exact content of issues. Yet they matter, nonetheless. Organized interests, ranging from attentive constituent confidants back home to institutional lobbies in the capital, *are* expected to do the more precise defining of what needs to be done. And those interests are also expected to be informed enough, tied enough to the public, and in agreement enough among similar interests to be generally reliable—not always correct, but still reliable indicators of what relevant people have preferences for doing. For those reasons, gatekeepers follow far more of a representational rather than an analytical approach to defining good issues and passing more rules and policies. Gatekeeping by ambitious public officials is less about determining what will actually solve social and economic problems than about deciding what citizens like to see.[29]

Good Issues and Compatible Public Institutions

Governance in the United States has been characterized frequently as driven by ambitious men and women. That's surely accurate to at least a point, for successful lobbyists need to be ambitious, or else the sheer bulk of what they have to do drags down their public affairs efforts. Lazy people really shouldn't apply. And, of course, public officials are often ambitious as well, particularly those who run for office or who aspire to ever better appointed offices. These are all individuals who need to play politics well, just as do lobbyists. And, they need to play it in a very public arena of policy users.

It would be a mistake, nonetheless, to think that ambitions run rampant, that the successful just walk all over anyone they can, any way they want. As this entire book has emphasized, that's just not the case. There are more or less distinct rules to politics, protocols to follow, expectations to meet. Ambitions are then kept in check to some degree. The ambitious are mostly reacting to and keeping others happy or content.

In explaining American interest politics, it's necessary to look at the confining effects of public institutions and their structures, as well as the drive of personal ambitions. The two work together. Institutionalization within policy bases and in government operations does much to define good issues, as has been seen in the previous pages. Good issues create a fit between interests and society. Well-developed lobbying by ambitious interests, which meets the needs of ambitious public officials, does the rest. Chapters Four through Six underscore that premise.

But isn't there more to describe about the institutional conditions that make for good issues? More to understand about that fit? So far the emphasis has been on privileged interests and the criteria developed by reactive gatekeepers. Why institutional rules clearly matter in both instances, is that all? Is there an interest perspective on institutions and another held by public policymakers? Yes, there is more.

Let's look at three closely related institutional conditions that define the broader political environment in which successful interest politics takes place. While there are many more institutional effects on American politics, these three are the ones that most influence organized interests, their public policymaking, and distinctions between good and bad issues.

First, the American states and nation-state itself are comparatively weak.[30] There's absolutely no one in charge of any of them. Nobody can make public policy all by herself. President Reagan showed that with his Economic Recovery Tax Act. Beyond that, those who share being in charge have very limited solidarity with one another. Not many binding linkages exist. U.S. government has a "hollow core," and those who surround that core exercise their interests quite narrowly.[31] Second, as representative governments that bring up recollections of market economies, American institutions are all about—as seen above—providing incentives to the public.[32] Or, more precisely, they're about bringing incentives to parts of the public, one at a time. Without such incentives, the public would always be inherently unhappy and politics would be unstable, and so subject to massive swings. There would be standards to apply in judging acceptable government. Citizens would always be shopping for something brand new, or worse yet, they'd be following charismatic crackpots. With no one in charge, though, providing public incentives is far from easy.

That's where transaction costs enter, especially in a capitalist economy where tons of private interests form.[33] The third environmental condition of American politics is the constant and ongoing battle in the face of escalating demands to keep the cost of political transactions—exchanges or negotiated bargains that bring incentives—as low as possible. Like doing the limbo, policymakers want to see how low they can go. They want to bargain with the fewest players over the least significant matters and make the fewest changes they must as quickly as they possibly can, if it's even necessary to make those changes or provide new public incentives. That's the process that brings the incessant and, to many, maddening tinkering with the existing policy base. American politics is about cooking stuff up for the privileged—that is, the most potentially disruptive—to keep them happy.

What does all that mean? Simple. As Douglass North pointed out, institutions of government have been put in place to reduce the uncertainty of everyday life.[34] In terms of interest politics, bad issues are the ones that produce especially uncertain or risky results if enacted into law. So institutions work against them. Good issues, quite obviously, reduce the uncertainty and risk to the immediate institutional relationships among those who govern, those who actively want things, and those who get things—for policymakers, interests, and the public.

Let's see all this at work with those interests that have good issues. Each of these interests with good issues enjoyed a useful advantage. They all had numerous policymakers to contact in order to facilitate their respective demands. Neither environmentalists nor Right to Life organizations aimed at finding specific or specific types of champions inside government. On the contrary, both proceeded patiently until public support swept up numerous ambitious public officials.[35] The same was true of farm interests. The Agricultural Adjustment Act wasn't possible until southern members of Congress representing southern crops fell in line with members from the Midwest.[36]

When the Reagan administration wanted unappealing new tax reform, businesses were relieved to find many policymakers who supported the idea but not the plan. The proliferation of diverse policymaker preferences created a momentum in favor of producing a bill of many colors, with plenty of stuff for specific interests. In contrast, labor was disadvantaged in its reform bill. Basically, liberal Democrats were the only labor proponents. When challenged by a risky situation, this particular tribe of policymakers was simply overwhelmed by the assault of numerous other tribes. There was no single foe to battle. As the architects of health care reform in the 1990s, the Clinton administration was in the same fix as Reagan and labor had been earlier. Interests with good issues hit Clinton from the left and the right, as well as the middle. Not many came to Clinton's defense. Why get hit too?

Of course, with each of the good issues, there was more for their interests to fight *for* rather than *against*. Each issue specifically rewarded those who joined or patronized the organized interests and who felt quite intensely about what each wanted. But they didn't have to be the sole beneficiaries of a policy service, gaining selective rewards from the outcome while others did not. Right to Lifers and environmentalists still felt good about winning. The institutionalization of such positive incentives into the structural responses of government certainly meant that it made more sense to lobby well, in a cumulative and multifaceted manner. So solid lobbies evolved.

It also made more sense for gatekeepers to give in to the public policy wants of good lobbies as a result. Those who successfully offered rewards in a political marketplace of competitive job seekers win endorsements, votes, campaign funding, good evaluations, solid reputations in Washington or the state capital, rewarding and résumé-building experiences, and, more generally, peace on their various political fronts. They haven't irritated those who might otherwise make the most political noise about poor governance. In consequence, good issues have brought a succession of environmental regulations, limits on abortion, farm subsidies, and business profits. But they've not yet been converted to health care issues, where loser lobbies, it seems, are hopelessly fragmented.

Interests that wanted incentives have always been advantaged by making demands that were comparatively easy to win

over time. Because of previous policy history, which had set precedents for interests such as business and environmentalists, none of
this was totally new rule-making. It wasn't something, or somebody, new for public policy to serve. None of it reversed long-
standing public policy directions or robbed revenue from competing public programs. For each of these emerging good issues,
things were already institutionalized in superb fashion. Just tinkering, then, was the order of each new policymaking day.

Those circumstances meant that there existed viable points
around which to both lobby the public and build multi-interest
coalitions. Moreover, the coalitions satisfied most of the participants. Generally, each player won goodies: an expanding progression of regulations to protect the air on one hand, and endangered
animals on another; progress to the ultimate goal of eventually
banning abortion; programs for each major farm commodity; and
a huge collection of business tax breaks and government contracts
for grabbing a share of expanded public purchases from the private
sector.

It wasn't, therefore, too hard to negotiate public policy transactions after the lobbying paid its dividends. Transaction costs did
become low. Many public officials were involved. Yet coalition politics made it possible to craft agreements with diverse public officials because that politics brought diverse interests together. If the
lobbyists who wanted things could agree, why should policymakers mess things up? There was no reason to do so at all. Doing
so would just cause problems. So, on good issues, transaction costs
have proven as low as they can generally be in a most cumbersome
American politics. That's why easy decisions equate with good
decisions, easy issues with good issues.

Institutional properties of rules, then, mean that some issues
just fit the structure of public decisions far better than do others.
They're more politically feasible.[37] Good issues, through their
lucky advocates, play politics both at the margins and in the mainstream. What does that mean? Good issues, of course, bring in lots
of public policymakers who aren't necessarily at the presumed or
publicized centers of American government. Those on the fringes
of day-to-day governance also come in on good issues. These issues
let fringe folks be players, which they like. Under the right circumstances, nearly any ambitious officials can then become gatekeep-

ers, only by using what blocking or advancing powers over policy they have.

But good issues need to fit more than that in playing with the rules. They need also to reflect enough mainstream values and traditional public policy approaches that the lobbyists who want them help bring those fringe players to the political forefront. That's when those gatekeepers really gain status—at least they do in these instances, until these particular incentives for the public are determined and distributed. All of that can be done for only some issues, not all by any means. Even Wilson would agree that winning on bad things is far more problematic, very much less likely.[38]

Summary and Highlights

There's nothing complicated about the point of this chapter. It's that some issues are better for winning than other ones. It's not because of their popularity, which plays only a partial role. Nor is it because some policy analyst or another likes them. No. The point of this chapter revolves around developing the most objective criteria possible for explaining why some issues win and others lose.

The explanation moves considerably beyond the notion that successful lobbying is doing numerous tasks well. Yes, we know what good lobbying entails. To win, though, something more tends to matter, as well. That's having a good issue.

To make that point—or is it two points?—Arthur Bentley's views get examined again.[39] As mentioned in the introduction, Bentley led academics to the belief that a few people can determine public policy by expanding their contacts and gradually winning supporters. It's grouping that matters, he said. Obviously, this book follows Bentley.

Bentley also said more, however. He called interest politics transactional, where things are related by what they do for the policy process.[40] With John Dewey, Bentley maintained that no single interest, or public official, or anything else *causes* a government decision.[41] It's a combined effect of many things coming together. That's precisely what brings about a good issue, not just its creation by a sound lobby.

So, following Bentley, this chapter has emphasized three sets of converging or intersecting criteria for understanding what makes for a good issue. These can be listed, but no matrix grid can describe them very well. First, good depends on what an interest wants. Is the desired issue socially preferred, or privileged? Does it correctly represent what the interest that wants it has an appropriate claim to have? Second, as its demands are set in motion, does the issue bring forward a solid and multifaceted lobbying effort? That is, does it seem like things are worth doing and doing well? Are public officials then satisfied with what the interest wants? Finally, are there constituents among the public who really want these policy rewards? Do the rewards go to specific and appreciative beneficiaries?[42]

A second set of similar criteria emerge from the worries of public officials, the gatekeepers who can, if they want, say enough already. Gatekeepers are best satisfied and even most united when three things take place. The issue, first, can be effectively argued as good for a diffuse segment of the public, or many people with different interests, in addition to just the specific beneficiaries. Second, the issue shouldn't irritate the public and lead to foul opinions. It's best for policymakers that the general public pays little attention to substantive specifics. If that public does become troubled, the gatekeepers, according to their third criterion, shouldn't have to take the blame for the negative reaction. That's why public officials want to reward well-organized and informed beneficiaries who can take any resulting political heat. Those three standards explain why an old political truism states that "public policymakers are 90 percent chicken."

This brings us to the third set of criteria for judging good issues. These, like several of the others, are linked to institutional factors already embedded in the structure of the policy base. But they exist as separate yet not distinct from the things that most advantage either an advocating interest or a cowardly and ambitious public official. Institutionalization advantages certain issues: first, if those issues bring forward diverse gatekeepers; second, if the resulting policy *offers* specific and negotiable incentives—not take-away items—that can be divided up among numerous claimants; and, third, if the settlements can be negotiated with minimal fighting, or low transaction costs.

The combined effect of these somewhat overlapping criteria reinforces what Shepsle said about the importance of a policy equilibrium in American politics.[43] Interests want new things. Great. But nobody likes to change existing things very much, either to obtain them or to alter institutions that govern them. While many Americans may be thoroughly irritated by the conditions of equilibrium politics, they don't refute that it produces, in some complex and transactional ways, good issues.[44] It just doesn't bring ones they like.

As North might say, that's the way American governments bring predictability and order, which of course are themselves valued commodities. But, as he agrees, those valued things aren't provided in a process that brings "built-in incentives" to lead organized interests to want efficient and fair results.[45] No, lobbyists and their organizations want, and indeed are set up, to win. As noted before, that's just the way the railroad runs, with lots of ongoing and renewed clamor, clamor, clamor.

8

What Some Interests Can't Get: The Losers

There must remain some skeptics. Aren't most Americans still carried away by the romantic idea that a great lobbyist can sell anything? Or, for the truly cynical, aren't they swept up in the sinister belief that public officials can be bought for anything, by any interest that's laden with sufficient cash? Either view is premised on the notion that there are, like kids at Boystown, no bad ones.[1] Bad issues are just so far unloved, still waiting to be hugged and understood. Well, maybe a little.

America's policy history, though, teaches that some issues are truly bad ones. Any thoughts that anything can be sold, or that the elected can all be purchased on any matter, are just in plain words baloney, or mythic. This chapter looks at some really bad issues that no one's been able yet to save, and probably never will. It looks at the underprivileged. Plus, it explains why they can't be saved.

The following pages pretty much duplicate the ideas in the chapter on good issues. It covers the same criteria. What will be emphasized here is identifying bad issues, explaining their institutional disadvantages, and analyzing their inability to muster good lobbying support. In reality, bad issues are those things that, for sensible reasons, people don't find of consequence. These issues aren't necessarily disliked. They aren't illogical. They're simply seen as irrelevant at best and politically threatening at worst, but probably both.

One difference exists between Chapter Seven and this one. Chapter Seven looked at several types of good issues. This chapter looks mostly at one type: rural policy. There are two reasons for the change: time and space.

Because of the complexity of identifying bad issues, it takes too much of both time and space to look long and hard at several policy areas. Rural policy, as a midget wrestler, gets the nod because its many issues have long been the antithesis of yesteryear's Ultimate Warrior, central city urban policy, as covered in Chapter Seven. While the midgets were indeed scuffling, they were doing it for chump change in torn leotards in some dirty and isolated tents. So were the rural policy advocates.[2] In contrast, urban policy proponents were once like professional wrestling's superstars: doing it in glamorous arenas, resplendent with glitter and media hype and in full and glorious costume.

What Are Some Bad Issues?

A list of objectively bad issues could go on at length. That list is hard for anyone to come up with only because no one takes its possible content as very serious. Yet the issues exist and have advocates.

What are some of these issues? Why are they so bad? A proposal to mandate diversity in sports teams is bad. Owners, coaches, and fans—who include policymakers—want to win, not be social workers. So nobody mandates an Asian left fielder or starting center.

Same-sex marriages make for bad politics, too. Literally everything in American society is set up with the little guy/girl couple in mind who stand stoically on top of the wedding cake. Two guys is too much. Much improved wage scales for fruit and vegetable pickers is really bad, especially linked to unionization. Nobody wants consumer prices for such daily necessities as fresh strawberries and asparagus to increase. Nobody wins by doing something costly for poorly educated migrants who perform stoop labor.

Environmentally mandated demands on either halting industrial production or for severely limiting economic growth are terrible issues. While they might solve obvious problems, they'd bring even more obvious ones with jobs, income, profits, and lifestyles. Governments are not going to do either, except maybe when everyone's living like *Mad Max* in a sterile dessert, though probably not even then.

Another bad issue in America is government coordination and control of economic planning. The Japanese do it with considerable effectiveness through their Ministry of International Trade and Industry (MITI). But not the United States. It reeks too badly of being against free enterprise, strategic corporate advantage, personal independence, private capitalism, and all the like. Maybe its socialistic, too. Worse, however, corporations would have to change their ways if a U.S. MITI ever came about. So it won't be on the public policy agenda anytime soon.

What's fascinating about each of those bad issues is that public policymakers have done a little to advance goals linked at least vaguely to each one of them. There's a tiny and related policy base for each. These are best called smidgen policies, tiny bits of reinforcement for the few who favor and make noise over such issues. These policies are brought to them by gatekeepers who want to be seen as truly representative of everything. As that implies, there also are indeed glimmers of advocacy on each of these bad issues, from around the country—but not very much. So there's not much policymaker response, mostly only some sympathetic clucking by officials who quite generally come to favor more African Americans in sports management, gays and lesbians and their rights, organized labor and its recruitment activities, enviro-driven public policy, or more socially responsible corporate economics.

All these may be things that get a little media air time. These are, though, issues that make network anchors Tom Brokaw and Dan Rather seem out of it or odd to much of the public. Because such issues get commented about with some seriousness, most public officials find the reporting journalists mindless interlopers. So, after the story, some policymakers bow half-heartedly and quickly move on to good and personally rewarding, and easier—or lower transaction costs or good—issues. That's why only a tiny bit, or a smidgen, of nearly every want goes superficially into U.S. policy bases. At least symbolically, America practices massive policy accommodation. But, even with the publicity and the bows, no big swirl of advocacy or public support is encouraged to come forward on bad issues. Certainly there are no major and socially central public policy initiatives advanced to really do these things. Madison was only semi-correct about many factions coming together.

As it has been for more than a century, that's the story of American rural policy: very little noise and periodic clucking, and then doing mostly something for somebody else. In 1909, there was the federal government's Country Life Commission, assembled by agricultural policy specialists at the urging of President

Theodore Roosevelt.[3] It spelled out very serious problems faced by rural residents and then strongly urged corrective actions by government. Most of those problems were linked to poverty, the same thing that later moved urban policy. But the proposed solutions were not so linked.

The Country Life Report essentially said that rural America was burdened by several social problems that affected all rural residents. Basically, these were problems of poor communications and isolation, too limited transportation, inadequate health care, and soil and other natural resource depletion. Such problems particularly and most severely, it was noted, bothered those who had not succeeded within an industrializing agriculture. Those who had *not* made their farms and ranches bigger, better managed, more technical, and more productive businesses were in trouble. These were people left behind by agricultural progress, or industrialization by mechanized equipment. Such progress had been advanced by public policies dating back to the 1860s and added to later: homesteading, farmer education, research, technical support, and railroad expansion.

There were lots of these folks who were left behind. They were left to live in poverty as subsistence farmers, periodically hired drifters, urban migrants, or just people living aimlessly in rural shacks. Maybe they were in the county poorhouse. For all practical purposes, they had exited the productive and progressive agricultural sector, disappeared both economically and personally.[4] They couldn't compete.

That, the Country Life Commission went on, was most unfortunate. Poverty wasn't just affecting people. It was also destructive for rural communities, settings that were socially and economically unhealthy because of the hangers-on. Poverty also hurt urban communities, where the displaced often fled to look for jobs and places to live. This wasn't a people-sensitive analysis.

Were there policy solutions? Well, they were *not* in developing rural community stabilization, nonfarm job creation, or giving aid to those displaced from farming. Agricultural experts from the land grant colleges, the Extension Service, and the U.S. Department of Agriculture, who made the commission's recommendations, not surprisingly simply renewed their commitment to the work of further industrializing agriculture. In their own interests, they wanted to build on previous efforts, expand considerably the existing agricultural policy base, and make agricultural producers

still bigger and better and more efficient. That's what their bureau-
cratic enterprises were about. The synthesis of the Country Life
report was that a healthy rural society depended directly on an
economically healthy and technologically advancing farm and
ranch population. People and communities both would win by
investing public funds in the best farmers and ranchers.

For the good of rural society, the poor were to be freed from
poverty's confining grip before, and only before, they exited farming. Agricultural institutions, as the homes of the gatekeepers, were
pledged to work that magic. But nobody suggested how to create
markets for generally oversupplied farm and ranch products, the
crops and critters. And nobody said a word in the report about
what to do with already impoverished people and deteriorating
small towns.

So what? That's not difficult to see. The idea of good issues,
and thus good policies, was reinforced.[5] Anything that had to do
with industrializing agriculture was a good proposal. It had ready
champions; provided incentives to already capable and politically
supportive beneficiaries, or larger-scale farmers; and did so by just
tinkering a wee bit more with the slew of existing public policies.
Farmers were put and kept first in line both for getting expensive
government benefits and for gaining stature as the curatives for
rural ills.[6] For the next two decades, as rural problems intensified
and rural economies moved into depression, agricultural policy
experts and lobbying advocates kept calling for ever more comprehensive assistance to the industrialization of agriculture—not for
rural relief.[7]

Of course, that meant there were, by definition, bad issues
being labeled, at least for federal programs. Direct investments in
nonfarm rural communities and people were bad. They wouldn't
have long-term social benefits. There was another reason: Were
agricultural professionals to have acknowledged the need for a new
policy direction for rural America, one apart from further industrialization of agriculture, they'd have created a threat to the credibility of existing policy and policy institutions.

It would have been seen by too many as an admission to
years of political and policy failure.[8] That would have led to policy,
policymaking, and lobbying turmoil. Nobody, then, really wanted
to change course. Rural issues for a rural society became bad ones.
Farm issues and agrarianism were still good. And the two policy

types—farm and rural—were not compatible with one another. It's as simple as that. Yet, to understand it all better, it's necessary to look a little more into institutional evolution, the emergence of an extensive array of farm champions in politics, and the effect of both on interest politics.

Institutionalizing All This Stuff, or Not

Institutions mattered so much in typing good and bad issues because there were, in agriculture, so many of them. Such a huge, mythically enhanced policy base existed. That base has been addressed in the earlier chapters on lobbying. From the onset, it had three forces driving its creation and expansion. The first was the American myth of agrarianism, the dream of an idyllic life brought on by producing for one's self on one's own property. Wow!

The second was agrarianism's close link to development and settlement policy, especially through westward expansion. There was lots of lobbying going on to advance those issues from numerous interests. Mark Hanna even helped. Third, to make development feasible, there had to be a large self-supporting commercial sector of people—people who would be consumers of some products, producers of others, financially sound enough to do both, and permanently entrenched. Farmers and ranchers, more than miners and lumbermen and moonshiners, fit those needs.

So agricultural producers gained substantial policy rewards. They won because an uninformed and inattentive peasantry, as rooted in European traditions, could never have supported modernization and development of the whole American continent.[9] They won because about half of the U.S. public lived on farms and, accordingly, defined an extensive block of voters and sometimes political activists.[10] These were a good set of people to keep happy with government.

Incentive- or reward-providing institutions were won politically from the beginning. And their farm bias was set in motion then too. The Act of Establishment of 1862 provided a U.S. Department of Agriculture (USDA) that was to find and then distribute any scientific information on improving farming, especially through better seeds and plants.[11] Rewards for producers were linked to better science. Farm science for farm people was the plan. And that dual goal stood for modernization and, later, industrialization of the sector. [12]

Other policy initiatives of 1862 were compatible with USDA's scientific tasks. The Homestead Act created more farmers with more needs for USDA to serve. The Morrill Land Grant College Act gave sites to each of the states for building schools that would teach both scientific farming and industrial technology and link them together. The Transcontinental Railroad Act promised producers a shipping connection to the rest of the economy. Farmers could grow more with what they purchased and then transport it out. Not surprisingly, both USDA and farmers began their scrutiny of the railroads and their executives' responsiveness.

The seven decades leading up to 1933 saw ever more institutionalization of rules and organizations linking farm and ranch services, science, industrialization, and economic assistance for development. The land grant colleges were created. Due to segregation, black land grants were added. In 1887, agricultural experiment stations were founded to bring together the scientific work of USDA and the educational capacity of the colleges. These stations did far more science than USDA had done by itself, even when the latter won full cabinet status and gained policy responsibility for all of rural America. The existing institutions all worked together to do even more. They helped create state departments of agriculture. And, in 1914, the Extension Service was formed by them as a federal–state partnership. Not enough farmers and ranchers were thought to be getting and using science and education, so local county agents were trained and funded to personally help farmers produce. [13] Better, more. Through science, industrialize with tractors and all that. Ditch any remaining peasant mentality. That was the prevailing view.

The Extension Service wasn't all. A federal farm credit system was created to provide low-interest loans for expansion and purchases. Farmers were allowed to set up farmer-operated cooperatives free from antitrust laws to process, market, and ship products as a group. The government endorsed and governed agricultural marketing agreements to help farmers negotiate more favorably with purchasers. To even better help farm finances, regulations also flourished: of stockyards, food manufacturers and processors, railroads, and other agribusinesses such as seed suppliers. [14]

For a laissez-faire nation, government was doing quite a bit for farmers. Many laws and regulations were theirs. Several agricultural experts were working only for them, representing them, and just plain giving them policy benefits. The collection of federal and state agencies, services, stations, and colleges was a dizzying array of organizations. Sometimes it seemed like all of government was intended solely to help American farmers and ranchers become commercially productive. No wonder all of this came to be called an "agricultural establishment," an organized interest in its own right, inside government.[15]

Yet the whole effort wasn't working out as hoped, which is ironically why it kept growing, establishing still more institutions. More policies were instituted. More farmer and rancher assistance came about. In essence, supplies of agricultural products in the United States had long outstripped demand. The public either didn't want or couldn't afford all of these foods and fibers. As farmers and ranchers grew more things through better science and mechanized production, oversupplies only escalated. Prices didn't drop far enough to sell very much more. As a consequence, farmers and ranchers were always in economic trouble. In all events, the least productive and least efficient were troubled.[16] Some of the troubled just languished. More and more producers, though, just quit producing. They sold out to their more prosperous and lower production cost industrialized neighbors. That was what the Country Life Commission commented on: resulting rural poverty for those growing few at the bottom and their resultingly inferior rural communities.

There was, however, too much farmers-first institutional structure in place to accept the prospects of severe policy change. Too many agricultural gatekeepers existed to ever emphasize investment in communities and poor people. That doesn't mean nothing was done for them—just never for them first. To modernize agriculture, several things were actually enacted to upgrade rural life. Rural electricity was provided. Very many rural roads were built, but mostly to get farm products to market when railroads couldn't. Telephones were eventually subsidized. Conservation was emphasized to upgrade worn-out land and soils. Ponds for irrigation and recreation were built. Farmers and ranchers were the reason for all this, of course. The experts said it was all necessary to make the sector healthy. And so, rural places were to be healthy, too. Other rural residents *did* get to use these things, if they could afford their small costs.[17] Many couldn't afford them, especially the poor.

Direct efforts to fix rural communities was then a truly bad set of issues. There was one small and useless initiative, the Resettlement Administration. It rounded up some rural poor, moved them in together, and gave them farm equipment. It failed and, bad of all bads, smacked of socialism anyway.[18] The institutions generally were just locked in on making development work and keeping more efficient farmers in business. They almost banged their self-interested administrative and scientific heads against walls to do it. But they couldn't. As a result, when the rural depression of the 1920s spread nationally in the 1930s, urban relief programs were passed.[19] Rural relief, in contrast, took quite a different tact on behalf of the same old producer constituents, through the Agriculture Adjustment Act (AAA) of 1933.[20] The government in AAA gave direct subsidies to farmers of major crops, or checks from government to stay in business.[21] Of course, farmers liked that.

And, in a strange but not illogical twist, the biggest government checks went to those farmers with the most land, who had modernized more, and who grew the most. Those producers, without a doubt, were the ones most likely to stay in business, and be politically active. They were the ones seen by agricultural experts and farm lobbyists alike as the best policy investment. They were the ones who could keep national development, agricultural industrialization, and sector modernization dreams alive. Existing institutions thus successfully helped keep some issues as good ones while preemptively closing the gates tightly on others. The rural ideas that didn't fit heard those gates banging shut.

Government's Champions

The institutionalization of an agricultural establishment, with its many services for producers, meant that a farmers-and-ranchers-first policy had tremendous support inside government. Support was inside Washington as well as the states. For decades, these literally thousands of administrators and specialists were forceful champions, as gatekeepers who ultimately defined good and bad. In an agrarian society, where people liked to hear the experts extol and enlarge upon agrarian values, having champions on the inside truly mattered.[22]

It wasn't surprising, then, that both Congress and the state legislatures worked well with establishment representatives. In the process, legislators became the prime gatekeepers. From place to place and through numerous sets of legislative rules, agricultural institutions were able to expand and gain modest operating income.[23] In Congress, agricultural experts won support first in the committee system, years later with the party leaders who increasingly dominated the committees, and once again with the committees when they made a comeback after revolts against strong party leadership.

This meant that a great many legislators throughout the country favored doing things for farmers and ranchers. No great presidential and precious few gubernatorial leaders got very active, but they tended to be supportive nonetheless. Sometimes, like Theodore Roosevelt with the Country Life Commission and Franklin D. Roosevelt with the Agricultural Adjustment Act, they demanded that the experts get on with it and work things out. That always lent executive credibility to efforts at modernizing agriculture. And they didn't provide much interference. Their tacit support also meant even more prominence for farm issues as good ones and, by definition, rural issues as bad ones. Not a single notable policymaker, other than Vermont's Democratic Senator Patrick Leahy, argued for generalized nonfarm rural policy relief—and that was not until the late 1980s and early 1990s.

A snowball effect, therefore, produced increasingly formidable political power for agriculture in the 1920s, and later with a rewritten AAA. Congressional leaders refused to go beyond supporting the existing agricultural establishment in the same old outreach ways, and were more focused on such hot partisan conflicts as trade tariffs.[24] But farm district and farm state congressmen rebelled in 1921, organizing the Farm Bloc to prevent congressional adjournment and move forward several pending farm bills.[25] After that win, the Farm Bloc continued to operate informally for several years and was even instrumental in changing congressional rules to restore committee power. After that, the agricultural committees, which had congressional jurisdiction over all agricultural and rural issues, simply stuck year after year with their farmers-and-ranchers-first business, even throughout the 1990s.

Public policy scholars didn't miss the implications of this concentrated but fragmented championing from the inside.[26] They commented frequently about how several networks of administrators and congresspeople worked together and piled up benefits for farmers.[27] Some of the champions' networks clamored for price supports, or the popular government checks. Others organized for conservation, education, research, extension, marketing, or credit, and for numerous other things. All, however, were interested in only one thing: distributing select public policy incentives to producer beneficiaries, especially the most modernized ones.

Throughout the years, direct nonfarm rural policy won few champions, and most of those that emerged just wanted to add to the farm policy base. Why back a loser, they reasoned. Such things as rural water systems, economic development assistance to rural local governments, and rural home loans all had a few agriculture committee champions. But, to avoid using up their always stressed political capital on nonfarm and nonranch issues, proposals were kept very small.[28] Such rural policy problems got the same small funding in the land grants, experiment stations, extension, and USDA. Again, nobody wanted to ask for too much, and few had the courage to say which agricultural—that is, farm and ranch—programs were silly or bad.

This produced another institutional change which hurt the development of rural policy. Committees and agencies dealing with health care, welfare, transportation, communications, the environment, and education took up small pieces of some neglected rural problems and worked them into broader policies.[29] Education and roads are examples, though the federal government role was small. This activity never led to a cadre of nonagricultural rural champions.

Quite the reverse happened. People and communities that were explicitly and uniquely rural weren't on these particular policymakers' agendas. And these legislators never wanted to work together across House and Senate committee boundaries. As a consequence, nobody was shaping specific incentives to develop and reward rural residents or their community leaders. Only a comprehensive, systematic, and assistance-laden rural policy bill would have done that, which, of course, was absolutely taboo. So, in the words of a former member of Congress, "Don't talk about that rural policy shit. I've got a farm district." It was a district with far fewer farmers than other rural residents, by the way.

And No Rural Lobby at All

In a Bentleyan transactional political world, several things emerge and work together, so it's not surprising that no really well-organized and multitalented rural lobby ever existed. Larger political forces weren't encouraging one. It's painfully obvious that no big advocacy effort was shaping rural policy. A combination of institutional and representative factors made rural policy an unrewarding choice in which to invest lobbying resources. Only the truly zealous signed on.

Farmers had the organizational advantage, or high road, as *the* rural spokesgroups.[30] Several thousand local and regional farm self-help groups populated all corners of rural America in the nineteenth century.[31] Farm protest movements frequently appeared. All spoke of farm policy as synonymous with rural policy.

So did the big and enduring and quite multitalented farm lobby that covered both Washington and the American states. Groups made up of all types of producers, or the peak associations, advocated—most especially—production price intervention, those government checks. There were four major peaks, representing varying ideologies. All but the Grange emerged early in the 1900s. Later, individual commodity groups became the most active interests. There were some two dozen of these, representing everything from pigs to wheat. And again, they were all for direct farmer assistance. They were also all yelling loudly that they and no one else spoke for rural America. Following the lead of the agricultural experts, the farm lobby never did anything but claim to be best for all things rural.

Some of this farm interest activism was inspired by the agricultural establishment and its institutions. The American Farm Bureau Federation, which for decades dominated peak associations, grew out of the Extension Service and its county agents.[32] Created through federal legislation, the cooperatives similarly organized southern farmers, and they provided a grassroots voice tied directly to southern congressmen. Not coincidently, these were the major interests shaping farm and rural policy in the 1930s.[33]

So, the rural communities lobby was, and stayed, a small and motley yet still often talented crew. When, that is, it was even there at all. Several reasons explain why this was so. Rural society presents problems for its communities and people. First, they lack the closeness and integration of urban places. Communities aren't usually geographically close enough to work together.[34] Second, local rural organizations have long tended—outside of churches, downtown businesses, and a few service clubs—to be few and far between. And as rural communities declined, these institutions became fewer.[35] Their momentum has been directed toward home anyway; and they've never had an abundance of resources to spare on political mobilization in some distant political capital. Farm groups were an exception because of their service orientation and, of course, they won. Third, there isn't much to organize around, even if distance and community structure weren't problems.

Doing things for rural America has no real encompassing constituency.[36] The issues are unclear. Do what? For whom? Only the why is known, not the precise beneficiaries. So rural policy solutions are always inexact and not supported by a popular consensus. In short, there aren't any obvious incentives around which diverse rural residents can organize, or well-intended financial patrons can rally. Policymakers, then, find general rural issues uninteresting and a burden. One even said, "Why spend money on people who don't seem to care about it?"

Rural community policy just offers selective rewards to very few who will, in turn, lobby hard for them. For decades there was but a single exception. County governments organized together to lobby for roads and public utilities. Because so many county commissioners in so many places were farmers and ranchers, this only continued the agricultural development bias. These were generally pretty conservative folks who didn't think it appropriate to get all worked up about welfare, finding jobs, community development, or improving education. They weren't a big rural lobby then.

In the 1970s, things evolved. The federal war on poverty and congressional reform both encouraged some activism. It looked at least possible that major rural investments might occur. Four separate efforts were made from 1977 to 1995, all by people who screamed loudly that farm policy wasn't rural policy. As an old poor people's advocate, Clay Cochran formed Rural America and became the rural guru of the 1970s. But he did it with foundation money—and not much of it, in fact. With the Aspen Institute and with funding from the Ford Foundation, Susan Sechler took on an activist role in the 1990s, giving away grants and badgering policymakers. Bob Rapoza used his money well, actively sought to build coalitions with such interests as construction contractors, and became the most recent big rural policy point man. Working in a very tiny office.

Each of the three won a few things, of course. That's the nature of policy accommodation. But they didn't win much, and certainly no encompassing rural policy bill was passed. Bills were planned and designed, however. Cochran, Sechler, and Rapoza built on old political contacts and found easy access. But, with small lobbies they lacked a cumulative policy impact, and never really were able to reinforce their negligible presence. Each was easily ignored later, as gates once again clanged shut on rural ideas.

What they won were the most expected of all policy benefits: water systems, community grants, and housing programs. These were all things that went to designated beneficiaries in local governments or the construction industries. And, regardless of the era, it wasn't that these three main rural spokespeople sealed the deals. Established lobbies such as the National Association of Counties finalized that task.

As one of Sechler's and Rapoza's congressional friends laughed: "Nice people, and they know everybody. But what a piddly-ass effort. Issues like this are bound to flame out. They can't get organized enough to impress even me." In that transactional world, there's just not enough critical mass to generate a sufficient rural lobby. Bad issues make for bad interests.

Issues That Fit and Those That Don't

All this good and bad issue business seems to unlock a little more of the mystery about where organized interests fit in American politics. It seems that organized interests fit in a very tidy fashion only if their issues are good ones. Good, or highly acceptable issues, make for a strong and influential organized interest. It's not just that lobbying is generally well-received and appropriate. It's that some lobbying, on only certain issues, is very well-received and especially appropriate. The rest is much like spitting into the wind. The results only really get to the one crazy enough to do it, and they appear mostly as negative.

Good issues encourage a good fit in numerous ways, all of which are tied to observations from earlier chapters. Entrepreneurs find good issues easiest to market. Joiners, only when they get valued incentives, find them sound reasons for affiliating. Good issues make politics matter. Not everything is actually

sound political stock in trade. Even idealistic institutional interests, from churches to charities, don't tend to bog down the
policymaking process with bad issues. There's some cleanliness
and sensibility to that busy game of politics, then. It doesn't get
easy, just not inherently fruitless. Most of the political dancing
about is around credible, or potentially credible, things that government might well do. The incredulous issues and organizers get
short shift, or not much work.

Why is this so? Neither the public nor the media will listen to
any improbable idea for long. Only the good issues or appealing
things turn public heads, even for entertainment purposes. And if
the public isn't paying attention, or finding policy ideas and problems relevant, the media moves on to something else. Journalists
need an audience. Once neglected issues can still be, and often
become, good issues. Their time just wasn't right until interests
made them so, and more importantly, times simply changed.

Knowing that organized interests can help bring an issue to
its time, policymakers certainly give lobbyists all sorts of chances—
maybe every chance sometimes. Gatekeepers test the waters. Information exchange, or the contact game, goes on. Often its result is
dramatic. Institutional transformations within government have
been frequent. In large part, such changes occurred as new issues
and new values were coming forward in society and old institutional arrangements were holding them back. Interests with good
issues changed institutions that weren't working, though not
always. But they did often enough to be encouraging as outside
interests suddenly found their representatives on the political
inside. And once good issues went to the outside, or at least their
lobbyists charged that they did. Nothing is a better example than
the eventual passage of numerous industrial and commercial assistance policies as the economic mix of America changed. Mathew
Carey was ahead of his time. Factories came to be seen as even *good*
places for many years.

Lobbyists who push bad issues also get little work because
other interests tend to avoid them (and they certainly don't share
with them).[37] They don't get asked to the spring coalition. Or, if
they do, it's to play a sacrificial role—largely cast out when the
time to divide up the possible goodies is near. They don't get
asked, even then, to lead the first dance, as was the case with rural
policy, where farm groups supported rural development in recent
farm bills as long as it didn't get in the way of anything else.

Things that cost farm program budget dollars were out. So what's nice about the good issue fit is simple, at least from the perspective of the interest community. Quite conveniently, there are innumerable ways of getting rid of those dumb issues and their lobbyists before they really muck up the process and confuse everyone. Through its little villages, the community takes care of itself.

Everything about interests in the policy process, then, revolves around the appropriateness of good issues. Interest politics fits the American policy making process so well because it respects policy institutionalization, finds extensive and enthusiastic political champions for only some things, and isn't amendable to all types of organizations. Interest politics has a far more manageable handle for purging negative pressure than some might suggest.[38] This undoubtedly, and quite justifiably, irritates the bad-issue folks. And it also makes many other Americans a bit sad that not all ideas have a chance.

Summary and Highlights

Once again, it's an easy chapter. Its emphasis is on explaining why some issues and types are objectively bad ones, why they're not good for winning much. What was identified here needs not more elaboration, but just to be pulled together a bit. Let's look specifically again at the three sets of criteria considered in Chapter Seven.

First, what are the general conditions for an issue to be a bad one rather than good one? A bad issue has no preferred or privileged social status. As with rural policy, it also claims to solve problems that those with privileges, such as agrarians, already purport to do best. Those that represent bad issues, accordingly, have little in the way of legitimate and credible claims. Central economic planning for business in America is, so far, against the political grain. As a consequence, it's hard for the advocates of bad issues like this to mount a solid and multifaceted lobbying effort. Nobody, or next to nobody, believes that those things should be done in the advocated way—not the public, not policymakers, nor other lobbyists. Such bad issues bring few hints of being politically satisfying to anyone. They're rather like being on the receiving end of a congressional investigation: The invited aren't there for the honor.

The second set of criteria for a bad issue pertain to the worries of gatekeepers. Bad issues cover only a small segment of society, such as things rural. Bad issues irritate the general public, or important segments of it, as does championing gay rights or threatening environmental policy. These things can't be passed, hidden, and forgotten. Too many watchdogs exist for that to be possible. So championing bad issues leaves the gatekeepers as the ones to blame if things go wrong. On bad issues, public officials can't blame a strong lobby or irreversible public sentiment. They can only blame themselves for doing it, and they understandably hate such vulnerability.

Third, the last set of criteria for being a really bad, rather than good, issue relates to institutional status within government and its existing rules. Bad issues elicit very small numbers of concerned gatekeepers in very few offices. Not many officials have a serious stake in them. The worst issues create no intensity at all in government, not even from the most iconoclastic member of Congress. Once again, rural policy failure is revealing: "What horrible ideas! Give scarce money to small, underappreciated, isolated places for no apparent purpose." Obviously, that particular congressman thought rural policy a bad idea.

Bad issues also have few specific incentives built in to give to designated beneficiaries, so next to nobody wins from them. That's another factor that makes a solid lobby so hard to create. Why support such things, even if there's appeal there somewhere? No good reason can be found.

Finally, bad issues have high transaction costs associated with them. They're hard to change; policy bases need to be substantially altered in order to do anything; there's no previous institutional base to build on; and plenty of policy enemies show up if desired changes are proposed. Ongoing public policy equilibrium is threatened. Doesn't that summarize the story of rural policy? And of migrant policy? And generally of gay rights? Yes, on all counts. They're all bad issues for which policy clamor necessarily remains minimal.[39] And the results arguably remain quite unfair, inequitable, and biased.

9

Revisiting Niches, Networks, Domains, and Other Scary Things

Two themes were developed in the earlier chapters. First, in order to be sound and to have its greatest impact on public policy, lobbying usually involves numerous interrelated tasks with several targets. All-directional strategies abound as well, with some interests hitting all the targets with great frequency. Such strategies are old ones but becoming considerably more commonplace. Second, however, sound lobbying, almost by necessity, evolves from good issues. Good issues are winnable, comparatively easy. So both what goes on and what's represented go hand in hand to make for lobbying success.

As this book comes to an end, there's an obvious need to explain more about the relationship between lobbying success and good issues. That's the purpose of this chapter, and it gets a bit abstract. Specifically, it asks, why do most interests look for good issues? And how and where do they find them? Why not just lobby all of government and society for years to create good issues, as done by environmental activists? But even the enviros didn't do that, as emphasized earlier. They didn't start all over, far from it. And they didn't lobby just anyone. As this chapter will make clear, successful interests have lobbied the appropriate political targets, those players already potentially interested.

Environmental lobbyists built on an institutional structure and a policy base which they at least intuitively understood to represent already good issues which could be expanded over time. Along with allies in office, these lobbyists eventually corralled some of the minimally bad issues by first getting the good ones into their victory column. Sort-of-bad issues evolved into good ones as environmentally friendly institutions further developed. But, of course, environmental activists continue to avoid challenges that engender widespread social opposition. For example, they don't argue for shutting down Gary, Indiana, steel mills. That issue is far too bad, as bad as lobbying the U.S. House of Representative's National Security Committee to impose sanctions against defense pact allies whose governments, such as Turkey, dangerously deplete water resources. That issue is also in the wrong place with the wrong goals and the wrong foes.

To better understand the avoidance by strategically sound interests of bad issues in bad places, the traditions of interest studies need be revisited. Those traditions have been a bit like fixations. The prevailing fixation with interest politics has been to divide up the whole of the interest community into compatible pieces, with the whole of government broken into parts. As was explained in Chapter Five, observers started this fixation by conceiving of shapes and sizes as metaphors for bringing forth knowledge about who really does what with whom.

Quite simply, the search was for order, not chaos. It was for simplicity, not complexity. Scholars emphasized manageable proportions and explanations, not infinite variety. And as this book exemplifies, they liked analogies. What this tradition creates in interest politics is a whole collection of somewhat scary concepts: iron triangles, cozy little triangles, subsystems, triple alliances, subgovernments, and whirlpools of activity. There also are issue networks, policy networks, sloppy large hexagons, policy domains, and amorphous clouds. And issue or policy niches, as well as hollow cores, probably fit this collective genre as well. These concepts are scary because none of them are real things, as are interest groups and issues. They don't say enough about real politics, only abstractions about the means of organizing and winning.

Let's not be too harsh, though, on policy making observers who've assembled this array of catchy terms and phrases. Criticism is not the intention. On the contrary, the work of previous scholars has indeed been done with a purpose that's akin to the effort in this book to explain public policy.

That kinship pertains to the long-felt need of interest representatives to be selective about their targets. It's a need to be selective about whom they lobby, with whom they work, and of course, which issues lobbyists will address with which policy-relevant participants. Interest scholars have, for years, intuitively grappled with ideas of who does what and why to the notion of which issues are winnable. Or, they've long looked to explain the search for the right issues in the right settings. It's just that interest theory has sought to be too simple, too tidy, too logical, and too fixated on the shapes of things. Accordingly, there exists only the rudiments of an interest/policy theory.

Triangles: The Scariest Idea of All

Poor old Arthur Bentley. All he did was to observe that small groupings of interactive participants make public policy.[1] Saying it, though, gave theory builders a chance to go explore while actually being grounded in some previous logic. Identifying the configurations of the groupings, or their sizes and shapes, was a somewhat consuming pursuit.

This pursuit was thoroughly explained in Chapter Five. But let's recall it a bit. Insider politics was discovered.[2] Transactional arrangements among interests, congressional committees, and public agencies were then identified.[3] And triangle theory was born and widely accepted—it became practically an unauthorized religion. Remember specialized decision making, emphasis on the contact game, dominance by experts, internal negotiations among the few, client-centered politics, neglect of the public interest, narrow public policies, reciprocity between various triangles, and lack of systematic oversight? Politics that mattered policywise was seen as both exclusive and exclusionary. The rest of government and society didn't get to play, or just weren't organized to do so.

According to triangle theory, American politics was a logical but undemocratic mess. Neither being so logically structured nor being so undemocratic seem likely to be possible. There's too much inconsistency. Whereas organized interests fit well the conditions of American politics and society, the silly old triangles seem not to fit at all. Can you imagine a completely inattentive public with its collective head in the sand? Or politics without conflict between policy areas, with welfare unaffected by defense? Not for a minute.

There are, indeed, important elements of truth to triangle theory, as well as to both of the above unimaginable conditions. More accurately, there once probably was some truth to that theory. Yet as a description of the historically prevailing tendencies of

American politics, triangle theory, or whirlpooling or subgovernmenting, is just too bizarre, and for three reasons: As James Madison predicted, Americans love to form factions, and diverse factions will, indeed, tussle like children or puppies.[4] Americans have never liked to let others govern for them and do whatever they want for those whose values are in conflict. It's too easy to get involved in politics and play the game. Despite the myth of social integration, the country has always been a boiling pot, not a harmonious melting pot.[5]

It's also too much to think that an open, democratic, representative, and republican form of government—with its separated powers, checks and balances, and federalism—is going to be as orderly as the triangles suggest. Why should all those gatekeepers who are empowered to decide merely reciprocate with the others? And why would they never try to defeat those they dislike? Even the thought of it seems slightly off the wall. And if it's true, when did the lobotomies of public officials take place? Never, not even in an institutional sense. Officials weren't totally dulled and overwhelmed by the American rules of openness.

Finally, the unlikeliness of triangle theory becomes obvious in the way it assigns policy-making responsibilities, within policy areas, within the structures and institutions of government. Does anyone really believe, for even a second, that all policies and their public rationale have been planned and executed by expert administrators? Or that the same is true for other policies, with only the faces of the players changing? Not likely with a Congress. As another example, does anyone believe that the executive always proposes and the legislature disposes? It's never been that simple. John Dewey and Bentley were correct in calling policy-making transactional, where things happen without attribution to any single participant.[6] In transactional situations, the parts all finally come together from miscellaneous sources and with miscellaneous results. It's not like an economic market. Old Clay Cochran said it well: Neither coral beds nor public policy can be planned. Someone plants something, and both flourish in unpredictable ways.[7] There's action, a check, and a countercheck, and pretty soon the transactions create an end product. That's why lobbyists have always lobbied so very hard to influence the public, many different policymakers, and other interests. They needed somehow and in any way to control some of what flourishes.

There's always been far too much going on in American politics for triangle theory to be accurate as a whole. And the goings-on have always been so disorderly, almost chaotic. That's why triangles have always been the scariest idea of them all. Triangle theory presents to those who want to understand American politics a horribly warped view of political agreement, institutional logic, and the capacity of government to systematically mute conflict. None of that is real. And it's hard to see that it ever could have been real. It just doesn't fit with what, in contrast, has been so prominently visible.

So where did the silly notion originate? (Not with whom—that was Griffith, it seems.) More precisely, what elements of triangle theory seem true enough to let it be spread so thoroughly as a political myth? What's been going on? Triangle theory was nothing more than a commentary on the strategies organized interests employed to lobby the right targets on the most winnable issues: keeping things easy, that is. Beyond that, it got completely out of hand. It became tremendously exaggerated, all for the sake of trying to simplify something that was too complex for orderly minds.

An example can best explain the strategies of organized interests. Let's say that the National Education Association (NEA), as a professional employees union, wants to protect federal collective bargaining rights for teachers, as it so often needs to do. There are, indeed, some obvious political places to begin: the Senate Labor and Human Resources Committee, the House Subcommittee on Employer–Employee Relations, and the U.S. Department of Labor. It's clear that NEA lobbyists don't just walk aimlessly the streets of Washington and talk things over with all passersby. That's much too hard—too, too transactional, and inane.

But neither does the NEA merely go to those obvious places and work things out in the mythic corridors of triangle theory. Doing so would be deplorably risky; not enough political bases would be covered. Any foes can check the NEA in other places through other policymakers. So NEA lobbyists go to a Democratic White House, where they've long had political alliances. They also go to the Department of Education, where some school labor issues are considered. The jurisdiction of still other congressional committees are scrutinized and visits made to their potentially involved members of Congress. And, without a doubt, members of Congress with supportive labor records and lots of NEA influence at home get lobbied.

All that isn't enough to do, enough places to go, however. Public and media fears that teacher unions hurt education are necessarily addressed, and coalition partners in education and among other labor unions are sought for support. A big push to get NEA members politically active always goes on during such threatening occasions. Teachers are encouraged to work on electoral campaigns and contribute funds to useful or friendly candidates. Plus, policymakers get daily reminders of these contributions: "Be grateful" is the message.

This all-directional strategy, of course, reflects the history of American lobbying that's been portrayed throughout earlier chapters. It's just more all-directional today, in a busier world. The Farm Bureau acted much the same in the 1930s. This isn't anything dramatically new, although it has become far more pronounced as things have evolved. After all, public policy-making rules and circumstances have become considerably more open.[8] So the contemporary NEA and the history of American lobbying both belie triangle theory, even on most narrow policy issues.

Yet, the example does demonstrate certain truths that call the old triangle metaphor to mind. Four things occur, all of which are integral to a more encompassing theory of interests and policy. First, sound lobbying efforts gravitate initially toward the obvious places within government, not toward everyone. Second, lobbyists emphasize both those who write legislation and those who do technical policy work, but they don't treat them as exclusively different. Third, the reason lobbyists do such targeting is to save as much as possible on scarce interest resources of time, energy, effort, manpower, and money—and to avoid irritating anyone who matters and who might otherwise feel neglected or slighted. Fourth, then, organized interests *do* seek consensus and agreement rather than conflict. Lobbyists *do* like to have the coziest political relationships possible. They don't want needless conflict, and they'll try to avoid it by allocating resources where conflict would not arise.

In summary, organized interests always want to lower their costs of transacting public policy business. They wish to be frugal with their resources and do things in the easiest ways possible. In other words, they want to spend the least of what they've got. So some obvious lobbying patterns and routines develop.

Yet, most importantly, organized interests want to win. And very rarely have they ever been able to win even modestly big things by following a simplistic and easy triangle-like strategy.[9] To lobby soundly, organized interests need to go more places, see more policy participants, win more friends, engage in more tasks, do more things, and raise at least a little more hell. Lobbying and public policymaking aren't nearly as neat and orderly as has been implied in the triangle metaphor, nor were they ever. It's very misleading to think about American politics any other way.

The Fallacy of Networks and Domains

Others have also noticed the inaccuracies of triangle theory.[10] In this case, a whole generation of observers sought to explain things better. Unfortunately, most of those who've critiqued the triangles still get hung up on the theory's several metaphors.[11] And they still emphasize the exclusive and exclusionary in politics, not the inclusive. They forget that everybody in America can play to at least a modest extent. The critics seem to wonder that if things aren't quite so tidy and simple, what are the variations and how are they best described? More size and shape ideas result because the starting point is wrong. More dividing up the whole into smaller wholes isn't the answer. As a consequence, even this next scholarly generation hasn't gotten on with the business of developing a useful theory of lobbying and policymaking.

However, these critics have provided some more useful concepts with which to fiddle in doing theory. Two of these concepts stand out: networks and domains. Policy networks have been used to describe triangles and such that have exploded—exploded with more participants, from more places, with more issue concerns, and with far more internal conflict.[12] This somewhat better fits the open nature of American politics than do triangles. The tendency is to blame the explosion of triangles into networks on representative changes within government and a proliferation of organized interests.[13] As repeatedly observed, both created increasingly more active policy participants and certainly raised hell with looking at politics as tidy, reducible to the simple, and aptly described through any single metaphor. But there was probably always more going on than the triangle partisans discovered.[14]

Nonetheless, networks are nice because they suggest that numerous little villages of people persist in policy making, that all will share a common political intent but still have their own issues, that those folks need to come together and transact business, that they can come and go from one another as their policy business is done, and that they can serve as places to meet for interests that are both friends and foes.[15] Every lobbyist who's held her position for more than a week can describe her current network. Networks, though, are very Bentleyan, especially in being vague about who exactly groups together and why they do. Ya'll come, or is it by selective invitation for the very cooperative? How big can networks get before they encompass the whole capital? When is a network just another name for coalition politics, or Washington, D.C.? Or for all of American politics? As Robert Salisbury emphasized, networks have no order. They're just ongoing interaction.[16] The idea of networking is so darned obvious that it explains very little of what lobbyists actually do in policy making. So what if liberal campaign reform groups won't cooperate on a bill with a recalcitrant American Civil Liberties Union? Will the Union disappear, will its lobbyists cry? Real answers are avoided in network analysis.

That's why scholars conceived of policy domains. Policy participants network mostly within them. That's the view. A domain is nothing more than a well-understood and established policy area, or a community of players or sector. As a lobbyist once said, "What do you mean by asking what I do? I make health care policy. My wife, who is another lobbyist, makes energy policy. Or we try, anyway, to do those things." The domains provided them referents in that big universe of politics. They labeled their jobs.

Domains are, indeed, handy as such points of reference, at least as ideas.[17] First, domains and what they do within them are understood by public officials. They can talk about their work in each domain, and people can talk back to them about their domain activities. The health domain is a different place from the labor domain in federal policy making. Second, domains give meaning to a common set of problems, such as higher education or welfare. Domains, in that sense, have integrating properties. They're like a sticky glue, but not super glue. What any one advocate within the domain does may have transactional effects on the other participants. Within the labor domain, a proposal by the United Auto Workers to negotiate employee layoffs causes a ripple among all of organized labor. Its lobbyists want to understand the likely effects on them, too. So, especially for lobbyists, intense observation and scrutiny go on within domains more than across them. Third, domains house institutional policy bases. That huge base of agricultural programs sticks largely together and governs farming and ranching mostly from within the agricultural domain. Almost all labor policy is written down within that domain, as labor law.

Domains then seem, at first glance, dandy ways to simplify and order parts of political life. They're understood, practiced, and institutionalized. So what's the problem? That's easy: All those things are only partially true. Domains are very much an overly idealized fit with how American government is practiced and divided.

Domains, first of all, are not mutually exclusive. Is food safety part of agriculture or health care? Second, all issues needn't fit only one domain. For example, water protection fits policies of the agricultural domain, as well as those of commerce and manufacturing, and pretty much everything else. It even fits health care, where disposal of toxins and used medical supplies is big business. As a consequence, very few organized interests are participants in only a single policy domain, or even at only a single moment in time. Nor, necessarily, are their issues at play in just those places. Interests, then, can't be kept from playing, or lobbying, just because they're not of a domain. Universities, for example, are affected by a wide range of issues. They necessarily lobby extensively across any imagined or institutional domain boundaries, even while talking about higher education policy.[18] The University of California lobbies on policy items from minority admissions, space research, treatment of laboratory animals, and more. Higher education lobbyists follow the action, not the boundaries of sizes and shapes.

The concepts of networking and domain, therefore, have limited utility in explaining where lobbyists go and what issues they take to those places, or with whom they transact business and why. A domain, like a network, is not a kind of exclusive political marketplace where one-on-one exchanges occur. Neither concept helps clarify very much about any underlying dynamics of how organized interests fit the structural, and thus representational, dynamics of American government and its politics. They don't define any established order, or even consistent patterns of behavior as some suggest. But, like triangle theory, they do help a little.

Four contributions *do* stand out and should be added cumulatively to interest/policy theory. First, lobbyists do have to interact widely—or network—as a central part of their strategy. At worst, it's merely for intelligence gathering; at best, it's for making winning alliances. Second, networks should be understood as short-term and situational, not as permanent or with a life of their own. Lobbyists try to keep their own organizations moving forward and alive. Their networks, and their allies, only contribute to that end. These are not, nor can they be, faithful people in their relationships.

Third, lobbyists nonetheless do have to identify with the domains in which they do business, even if there's overlap. Why? It's important for them to understand the institutionalized policy bases and self-identified stakeholders within each domain. Everyone in health absolutely must know that the American Medical Association (AMA) has lost members, much physician respect, and allies, and thus political clout. AMA can no longer even dictate federal physician standards. It must compromise widely. Without knowing such things, there's no way to pick good issues, to differentiate them from what are widely seen as bad ones. The AMA can be judiciously criticized more than many people realize. It may not be able to move an issue as many expect, even in its greatest area of expertise. Domains are a nice place to be, though, and it's great to have credibility within one or more. Fourth, and finally, lobbyists want to focus primarily on their *own* issues, the issues they've picked as winnable—not those of the other guy. They stick to them, and stick them whenever possible into the acceptable context of domain politics. That's obviously the easiest transaction. More familiar and understandable groupings exist if they do. Lobbyists don't usually network for the fun of it. They do it to advertise and advance precisely what it is that they want, in order to smooth those transactions. That has to be the subject of any interest analysis that explains policy making.

So, it's not accurate to say that networks and domains define and order politics. It's just that they help do so and, thus, contribute to theory. And because the boundaries of each are so permeable, neither helps create all that much order. They do yield a bit of it, though. They're just not the stuff an interest can absolutely rely on. But is anything?

Niches: Getting a Little More into It

If interests can't count on triangles, networks, or domains for maintaining their importance or relevance as political factions, on what do they rely? Themselves, of course—their relationships are but strategies that organized interests chose to create. They create relationships based mainly on their own chosen issues and their own adaptive strategies. It's like life for an alcoholic. The family, whose inner circle resembles a political triangle, can help sort things out. Alcoholics Anonymous can provide a supportive network. And if the troubled person doesn't hang out in unfriendly domains, such as bars and opium dens, that also helps sobriety. Nonetheless, drinking and partying can persist, and the reason for it lies only with the weak resources of the person with the problem.

The most suggestive recent interest/policy research has emphasized blaming the interest when things go wrong. It's very accurate, if one isn't too irritated by the idea that not all interests, issues, and strategies should have a fair shot. Interests can choose badly, both what to do—what tactics—and what to do it on—what issues. Without a doubt, many will make mistakes, often just by not wanting to play the game in such acceptable mainstream fashion. As seen in the last two sections, some points become obvious in avoiding mistakes: Go to the most likely involved political participants but still network widely. Those are two of the eight lessons seen thus far. However, it's time to move beyond shapes of interaction, sizes of alliances, and overly familiar friends and foes. It's necessary to understand the interest itself. The concept of issue or policy niches gets us a bit closer.

The first foray into interest niches emphasized the need that lobbyists have to create a highly specific identity.[19] Perhaps most of the need is internal, for maintenance.[20] Members have to know what interests they're joining and patrons need to understand who they're funding, but niches also have policy consequences.

No other policy participants are going to work with and provide cozy relationships with people they don't know. Blind dates have never been too appealing. Since most lobbyists, with the exception of some contract employees, gain their reputations from those they represent rather than for who they are personally, it's the interest that needs the identity. There are two ways to get one, both of which tend to be followed by the soundest lobbies.

To have a niche, first of all, have a recognizable issue and *stick with it*. Or at least have a small set of core issues necessary to that interest. That's where issue selection becomes so important. A good issue will be around for a long time. A bad issue won't be. Second, to have a recognizable niche, an interest needs to play politics in a predictable way, a way that other policy participants expect this particular interest to behave.[21] A lobbyist who had just won on changing federal pesticides regulations said it most specifically: "For us, it has to be done in a way that is not shrill, emotional, nor bombastic. . . . It happens slowly, you just grind it out."

A major opponent of his group, in contrast, was known for a quite different style. It played to the media, worked to frighten people through shocking statements, and mobilized public protests. Gatekeepers respected this group because they understood that it could gain public responses quite handily. It seldom lost.

That distinction, of course, limits some of the possible tactical options for both of those interest groups, as do the actual resources they have available. But they can still do plenty, as long as their respective stylistic images are left intact. They still can be all-directional. The first group has been known to encourage demonstrations against government, but not by overt means, nor as a primary strategy. The second group has its allied insiders with whom it also plays the contact game. Occasionally, however, group lobbyists continue to blast these friends in public: "It helps with our independence."

The reasons for developing a niche should be apparent by now.[22] There are more active interests out there in politics. That creates competition for time and attention. It's not so easy to win access. Recognizable and predictable lobbies get in first. They get invited to more coalitions during the season.

Also, as mentioned time and again, political relationships within structural institutions, from Congress to the White House, have changed, broadened in participation. A wider range of attentive policymakers means that interests, by necessity, are more likely to be lobbying those who don't know them well. Jumping from one domain to another, as is so often necessary, enhances that problem. A reputation that's both predictable and as widely understood as possible only helps with such strangers. Even without these evolutionary happenings, though, a third factor exists. Public officials have always wanted to know with which interests, from among the several options available, they can most comfortably deal.[23] If an interest group stands for something consistently over time, and does things a certain way, that question has far less relevance. It's pretty easily answered. Transactions with them are predictable, safe, and even welcome. As a consequence, for example, the United Auto Workers (UAW) sticks to issues that its lobbyists might like to dump as bad ones. But not championing all union rights would make the UAW too much of a loose cannon among both friends and foes.

The niche idea suggests that organized interests are, in keeping with the earlier lessons, averse to political risks. Good issues are winnable ones, remember. Winnable issues are most likely those that are familiar and widely seen as relevant. They're those where the problems that interests address persist over time and ones to which public officials have previously given their attention.

Why is that so critical to organized interests? It's critical for reasons beyond just winning. Morbidity in politics is high.[24] Interests can easily be hurt by following risky strategies. Some are even so wounded that they exit lobbying for a time. Mortality for interests is also common, and rarely do interest staff and lobbyists want their organizations to die. Very few American interests stay around for many decades, and certainly not by merely lobbying. Virginia Gray and David Lowery, in the second foray into niches, gave a clear analysis: Niches occur as an attribute of an interest so that its followers can, as much as possible, have a fitting relationship with their entire environment.[25]

The entire environment matters—not just some part of the whole. Rabbits weren't good for Australia's environment because they, as exotic imports, had no predators. So there was much suffering and damage. A former senator expressed it in much more explicitly political terms: "I took care of my state. McDonnell Douglas Corporation was there, so I got them aerospace contracts. But only when they needed them and could logistically manage them, not when they'd be too busy to produce a good product and kill the quality reputation of the firm. I had to watch out for greed." Quite frankly, he didn't want any sickly rabbits or diseased defense contractors in Missouri. They'd be too much hassle, what with unemployment, federal investigations, and lawsuits. As a Democratic Speaker of the House, Jim Wright did much the same thing in his Texas district by selectively taking care of General Dynamics. When it needed a new aerospace contract, Wright helped get it.

What are the implications of niche politics for public policy making and its processes? Beyond the eight earlier lessons, two new ones stand out. First, and obviously, interests try to take their own unique slice out of the entire, or the encompassing, policy base. Nichers don't try to influence everything. Issues are kept as narrow as possible, given the several goals of the organization. An organization such as the Center for Science in the Public Interest exposes unhealthy things, especially popular foods. That's its self-defined job. Others in politics accept its searching for a few nice bans. After all, these people are the food police, not much else. So the Center doesn't extend into some related and possibly logical issues where it's not accepted.

Its staff doesn't develop a healthy diet for all Americans or involve themselves in teaching the public about what to eat. Nor does it lobby for either. Those things are too risky. They're not the Center's job as it has been defined. Were the Center's niche to be expanded, its relationship to the entire political environment would have to be reexamined. The Center for Science in the Public Interest couldn't survive and have policy relevance as just another cookbook publisher. There's too much competition among fad-diet designers, and too little public respect for them as well. Through its existing niche as the food police, the Center both survives and gets listeners quite successfully.

Second, in trying to avoid risks, and thus become labeled a loser interest, niche followers try to select issues that others ignore. This not only minimizes competition among those who represent related things, it also makes it more likely that an interest can win. If nobody cares much, few other organized interests go on the attack. Or, if the issue is so overpoweringly good, potential foes elect not to fight it. That's yet more reason why the search for the right issue is so intense for any interest.

Major League Baseball provides an excellent example. After massive public dissatisfaction over the 1994 players' strike, members of Congress saw their own rewards in removing baseball's antitrust exemption. At first, there was impasse. When policymakers proved serious, both player and owner interests decided to compromise. At the end of negotiations, Congress quickly passed a split-the-difference bill. Players won their core issue, a removal of exemptions on labor negotiations. That related directly to improved player salaries. Team owners, as an interest, also won their core issues, and a substantial amount of antitrust protection. Since the two opponents split the essential differences, the owners' organization was free from antitrust lawsuits for relocation of franchises, broadcasting issues, and player development. All those issues were central to owners' reasons for being in baseball's game. It was their collective niche.

The Animal Protection Institute (API) did a great job developing its niche and picking an easy issue. As a defender of animal rights, API restricted its issues to domestic dog and cat abuse. Furthermore, it picked specific issues that could hardly be contested by any credible interest. Puppy mills, or breeder kennels with inexpensive production and unhealthy conditions, were a great choice, as was the encouragement of spaying and neutering for dogs and cats adopted from animal shelters. Who's going to claim that API isn't riding the high road? Nobody that matters does.

To further avoid conflict, API did even more by doing little else. Animal rights activists generally have reputations as troublesome. Some talk about new ethics of food consumption, an animals' bill of rights. Others want to make feedlot operations for cattle more sanitary, and much more costly. Others lobby against exotic animals in homes. API generally avoided all that. Its staff kept its lobbying arena simple. No foes were encouraged. Few idiotic or contentious statements were made about non-niche issues. One lobbyist explained the strategy: "We love cows, ferrets, and all living things. We'll say it, too. In reality, we lobby for dogs and cats who get abused. People love us as a consequence." Or, if people don't, they keep their mouths shut.

Niches, though, aren't just the creations of highly professional and skillful groups such as API. Less resourceful interests look for them, too. Maybe for them a niche is even more critical. When the Sokaogon Chippewa tribe feared Exxon Corporation's move to buy Wisconsin mining rights, this poorest of Native American groups didn't try a broad-based legislative campaign against corporate America—far from it.

The Sokaogons opposed only the dumping of mine wastes in a local river. Alliances with the public and with environmental groups were quickly won. Such dumping was easily seen as bad; it wasn't hard to support the issue. And the Sokaogons' style of lobbying also won friends. To block Exxon, the tribe emphasized just one thing: a well-backed and popular effort to challenge the state Department of Natural Resources' granting of a mine permit. These allies put the tribe in position to do some all-directional lobbying. In response, Exxon couldn't turn the issue into one of jobs and economic growth. The tribe had already staked out the simple parameters of the issue: Water pollution is unhealthy and wrong. That was the end of the discussion over the meaning of the issue.

So, to affect public policy considerably, interests try to lobby from a niche. They like to ask policymakers for a manageable and acceptable amount of what it is that they represent. They like to go to the public with clean and simple messages. They network and build coalitions with interests that can help them, without duplicating the representation of their wants and forms of expression. Nobody wants to be the Australian rabbit of the lobbying world.

This means that successful niches are not only relatively narrow, they're also incredibly difficult to capture—or to create. While anyone can play, not everybody can win a niche or a place in the general public policy environment. Gray and Lowery discovered something vital: Not all interests that might want a niche ever realize a niche.[26] As a result, there are many organized interests wandering about without a niche, wondering what to do and how, having little or no policy impact in the process. That's why a group such as the American Civil Liberties Union (ACLU) clings so hard to represent freedom of participatory rights, which is its niche issue. Even when liberal allies get angry, ACLU sticks to its position.

The reasons for being without a niche or even losing a niche are many. Sometimes the lobbyists are unskilled. At other times they're just too eager to influence. So they meander, they don't look for what they can actually win. Sometimes interests are too trapped by their once productive pasts, and as conditions change, the group or firm lapses into irrelevance. Some of them simply buy into the glamors of lobbying, thinking that these people alone define what's winnable. So they just go for it. Others are out to attack everyone they see as the crooked weasels who run government, and then they come away wondering why no one on the inside cooperates with them.

What's clear of the non-nichers, however, is that they're not fitting adequately into the environmental circumstances in which they find themselves. They're not reading their surroundings accurately. For example, the American Medical Association tended to talk about everything in not very exact ways, long after others had stopped listening to it all. AMA simply didn't appreciate how many more informed interests were appearing in the health policy domain. The interests of such groups aren't planned well for survival, or to make a profound impact on even the narrowest pieces of public policy. They choose badly about what to want, who to want it from, and how to get it. Greenpeace discovered this in 1997, and downsized dramatically. Hundreds of workers were fired, many offices were closed, and the number and range of issues addressed by the organization were restricted. Greenpeace found out that if an organized interest tries to be too much, nobody knows what it's about. Then nobody cooperates.

Is this true of all interests? The fitting business certainly matters to all. Yet, it seems, there are some variations from one interest type to another. Two exceptions stand out. Media talk show hosts with issue agendas certainly thrive off conflict—at least they thrive off fighting with some interests. That's the nature of their environments. There are niches for these folks. Paul Harvey niches his way through "common man" criticism of big government.

Legislative enterprises are another exception, particularly since staffs wander through domains and networks rather haphazardly in pursuit of constituent pleasures. They each seem, however, to occupy some sort of issue niche in the eyes of people back home and in the Capitol. It's probably through the nature of who they see as their main constituents, such as taking care of the oil guys back home. But maybe there's more to it than material constituent service. Oregon Senator Ron Wyden, a Democrat, is known far and wide for restricting the width of his niche. How does he do it? He'll do anything that gets publicity through the advocacy of the personal rights of those who've somehow been screwed. That's his identity, and not much else is on his issue agenda. U.S. Representative Dave Camp, a Republican, does homestyle stuff linked mostly to constituents' economic and finance problems. That's his quiet and pensive style. There are, then, some niche characteristics that need further exploration.

Can There Be a Theory of Interests and Policy?

Sure there can, and this chapter offers a better start than those theories that emphasize power, money, and coercion of public officials. As expressions of private or extragovernmental factions, organized interests do a great deal to structure both the content and direction of U.S. public policy. The reasons why can be seen by putting away triangles, networks, and much of the assumed exclusiveness of domains. They're not the right place to start. Rather, let's start with issues and interests.

What's been learned from the earlier sections? Forget the metaphoric paradigms, or the just plain jargon; look only at the lessons. And go back once more to Bentley, those glorious days of yesteryear, to a theory of transactions. First, lobbyists who want to make public policy form loose groupings; they get together.[27] Second, they do so under transactional circumstances where the contributions of any single participant are tough—perhaps impossible—to evaluate. What matters are the common interactions of those who group together.[28]

Out of that milieu, nonetheless, come exchanges among the participants.[29] But given transactional circumstances and the variety of participating players, those exchanges are undoubtedly not one-on-one—nor are they made by each interested player with every other one. So they're a kind of nonmarketplace exchange, not simple, rational, choice-based trades. The participants benefit from the grouping, not necessarily through each interactive partner. This is more an investment theory than an exchange theory. The lesson is: Invest all together in the grouping, then extract your individual wins from it. That's why coalitions aren't common entities but, rather, groupings of several self-interested players.

Accordingly, all who can actually contribute to some public policy get to play. That is, those who have resources can play. But those with little promise of contributing, or those who are seen skeptically, get excluded. They are, for all practical purposes, shunned—for their own faults, even if blame shouldn't be attributed. This happens in politics because, like life, most of the environment of policy making is informal and situational.[30] Nonetheless, the environment still provides a significant structure for getting on with and doing either personal or political business.[31] The legend of any interest that messes up big time will live long.

Thus, other things structure that business in far less temporary ways. Relationships among the policy participants are also affected by the public institutions surrounding those who are targeted for policy change or support.[32] Rules, public organizations, and existing policy bases all matter. Mostly they matter by their confining effects.[33] Policy participants can't just do—or transact—what they want; they must do things in a governmental environment that's formally rigid and rule-bound, as well as often informally structured.[34] As a result, there are real costs involved in those groupings that are transacting public policy results.[35] The costs can kill some organized interests before they gain influence—or even after a long run of success, if they don't evolve in relevant ways.

So what? Here's the easily understood part for creating a workable yet rudimentary theory of interests and public policy: Those involved in making public policies, including all the privately organized interests, don't *want* to informally group with those who increase transaction costs.[36] They won't unless they must, which is rarely the case. Lobbyists who want to change a great deal of existing policy, wipe out beloved programs or rights, spend lots of money, go against conventional wisdom, or affront social values get shunned. Those who want to fill the "hollow core" by integrating all of a policy base—or, worse yet, *all* the policy bases—really get shunned. So do the interests they represent. Those interests fail because of bad issues, bad choices, and maybe inappropriate behavior, as well. But it's their fault.

There is, then, a political economy of grouping. And since interests have to group, or network, in order to matter at making public policy, lobbyists need to behave and make choices economically, both for themselves and for those within their environment. Interests perform a lot of appropriately interrelated tasks and select good issues in order to gain an accepted policy niche. Their representatives desperately want that niche in order to be in the "in-crowd."[37] That means that these interests at least semipermanently fix their resources on affecting certain specific issues which they hope to claim as their own. Each lobbyist darned well understands being in, even if as an outsider.

Obviously, as parts of the overall environment vary even within American politics, there will, indeed, be some variations of this general condition. Also, environments change with time. And some national policy domains are institutionally less structured than others: agriculture is; labor is not. Interests within the latter don't face such intense competition for access.[38] Some states have less developed governments and policy bases than others. They tend to have fewer organized interests, or less interest density, as a result.[39] Iowa doesn't have lots of organized interests; Michigan does. Therefore, the ease of successfully developing a niche, and even the idea of the essentials of a niche, will vary somewhat from setting to setting, domain to domain, state to state.

Still, however, public policy making in American politics is generally affected by organized interests in similar ways. Here's the heart of a theory of interests and policy: Organized interests do matter—a great deal. They're instrumental in producing public policy, particularly as parts of larger interactive groupings.[40] But not all interests are so chosen, and not all get to be so exclusive. Some mess up and no longer fit processes of their environment. Those that don't mess up do matter in what truly *is*, then, a most exclusionary process. They play in a wide-open process, but they fail to lobby well. Or, that is, they get to play, but they don't get to matter much. This is not the exclusiveness portrayed in triangle or network metaphors. Usually, groups and institutions are excluded because their issues are, themselves, bad choices. So they then lobby and organize poorly. Those interests suffer high rates of morbidity, mortality, and rejection because, quite simply, they don't fit very well their immediate circumstances. They've not found and kept a realizable niche and fixed their resources and identity adequately within it. Alternatively, they've fixed things so well that they can't successfully evolve. The Grange is a good example of this.

Summary and Highlights

This chapter is a little too abstract and esoteric to be very much fun because the study of interests and their policy making has been dominated with too many size and shape metaphors. That gets tedious to discuss. The review, however, was necessary for getting to a theory of how and why only some organized interests help produce public policy results. Triangle theory was mostly inaccurate, but it did teach four lessons: that interests do gravitate first to certain public officials; that legislators, alone, aren't the targets of—or even partners with—lobbying; that interests must try to conserve resources; and that lobbying does involve a search for relatively cozy relationships.

The concepts of networking and domains are good ones, but despite their efforts, they are just not sufficiently well-ordered to explain much. Proponents have just tried too hard to be neat and tidy. But they contribute four more lessons: that grouping together is vital for successful interests; that those groupings are largely short-term and situational; that lobbyists need to fit the expectations of those domains and other places where they do business; and that, with all that, they still need to take care mostly of their own business and issues, not look after the other guy's business or issues.

The two lessons from niches followed: Interests tend to pick issues as narrow as possible. And, also as much as possible, they pick issues that engender the least conflict. That is, they pick advocacy proposals which best fit their environment, or daily circumstances. Those are good issues. Other issues that don't fit tend to be bad.

Finally, this chapter proposed the rudimentary outline of a theory of interests and public policy making. By building on earlier chapters, it emphasized transactional relationships, the political economy of grouping, and the confining effects of existing public institutions of the state or nation-state. When successful, organized interests are mostly about affecting public policy by lowering the transaction costs of what their representatives want from government. Doing so lets these lobbyists play the game well with many others and not be excluded from, à la Bentley, transactional groupings. If they do their work well, they stay in the game. Interest theorists have long missed the real meaning of lobbying exclusion and the exclusionary nature of policy processes.

Thus, interests can't demand just anything from their targets. The losers, indeed, often try, and they get shunned for their efforts. Other interests get integrated into the process and produce public policy, at least in a collective sense with others. Maybe they don't win exactly what their own representatives, their members, and their patrons want. Maybe they don't even try for such goals. But they are, nonetheless, still the winners, and all because they fit their environment. They've invested in it well and extracted some nice nonmarket earnings from their fit.

10

A Wasted Process? Or Running (Ruining?) Things?

The case has been made and this conclusion will be short, so keep reading. This chapter only intends to draw from the earlier presentation. The questions posed in the introduction will be answered, and their meaning hopefully made more clear. After all, those questions have been the bases of what has so far been written.

Four things were asked at the onset. Where do interests fit into the policy-making process and, very importantly, into society? What do they do to fit? How do they do it? How much have organized interests adapted over time and with new circumstances in order to fit?

The Matter of Fit

Critics of organized interests like to charge somehow that they don't fit America. How silly, of course they do. E. E. Schattschneider had wonderful insights into interest politics, but he was undeniably wrong on one. He believed that regular people weren't taken into policy-making account. He felt very strongly that only wealthy interests really run things.[1]

Schattschneider was actually saying that the effects of interests on public policy fail to fit his preferences about which issues should win, about who should win. Loads of other critics evaluate things in the same way.[2] That's okay, but they shouldn't say that organized interests don't fit American politics or society values. On the contrary, they epitomize a close and proximate fit, and they always have. Certainly, organized interests don't fit an America of dreams, grand aspirations, philosophical ideals, and pie-in-the-sky.

This book would be a terribly overly optimistic and Polyannaish analysis if there were any claim to interest politics fitting the ideal of how American politics ought to work under the most fair rules. As it is, this text is only optimistic in saying that politics reflects some happy mainstream. But interest politics does fairly well fit daily empirical reality. And daily American political reality, throughout the society, is dominated by factionalized selfishness and narrow visions. Every so often it does create quite new policy ideas and sees them spread.[3] Once again, however, it's most generally for selfish reasons.

The strategies that sound lobbyists follow have long accomplished four things. First, they've placed policy ideas in the context of mainstream American popular images. And, while they've spun their good and still idealized stories, lobbyists haven't sold much that the nation as a whole found either anathema or absolutely wrong at the time.

But those lobbyists, of course, have sold ideas that many ideologically inclined political observers find offensive.[4] And the lobbyists have blocked policies that observers think should have passed.[5] Pluralism, as a theory of all interests and issues legitimately coming together for negotiated agreements, wouldn't have expected that.[6] Big deal, for those in politics daily. Who in heck, they question, are pluralist critics to think that their beliefs should call the shots? A lobbyist once said of them: "Critics are people who either lost or who didn't have to deal with the realities of playing the policy game anyway." That's true, but it still misses the pluralists' point of society's need for ideals.

Second, organized interests have long done comprehensive, or even all-directional, lobbying, and for a reason. Frank Baumgartner tells a great and most apt story about President Charles de Gaulle during the days when France had a foreign policy of ardently pursuing its own national interest. When asked where France had its nuclear missiles aimed, de Gaulle said that they were pointed in all directions. That irritated Americans, but not the French. France still, however, fit the world order.

When organized interests aimed at targets in order to sell their marketable ideas, the targets were the public and the media, various public officials, and, of course, other interests. Nobody who mattered was forgotten and some elements of each of those targets were always of policy-making significance. By following their own interests, factions realized right away that they couldn't go very far against the wishes of any important part of a complex policy process that had its roots deep in public values—though not necessarily in the ethics of right and wrong, or morality. For the American public, it was nice to develop the West and displace, through war, Native Americans. It wasn't nice only in the eyes of Thurlow Weed and Mark Hanna. The Indian tribes didn't count. They had no legitimate American social niche. Those without a social niche were labeled savages.

Third, lobbyists have always sought strategically good issues and avoided bad ones. Good issues fit U.S. or state policy traditions and the institutional structures that democratically govern them. They are relatively easy to win. The central texture of American public policy has always had a specific grain, a way to do things. As good craftspeople, lobbyists have always shaped things with that grain, not against it. Interests with incompetent lobbyists went away, just as did shops with bad craftspeople, as later did shops with good craftspeople when far fewer of the public wanted to support quality furniture and its high prices. They disappeared when, it seems, the width of the transactable craft niche narrowed dramatically.

Fourth, in a very complex way, the most successful of American interests have long fit their own environments. They've sought to be identified circumstantially as legitimate and credible policy players, to fit. They've picked issues on which they could win. And they've stuck with them whenever possible. They've also played the policy game within their own environments in a recognizable and generally appropriate fashion. As factions, they've had to be known and predictable, and therefore able to win a response from those who make policy.

So organized interests not only fit the moderate pace of the U.S. policy process and mainstream American society, they also fit specifically because of what their lobbyists do with the resources they have. Successful factions have won in politics and policy making not by forcing narrow values on the rest of the nation. Rather, they've won largely by reflecting the sentiments, values, institutions, and accumulated policy traditions that make up and support American governments. And they've won by asking only for some part of it all, for example, more rights for women.

Theodore Lowi once suggested that liberal traditions—or the let's-have-lots-of-public-policy views—of American politics essentially meant tit-for-tat.[7] That's sort of true. If an interest that wanted a tit saw it necessary, its representatives tended to let the other players win a tat *if those players could do it*, even if the first guys hated tats. But tit-for-tat wasn't a cabal or a conspiracy, or a big secret society. It was just letting another interest that found a fit get what it probably would anyway, only with less of a battle, or with fewer transaction costs for everybody.

Adaptation by Interests

Do organized interests change? There are several specific responses to that question. We'll begin with the big picture and go on to the smaller, and the smallest.

Organized interests, as a universe of groups and institutions, don't appear to be inherently different in what they do and how they best fit politics.[8] It's the political process that's quite different indeed. So is society. Quite obviously, as a consequence, lobbying has evolved, and it has evolved regularly. New technologies and new institutional rules, as they emerge, force some degree of change in how lobbying takes place. Computers and congressional reforms of the 1970s are two obvious examples. Yet the essential targets, and the emphasis on being ready to lobby in all directions through numerous tasks, surely aren't new. Traditions are involved.[9] Now what if Daniel Shays *would* have hanged a few public officials?

More interests, more actively involved public policymakers, and more issues just produce more of the same stuff, and all in the context of *very* expanded public values. That certainly mucks things up a considerable bit more. So many players and wants make a difficult process with difficult rules even harder. Relationships in today's politics are far more fragile. There's just a lot more politics. But, in general, in order to adapt and wade through all that politics, lobbyists have probably gotten more talented and more skillful.[10] That may either help or hamper that slow, hard process. It certainly means fewer bills out of legislatures. But it also means bigger bills, as in larger or omnibus ones.[11] Interests and gatekeepers want more goodies in each package, more winners in each one.

Individual interests are pretty adaptable, too. Mostly they change as their environments evolve. They pick new issues if they need to do so. They adopt more strategies, as was the case when everybody decided that they were outsiders for strategic reasons. In general, however, lobbyists do like the status quo—their old issues, their old benefits, their old ways. And they'll defend them all as long as they can hold on to their current realized niches and not become irrelevant.[12] Lobbyists hang on because they don't want to make an ever more difficult process even harder by increasing political uncertainty. They worry constantly about keeping the costs of transactions manageable. So even the most high-minded of active advocates don't try very hard to change the ideals of American society, or the system.

Also, interests are very adaptive to new things, especially to toys of the trade. When a new and upgraded computer comes out, everyone wants one. When the ease of communicating with the grassroots is enhanced, every business interest wants a boiler room from which to make contact—from which to read lists, dial phones, and be persuasive to the regular folks. When more members of Congress can influence a bill, lobbyists find the ones who've recently gained entry—quickly.

Adaptability of organizations can be seen, as well, in the emergence of new interests, which goes on all the time. As the environment changes, organized interests come and go in politics. When more public officials exist in an environment, there get to be more organized interests.[13] What most frequently happens is one of two things. Either an existing organization, such as Microsoft, with its desire to alter participatory rules, adds lobbying to its chores. Many organizations go from a group to an interest group in these cases, or from a mere firm to an organized interest. That's the pattern. In response to social or economic changes, existing organizations also found, prod, and support brand-new interest groups, sometimes by patronage. Sometimes they do it by buying or renting help—really by any means legally possible.

Nowhere is this second pattern more obvious than with communications technologies in general, and the Internet in particular. With the great popularity of and media attention to the Internet, an untold number of new organized interests have sprung up. Many are so short-lived they can't be accurately counted. Opportunities, though, abound: to link suppliers in trade associations, to assist and protect users, to interject Christian values pro and con onto cyberspace, and so on. And because factional values vary, as do component parts of the Net, there are a number of groups in each category. Many more niches are continually being created and aspired to. There are no definitive limits here, but the environment and fitting within it is certainly a constraining factor.

But niches are also disappearing, and with them organized interests that had niches. The need for social fraternity among out-of-the-way rural residents and small farmers has pretty much disappeared. Accordingly, the once esteemed Grange no longer has a niche, no fit with politics or with society. So, as a lobby, it's now a joke. These last hangers-on were *not* players, *nor* active, *nor* any longer even possessed of policy goals or issue interests. They weren't a part of the Washington policy-making environment, at least realistically. Like so many once vital interests, the Grange adapted and, for all but the final ceremony, died.

Without question, then, organized interests are quite adaptable. They need to be in order to fit their environments, the policy process, and public expectations, especially since these are all so evolutionary. But because of the slowly changing nature of political environments, organized interests should better be understood as semi-adaptive, rather than as innovatively so. They're not much ahead of the evolutionary curve, if indeed they're ever out front. That's not their job. They do day-by-day politics. So organized interests are each what they are—not everything to everybody or out trying to save the world. Interests, lobbyists, and their tasks only change when they must. And sometimes that's either impossible or too late, except, that is, in acquiring newly available toys.

How Much Does Lobbying Matter?

It's noted in the introduction that asking to quantify influence is a deplorably bad question. Too many problems of both measurement and values get in the way. A U.S. senator said, "Obviously [that lobbyist] is one of the most influential in Washington. How do I judge? What he succeeds with regularly makes me angry, that's how."

After carefully looking at the fit of organized interests, it seems possible to judge their importance to public policy making. If interests fit so well into a slow-moving process, whatever slowness they add is both logical and a display of their prominence. They exaggerate and help give meaning to basic constitutional tendencies.

Interest politics, then, is not a wasted process by any means. When Republican legislators, after nearly a three-year effort from 1993 to 1995, helped kill health care reform, they were responding to interests that identified with those partisans.[14] Democratic members of Congress also did their part to seal health care's coffin. Why? They were responding to organized interests that fit their portion of their legislative party and its political goals. Additionally, despite giving their tacit support, other interests wouldn't get active for the Clinton administration's plan. It wasn't really to their liking, their lobbyists argued. So they didn't lobby much, if at all. Health care reform, in a democratic and Madisonian sense, richly deserved its fate. No one should complain about its inability to fit consensually into politics.

Further evidence of the contribution of lobbying and interests can be seen in what they succeeded against with health care reform. In public opinion polls, approximately 70 percent of the public favored the major tenets of the Clinton plan: health insurance for all and employers paying for it.[15] But had the *public* spoken?

As Haynes Johnson and David Broder concluded, "Public opinion is more often than not a myth."[16] As evidenced in these polls, public opinion is transitory, short-term, abstract responses. Opinions are not necessarily thought-through in context, not an indicator of policy salience, not usually an indicator of ranked policy preferences. They're the basis for general agreement, with few, if any other, factors taken into account—pretty weak, or risky, stuff on which to pin a major public policy. So public opinion polls don't often define what gatekeepers see as the relevant, attentive public.

Does anyone, then, really wonder why public officials elect to listen instead to lobbyists? These are the people who, given a fight, will help inform public attitudes and mobilize constituents over very specific, real-life, everyday issues. They're tied also to their own constituents, who are constituents of public officials as well.

A Clinton health plan supporter grudgingly agreed: "The special interests were the only ones who successfully judged what the public was willing to swallow on this bill." No, what organized interests do is far from wasted.

Does that mean that organized interests run American public policy making? Of course they don't. Transactional relationships predominate, with organized interests and numerous public officials joining together to invest and produce policy ends, like coral evolves. Organized interests have considerable influence but not total control. The collections of them, or even their little villages, matter most.

Critics may scream at that comment. Look at all that money, those campaign contributions! Let's conjure up James Madison once again to begin quieting those critics.[17] As Madison explained in one of his lesser known texts in the *Federalist Papers*, factions aren't the only selfish creatures that would emerge in American politics. Individual public officials will be no less prone to pursue their self-interest, and no rules can prevent them.[18] But that doesn't mean they're crooks.

In a transactional policy process, there are thus two sides to campaign contributions. Fred McChesney noted the extortion factor.[19] Those running for office want money; interests have it; the officials go after it. As lobbyists are so fond of saying, giving campaign contributions is like paying for protection from the mob: "If you don't contribute, you're left out. Or you fear you will be." Money, then, just helps the fit of transactional groupings. But it doesn't control the fit. And some interests are so fed up that they don't care if money politics goes away. In 1997, General Motors announced that the corporation was all finished giving to national party organizations. Policymakers quaked a bit. Lobbyists, though, knew that whatever happened, they'd still lobby.

Organized interests don't win *only* by giving money. It should be apparent after all these pages that any such view is hopelessly naive. No one task provides a panacea. There's much more to sound public affairs work, as two impoverished Native American tribes found out in 1997. The tribes were trying to get federal officials to return Fort Reno, Oklahoma to them, to develop it as a tourist site. What did the tribes do? They donated $107,000 from their tribal emergency relief fund to the Democratic National Committee. After they talked things over with policymakers and didn't get their wishes, tribal leaders wanted their campaign contributions back. Sure, money gets anything anyone wants! It didn't in this case. It didn't even get some dry Oklahoma dirt.[20] But, it did get some nice talk, or access without reinforcement.

None of that refutes the substantial evidence that key people make things happen in politics. Some of them are lobbyists; others are not. However, all of them share one common characteristic: They don't do it alone. As catalytic policy entrepreneurs, advocates or lobbyists do matter—all because they sell their ideas to others, win wide support, yield part of the action to others, and let others win, too. They move from the specific interest to create a more diffuse American public concern.

A simple and convenient way to look at this is: Lobbyists try to wrap their issues in winnable policy vehicles.[21] Doing it is quite complex. Omnibus authorization bills, appropriations packages, regulatory reform proposals that cover many items, and court cases that fit a pattern of precedents are all examples of vehicles in use. Vehicle tactics are certainly more prevalent with more interests today, and more public policymakers are involved. But, as development and settlement interests demonstrated in the nineteenth century, packages of bills are put together over time. In that way, several interests cooperate and get a piece of a shared set of interdependent policy benefits.

How does this go on? It works by tinkering together with existing institutions. Or it works by manipulating previous policy bases, the structures of government, and the rule-bound traditions of decision making. Interests need to be understood in terms of their issues.[22] But transactional groupings need to be understood in terms of the vehicles on which they're collectively working. Investing in the grouping hopefully gets a win for one's issue in return. As it's so well known, however, not all the vehicles win. Bills fail; litigation loses; and lobbyists continue—wishing that they really did run government.

But aren't those transactional groupings ruining things? Of course not, except maybe the national spirit. By definition, politics is about contesting values. There *will* be winners and losers. Some winning interests *will* consistently pick better issues than others. The environment of American politics *will* fit some interests far better than others. Congressional enterprises, for instance, will have an institutional advantage. Poor people's lobbies will not.

But none of these are reasons to disparage organized interests or those with whom they group. That broader fault is part of the constitutional design of American politics, and its evolution. As has been said before, politics isn't fair—nor can it be. Nor was it designed to be. Don't blame special interests for it, though. Even successful victims rights groups can be found today. Poor people's lobbies do fit better at the turn of the twenty-first century than they did at the turn of the twentieth. Interests of all sorts merely do their representative best in a complex political world. And that even meets, somewhat, that old grudgemudgen Schattschneider's OK—even though he believed in parties, while the policy-making game today is about believing in organized interests, as it has long been. Yet, as even Schattschneider said, one must judge whether organizational rights are apparent and whether interests can compete with one another in order to judge democracy. That judgment is generally positive.[23] And more true now than before. But it doesn't stop some lobbyists like Microsoft's Bill Gates from wanting to change the constitution to make it better fit an information age. And it doesn't stop some Americans from saying that too many are still left out of today's game too much. After all, these advocates don't want to promote mainstream issues that are easy to sell. They don't think those issues are what society needs.

A Concluding Word

Are all the conclusions and the speculation in this book correct? Has it discovered truth? Maybe, maybe not. Obviously the person who wrote it thinks so. His dog does too. Others, now, will have to judge that opinion, hopefully by undertaking rigorous tests of its findings and analysis. There's plenty of room for research on the relationship between organized interests and public policy. One particularly important research objective would be to clarify which types of organized interests best fit with varying circumstances and environments. So until these awaited scholars get on with it, there is indeed a definitive final word. See the reference to Jack White in Chapter Six: FIDO.

Notes

INTRODUCTION

1. Arthur F. Bentley concluded the same thing nearly a century ago in *The Process of Government: A Study of Social Pressures* (Chicago: University of Chicago Press, 1908).

2. The most clear statement of personal influence within institutions is by John Mark Hansen, *Gaining Access: Congress and the Farm Lobby, 1919–1981* (Chicago: University of Chicago Press, 1991).

3. William P. Browne, "The Third House: A Study of Lobbyists in Iowa." M.S. thesis. Iowa State University, 1969.

4. William P. Browne, "Spokesmen for Cities: Organizational Membership in Voluntary Municipal Associations." Ph.D. dissertation. Washington University, St. Louis, 1971.

5. William P. Browne, "Variations in the Behavior and Style of State Lobbyists and Interest Groups," *Journal of Politics* 47 (1985): 450–468.

6. William P. Browne and Delbert J. Ringquist, "Michigan: Diversity and Professionalism in a Partisan Environment," in Ronald J. Hrebenar and Clive S. Thomas, ed., *Interest Groups in the Midwestern States* (Ames: Iowa State University Press, 1993), pp. 117–144.

7. The start was a series of five edited books with the late Don F. Hadwiger, all supported by the Economic Research Service of the U.S. Department of Agriculture and done through the Policy Studies Organization: *The New Politics of Food* (Lexington, MA: D.C. Heath, 1978); *The Role of U.S. Agriculture in Foreign Policy*, also with Richard M. Fraenkel (New York: Praeger, 1979); *Rural Policy Problems: Changing Dimensions* (Lexington, MA: D.C. Heath, 1982); *World Food Politics* (Boulder, CO: Rienner, 1986); and *Public Policies and Agricultural Technology: Adversity Despite Achievement* (London: Macmillan, 1987).

8. William P. Browne, *Private Interests, Public Policy, and American Agriculture* (Lawrence: University Press of Kansas, 1988).

9. William P. Browne, *Cultivating Congress: Constituents, Issues, and Interests in Agricultural Policymaking* (Lawrence: University Press of Kansas, 1995).

10. Advocacy and policy change were the intentions of William P. Browne, Jerry R. Skees, Louis E. Swanson, Paul B. Thompson, and Laurian J. Unnevehr in *Sacred Cows and Hot Potatoes: Agrarian Myths in Agricultural Policy* (Boulder, CO: Westview, 1992).

11. Robert H. Salisbury picks up on this Bentleyan theme in "Putting Interests Back into Interest Groups," in Allan J. Cigler and Burdett A. Loomis, ed., *Interest Group Politics*, 3d ed. (Washington, DC: Congressional Quarterly Press, 1991), pp. 371–384.

12. The genesis of this theory begins with Mancur Olson, Jr., *The Logic of Collective Action: Public Goods and the Theory of Groups* (Cambridge, MA: Harvard University Press, 1971). David B. Truman addressed it less satisfactorily earlier in *The Governmental Process* (New York: Knopf, 1951).

13. Robert H. Salisbury focuses on mass membership groups in his groundbreaking "An Exchange Theory of Interest Groups," *Midwest Journal of Political Science* 13 (1969): 1–32.

14. This is best typified in J. Leiper Freeman, *The Political Process: Executive Bureau–Legislative Committee Relations* (New York: Random House, 1955).

15. See Hugh Heclo's refuting article, "Issue Networks and the Executive Establishment," in Anthony King, ed., *The New American Political System* (Washington, DC: American Enterprise Institute, 1978), pp. 87–124.

16. E. E. Schattschneider, *Politics, Pressures, and the Tariff: A Study of Free Enterprise in Pressure Politics as Shown in the 1929–1930 Revision of the Tariff* (New York: Prentice-Hall, 1935).

17. Raymond A. Bauer, Ithiel de Sola Pool, and Lewis Anthony Dexter, *American Business and Public Policy: The Politics of Foreign Trade* (Chicago: Aldine-Atherton, 1963).

18. Jeffrey M. Berry, *The Interest Group Society*, 2d ed. (New York: Little, Brown/Scott, Foresman, 1989), pp. 16–17.

19. Numerous voluntary associations don't specifically lobby, for example Rotary International and other groups organized around community service. They may, as will be discussed later, still wield political influence.

20. See Truman's use of James Madison, *The Federalist Papers*, no. 10, pp. 14–15.

CHAPTER 1

1. Jeffrey H. Birnbaum, *The Lobbyists: How Influence Peddlers Get Their Way in Washington* (New York: Times Books, 1992); Jonathan Rauch, *Demosclerosis: The Silent Killer of American Government* (New York: Times Books, 1994).

2. Myths are used to simplify complex situations and, thus, build social consensus on otherwise difficult issues. Harry M. Johnson, "Ideology and the Social System," *International Encyclopedia of the Social Sciences*, vol. 7 (New York: Macmillan and the Free Press, 1968), pp. 76–85.

3. Interview with the author, July 1986. Unreferenced quotes throughout the text are from author interviews as well.

4. David Knoke, *Organizing for Collective Action: The Political Economies of Associations* (New York: Aldine de Gruyter, 1990), pp. 27–45. Kay Lehman Schlozman reports that 79 percent of Americans joined one or more voluntary associations involved in politics in "Voluntary Organizations in Politics: Who Gets Involved?" in William Crotty, Mildred A. Schwartz, and John C. Green, ed., *Representing Interests and Interest Group Representation* (Lanham, MD: University Press of America, 1994), p. 71.

5. Graham Wooton, *Interest Groups: Policy and Politics in America* (Englewood Cliffs, NJ: Prentice-Hall, 1985), pp. 21–24.

6. This volume follows the logic of David B. Truman, *The Governmental Process* (New York: Knopf, 1951), pp. 16–44. Frank R. Baumgartner and Beth L. Leech wrestle with this matter of imprecision quite nicely in *Basic Interests: The Importance of Groups in Politics and in Political Science* (Princeton, NJ: Princeton University Press, 1998).

7. John Mark Hansen, *Gaining Access: Congress and the Farm Lobby, 1919–1981* (Chicago: University of Chicago Press, 1991), pp. 26–31.

8. Alexis de Tocqueville, *Democracy in America,* edited and abridged by Richard D. Heffner (New York: New American Library, 1956), pp. 11–12.

9. John Dewey, *The Public and Its Problems* (New York: Holt, 1927), p. 151.

10. James Madison, *The Federalist Papers,* no. 10.

11. This comment by no means refutes the analysis of Jeffrey M. Berry in *The Interest Group Society,* 3d ed. (New York: Longman, 1991), pp. 17–43. Advocacy has indeed exploded, but not just by interest group additions to the policy process.

12. Solon Justus Buck, *The Granger Movement: A Study of Agricultural Organization and Its Political, Economic, and Social Manifestations* (Cambridge, MA: Harvard University Press, 1913), pp. 106–122.

13. On latent interest groups, see Harmon Zeigler, *Interest Groups in American Society* (Englewood Cliffs, NJ: Prentice-Hall, 1964), pp. 68–75. Mancur Olson, Jr. also identifies latency in *The Logic of Collective Action: Public Goods and the Theory of Groups* (Cambridge, MA: Harvard University Press, 1971), p. 51.

14. Stephen Gill, *American Hegemony and the Trilateral Commission* (Cambridge: Cambridge University Press, 1988).

15. Stephen Gill and David Law, *The Global Political Economy: Perspectives, Problems, and Policies* (Baltimore: Johns Hopkins University Press, 1988), p. 91.

16. These scholars simply follow David Easton, *The Political System: An Inquiry into the State of Political Science* (New York: Knopf, 1953), pp. 126–128.

17. Truman, *The Governmental Process,* pp. 26–33.

18. Olson, *The Logic of Collective Action,* pp. 9–52.

19. Ibid., pp. 60–63.

20. Robert H. Salisbury, "An Exchange Theory of Interest Groups," *Midwest Journal of Political Science* 13 (1969): 30.

21. This mostly can be seen in the off-handed way scholars lump the groups together in their comments. See James Q. Wilson, *Political Organizations* (New York: Basic Books, 1973), pp. 42–43; and Schlozman, "Voluntary Organizations in Politics," pp. 67–83.

22. The analysis most commented on is by Terry M. Moe, *The Organization of Interests: Incentives and the Internal Dynamics of Political Interest Groups* (Chicago: University of Chicago Press, 1980), pp. 208–216. Lots of others followed.

23. See the literature on voting behavior and public opinion beginning with Angus Campbell, Philip E. Converse, Warren E. Miller, and Donald Stokes, *The American Voter* (New York: Wiley, 1960), pp. 216–227; and continuing through with Benjamin I. Page and Robert Y. Shapiro, *The Rational Public: Fifty Years of Trends in Americans' Policy Preferences* (Chicago: University of Chicago Press, 1992). See also Sidney Verba, Kay Lehman Schlozman, and Henry E. Brady, *Voice and Equality: Civic Voluntarism in American Politics* (Cambridge: Harvard University Press, 1995).

24. Paul Johnson, "Of Exchange and Environmentalism: An Exploratory Study." Unpublished manuscript. (Lawrence: University of Kansas, Department of Political Science, 1995).

25. Salisbury, "An Exchange Theory of Interest Groups."

26. Steven Rosenstone and John Mark Hansen, *Mobilization, Participation, and Democracy in America* (New York: Macmillan, 1993).

27. This was observed in writing letters to Congress, but it surely applies to joining as well. Stephen Frantzich, *Write Your Congressman: Constituent Communications and Representation* (New York: Praeger, 1986), p. 66.

28. Christopher J. Bosso, "Adaptation and Change in the Environmental Movement," in Allan J. Cigler and Burdett A. Loomis, ed., *Interest Group Politics*, 3d ed. (Washington, DC: Congressional Quarterly Press, 1991), pp. 161–165.

29. Olson, *The Logic of Collective Action*, p. 158.

30. Wilson, *Political Organizations*, pp. 39–45.

31. James Q. Wilson, *The Amateur Democrat: Club Politics in Three Cities* (Chicago: University of Chicago Press, 1962), pp. 226–257.

32. William P. Browne, *Cultivating Congress: Constituents, Issues, and Interests in Agricultural Policymaking* (Lawrence: University Press of Kansas, 1995), pp. 22–39.

33. Berry, *The Interest Group Society*.

34. Douglas R. Imig, *Poverty and Power: The Political Representation of Poor Americans* (Lincoln: University of Nebraska Press, 1996), pp. 25–39.

35. William P. Browne, "Benefits and Membership: A Reappraisal of Interest Group Activity," *Western Political Quarterly* 29 (1976): 263–265.

36. Buck, *The Granger Movement*, pp. 80–102.

37. Salisbury, "An Exchange Theory of Interest Groups," p. 12.

38. Murray R. Benedict, *Farm Policies of the United States, 1790–1950* (New York: Twentieth Century Fund, 1950).

39. Bonnie H. Erickson and T. A. Nosanchuk, "How an Apolitical Association Politicizes," *Canadian Review of Sociology and Anthropology* 27 (1990): 206–219.

40. Rosenstone and Hansen, *Mobilization, Participation, and Democracy in America*, p. 70.

CHAPTER 2

1. Belle Zeller, *Pressure Politics in New York* (New York: Prentice-Hall, 1937).

2. The best example is E. E. Schattschneider, *The Semi-Sovereign People: A Realist's View of Democracy in America* (New York: Holt, Rinehart and Winston, 1961).

3. The amount depends on which measures are used. Robert H. Salisbury, "Interest Representation: The Dominance of Institutions," *American Political Science Review* 78 (1984): 64–76.

4. Oliver E. Williamson, *The Economic Institutions of Capitalism* (New York: Macmillan and the Free Press, 1985), pp. 16–17; Douglass C. North, *Institutions, Institutional Change, and Economic Performance* (Cambridge: Cambridge University Press, 1990), pp. 3–10.

5. Richard Lehne, *Industry and Politics: United States in Comparative Perspective* (Englewood Cliffs, NJ: Prentice-Hall, 1993), pp. 101–105.

6. Michael T. Hayes, "The New Group Universe," in Allan J. Cigler and Burdett A. Loomis, eds., *Interest Group Politics*, 2d ed. (Washington, DC: Congressional Quarterly Press, 1986), pp. 133–145.

7. William P. Browne, *Private Interests, Public Policy, and American Agriculture* (Lawrence: University Press of Kansas, 1988), pp. 92–94.

8. Patrick O'Brien, "Economic Analysis and the Shaping of Public Policy: A 1995 Farm Bill Perspective," *Journal of Agricultural and Applied Economics* 28 (1996): 21–23.

9. Ralph Nader and Mark J. Green, eds., *Corporate Power in America* (New York: Grossman, 1973); Ralph Nader, Mary Green, and Joel Seligman, *Taming the Giant Corporation* (New York: Norton, 1976).

10. Williamson, *The Economic Institutions of Capitalism*, pp. 41–42.

11. Lehne, *Industry and Politics*, pp. 92–108.

12. Kirk Victor, "Being Here," *National Journal*, August 6, 1988, pp. 2021–2025; and his "Takin' on the Bacon," *National Journal*, May 6, 1995, pp. 1082–1086.

13. Andrew Shonfield, *Modern Capitalism: The Changing Balance of Public and Private Power* (Oxford: Oxford University Press, 1969).

14. E. E. Schattschneider, *Politics, Pressures, and the Tariff: A Study of Free Private Enterprise in Pressure Politics, as Shown in the 1929–30 Revision of the Tariff* (Englewood Cliffs, NJ: Prentice-Hall, 1935).

15. Raymond A. Bauer, Ithiel de Sola Pool, and Lewis Anthony Dexter review that tariff war and contrast it with later legislative battles.

American Business and Public Policy: The Politics of Foreign Trade (New York: Aldine Atherton, 1963), pp. 24–26.

16. Philip A. Mundo, *Interest Groups: Cases and Characteristics* (Chicago: Nelson-Hall, 1992), p. 89.

17. William P. Browne and Kenneth VerBurg, *Michigan Politics and Government: Facing Change in a Complex State* (Lincoln: University of Nebraska Press, 1995), p. 222.

18. Lehne, *Industry and Politics*, pp. 94–100.

19. Salisbury, "Interest Representation," p. 74.

20. Schattschneider, *Politics, Pressures, and the Tariff*, p. 84.

21. Salisbury, "Interest Representation," p. 74.

22. Arthur C. Close and various colleagues, *Washington Representatives: Who Does What for Whom in the Nation's Capital* (Washington, DC: Columbia Books, annually since 1977).

23. Christopher J. Bosso, *Pesticides and Politics: The Life Cycle of a Public Issue* (Pittsburgh: University of Pittsburgh Press, 1987), pp. 45–60.

24. Graham K. Wilson, *Business and Politics: A Comparative Introduction*, 2d ed. (Chatham, NJ: Chatham House, 1990), pp. 42–44.

25. Browne, *Private Interests, Public Policy, and American Agriculture*, pp. 121–125.

26. Ibid., p. 122.

27. Kay Lehman Schlozman, "What Accent the Heavenly Chorus? Political Equality and the American Pressure System," *Journal of Politics* 46 (1984): 1006–1032.

28. David Vogel, *Fluctuating Fortunes: The Political Power of Business in America* (New York: Basic, 1989).

29. Dan Bertozzi, Jr. and Lee B. Burgunder, *Business, Government, and Public Policy: Concepts and Practices* (Englewood Cliffs, NJ: Prentice-Hall, 1990), pp. 191–218; Thomas Gais, *Improper Influence: Campaign Finance Law, Political Interest Groups, and the Problem of Equality* (Ann Arbor: University of Michigan Press, 1996).

30. Jonathan Rauch, *Demosclerosis: The Silent Killer of American Government* (New York: Times Books, 1994), p. 38.

31. Sheila Slaughter and Edward T. Silva, "Looking Backwards: How Foundations Formulated Ideology in the Progressive Period," reprinted in David L. Gies, J. Steven Ott, and Joy M. Shafritz, eds., *The Nonprofit Organization: Essential Readings* (Belmont, CA: Brooks/Cole, 1990), pp. 374–394.

32. Hugh Hawkins, *Banding Together: The Rise of National Associations in Higher Education, 1887–1950* (Baltimore: Johns Hopkins University Press, 1992).

33. John G. Alexander, "Planning and Management in Nonprofit Organizations," reprinted in *The Nonprofit Organization*, pp. 155–166; Eleanor L. Brilliant, *The United Way: Dilemmas of Organized Charity* (New York: Columbia University Press, 1990).

34. Allen D. Hertzke, *Representing God in Washington: The Role of Religious Lobbies in the American Polity* (Knoxville: University of Tennessee Press, 1988), p. 101.

35. James L. Adams, *The Growing Church Lobby in Washington* (Grand Rapids, MI: Eerdmans, 1970); James A. Smith, *The Idea Brokers: Think Tanks and the Rise of the New Policy Elite* (New York: Free Press, 1991), pp. 24–45.

36. Bruce L. R. Smith, *The RAND Corporation: Case Study of a Nonprofit Advisory Commission* (Cambridge, MA: Harvard University Press, 1966), pp. 148–194; Constance Ewing Cook, *Lobbying for Higher Education: How Colleges and Universities Influence Federal Policy* (Nashville, TN: Vanderbilt University Press, 1998).

37. Daryl E. Chubin and Edward J. Hackett, *Peerless Science: Peer Review and U.S. Science Policy* (Albany: State University of New York Press, 1990); the other side, why policymakers like such grants, can be seen in William P. Browne, *Cultivating Congress: Constituents, Issues, and Interests in Agricultural Policymaking* (Lawrence: University Press of Kansas, 1995), p. 197.

38. Robert D. Calkins, *The Role of the Philanthropic Foundation* (Washington, DC: Cosmos Club, 1969).

39. Gary N. Scrivner, "100 Years of Tax Policy Changes Affecting Charitable Organizations," in *The Nonprofit Organization*, pp. 126–137.

40. Hertzke, *Representing God in Washington*, pp. 94–116; Smith, *The Idea Brokers*, pp. 167–189.

41. James A. Reichley, "Religion and the Future of American Politics," *Political Science Quarterly* 101 (1986): 237.

42. Kenneth D. Wald, *Religion and Politics in the United States*, 2d ed. (Washington, DC: Congressional Quarterly Press, 1992), pp. 222–278.

43. Browne, *Private Interests, Public Policy, and American Agriculture*, pp. 231–233.

44. Robert E. Lane, "The Decline of Politics and Ideology in a Knowledgeable Society," *American Sociological Review* 31 (1996): 649–662.

45. Gene M. Lyons, *The Uneasy Partnership: Social Science and the Federal Government in the Twentieth Century* (New York: Russell Sage, 1969).

46. Cook, *Lobbying for Higher Education*, chap. 6.

47. Ronald J. Hrebenar and Clive S. Thomas, eds., *Interest Group Politics in the Midwest States* (Ames: Iowa State University Press, 1993). See especially Michigan, where 11 percent of all registered lobbyists were state officials, p. 125.

48. Jeffrey M. Berry deserves credit for coining the phrase in *The Interest Group Society*, 2d ed. (New York: Little, Brown/Scott, Foresman, 1989), pp. 17–43.

49. William P. Browne and Robert H. Salisbury, "Organized Spokesmen for Cities: Urban Interest Groups," *Urban Affairs Annual Review* 6 (1972): 259–262.

50. Ibid., p. 258. More than five dozen to be precise.

51. Ibid., p. 263.

52. Glen Brooks, *When Governors Convene: The Governors' Conference and National Politics* (Baltimore: Johns Hopkins University Press, 1961).

53. Suzanne Farkas, *Urban Lobbying: Mayors in the Federal Arena* (New York: New York University Press, 1971), pp. 253–259; Donald H.

Haider, *When Governments Come to Washington: Governors, Mayors, and Intergovernmental Lobbying* (New York: Free Press, 1974), pp. 114–143.

54. Richard D. Bingham, Brett W. Hawkins, John P. Frendreis, and Mary P. Le Blanc, *Professional Associations and Municipal Innovation* (Madison: University of Wisconsin Press, 1981).

55. Beverly J. Cigler, "Not Just Another Special Interest: Intergovernmental Representation," in Allan J. Cigler and Burdett A. Loomis, *Interest Group Politics*, 4th ed. (Washington, DC: Congressional Quarterly Press, 1995), pp. 131–153.

56. Salisbury, "Interest Representation," p. 74.

57. Russell Warren Howe and Sarah Hays Trott, *The Power Peddlers: How Lobbyists Mold America's Foreign Policy* (Garden City, NY: Doubleday, 1977).

58. Thomas M. Franck and Edward Weisband, *Foreign Policy by Congress* (New York: Oxford University Press, 1979).

59. Ronald J. Hrebenar and Clive S. Thomas, "The Japanese Lobby in Washington: How Different Is It?" in *Interest Group Politics*, 4th ed., pp. 349–367.

60. Pat Choate, *Agents of Influence: How Japan's Lobbyists in the United States Manipulate America's Political and Economic System* (New York: Knopf, 1990).

61. William Martin, *With God on Our Side: The Rise of the Religious Right in America* (New York: Broadway, 1996).

62. Larry J. Sabato, *The Rise of Political Consultants* (New York: Basic Books, 1981).

63. Susan B. Trento, *The Power House: Robert Keith Gray and the Selling of Access and Influence in Washington* (New York: St. Martin's, 1992).

64. Browne, *Private Interests, Public Policy, and American Agriculture*, pp. 155–163.

65. Burdett A. Loomis, "The Congressional Office as a Small (?) Business: New Members Set Up Shop," *Publius* 9 (1979): 35–55; Robert Salisbury and Kenneth A. Shepsle, "U.S. Congressman as Enterprise," *Legislative Studies Quarterly* 75 (1981): 559–576.

66. Browne, *Cultivating Congress*, pp. 110–114.

67. Barbara Sinclair, *The Transformation of the U.S. Senate* (Baltimore: Johns Hopkins University Press, 1989); David W. Rohde, *Parties and Leaders in the Postreform House* (Chicago: University of Chicago Press, 1991).

68. David Whiteman, *Communication in Congress: Members, Staff, and the Search for Information* (Lawrence: University Press of Kansas, 1995), pp. 111–129.

69. Browne, *Cultivating Congress*, pp. 115–119.

70. Schattschneider, *The Semi-Sovereign People*.

71. Robert A. Dahl, of course, says this with far greater elegance in *A Preface to Democratic Theory* (Chicago: University of Chicago Press, 1956), p. 138.

72. William P. Browne and David B. Schweikhardt, "Demosclerosis: Implications for Agricultural Policy," *American Journal of Agricultural*

Economics 77 (1995): 1128–1134; James T. Bonnen, William P. Browne, and David B. Schweikhardt, "Further Observations on the Changing Nature of National Agricultural Decision Processes, 1946–95," *Agricultural History* 70 (1996): 130–152.

73. Salisbury, "Interest Representation," p. 75.

CHAPTER 3

1. Charles Miller, *Lobbying: Understanding and Influencing the Corridors of Power*, 2d ed. (Oxford: Basil Blackwell, 1990), pp. 156–158.

2. Jeffrey H. Birnbaum, *The Lobbyists: How Influence Peddlers Get Their Way in Washington* (New York: Times Books, 1992), p. 208.

3. Jeffrey M. Berry, *The Interest Group Society*, 3d ed. (New York: Longman, 1997), p. 6.

4. Elisabeth S. Clemens, *The People's Lobby: Organizational Innovation and the Rise of Interest Group Politics in the United States, 1890–1925* (Chicago: University of Chicago Press, 1997).

5. Allan J. Cigler, "From Protest Group to Interest Group: The Making of American Agriculture Movement, Inc.," in Allan J. Cigler and Burdett A. Loomis, ed., *Interest Group Politics*, 2d ed. (Washington, DC: Congressional Quarterly Press, 1986), p. 58.

6. Alan Rosenthal, *The Third House: Lobbyists and Lobbying in the States* (Washington, DC: Congressional Quarterly Press, 1993), p. 112.

7. L. Harmon Zeigler and Michael Baer, *Lobbying: Interaction and Influence in American State Legislatures* (Belmont, CA: Wadsworth, 1969), pp. 8–11.

8. Lester W. Milbrath epitomizes this genre in *The Washington Lobbyists* (Chicago: Rand McNally, 1963), pp. 297–304.

9. Mark J. Rozell and Clyde Wilcox, *Second Coming: The New Christian Right in Virginia Politics* (Baltimore: Johns Hopkins University Press, 1996), pp. 72–83.

10. Kenneth G. Crawford, *The Pressure Boys: The Inside Story of Lobbying* (New York: Messner, 1939); Karl Schiftgiesser, *The Lobbyists: The Art and Business of Influencing Lawmakers* (Boston: Little, Brown, 1951).

11. Raymond A. Bauer, Ithiel de Solo Pool, and Lewis Anthony Dexter, *American Business and Public Policy: The Politics of Foreign Trade*, 2d ed. (New York: Atherton, 1972).

12. Rosenthal, *The Third House*, pp. 121–123.

13. Ibid.

14. Kay Lehman Schlozman and John T. Tierney, *Organized Interests and American Democracy* (New York: Harper and Row, 1986), pp. 149–152.

15. Ibid, p. 274.

16. David Truman gets credit for it. See *The Governmental Process: Political Interests and Public Opinion* (New York: Knopf, 1951), pp. 264–270.

17. John Mark Hansen, *Gaining Access: Congress and the Farm Lobby, 1919–1981* (Chicago: University of Chicago Press, 1991).

18. Ibid., pp. 26–77.

19. Ibid., p. 77.

20. Birnbaum, *The Lobbyists*, pp. 59–61.

21. This can be seen best in the extensive public administration literature, where experts truly are supposed to plan and solve social problems. See, for instance, Steven Kelman, *Making Public Policy: A Hopeful View of American Government* (New York: Basic Books, 1987), p. 39.

22. William P. Browne, *Cultivating Congress: Constituents, Issues, and Interests in Agricultural Policymaking* (Lawrence: University Press of Kansas, 1995), pp. 206–215.

23. Ibid., pp. 142–150.

24. Matthew Josephson, *The Politicos: 1865–1896* (New York: Harcourt, Brace and World, 1963).

25. James Deakin, *The Lobbyists* (Washington, DC: Public Affairs Press, 1966), p. 29.

26. Thomas Gais, *Improper Influence: Campaign Finance Law, Political Interest Groups, and the Problem of Equality* (Ann Arbor: University of Michigan Press, 1996).

27. Larry J. Sabato, *PAC Power: Inside the World of Political Action Committees* (New York: Norton, 1984); Brooks Jackson, *Honest Graft: Big Money and the American Political Process*, rev. ed. (Washington, DC: Farragut, 1990).

28. Burdett A. Loomis and Eric Sexton, "Choosing to Advertise: How Interests Decide," in Allan J. Cigler and Burdett A. Loomis, eds., *Interest Group Politics*, 4th ed. (Washington, DC: Congressional Quarterly Press, 1995), pp. 193–214.

29. Browne, *Cultivating Congress*, p.114.

30. The seminal work is in Clement E. Vose, *Caucasians Only: The Supreme Court, the NAACP, and the Restrictive Covenant Cases* (Berkeley: University of California Press, 1959). Lots of research has followed.

31. William P. Browne, "Mobilizing and Activating Group Demands: The American Agriculture Movement," *Social Science Quarterly* 64 (1983): 24–25.

32. Miller, *Lobbying*, p. 177.

33. Rosenthal, The Third House, p. 126.

34. Hansen, *Gaining Access*, pp. 17–19.

35. William P. Browne, "Organized Interests, Grassroots Confidants, and Congress," in *Interest Group Politics*, 4th ed., pp. 281–297.

36. This is a suprisingly neglected topic. See, for a rare glimpse, Browne, *Cultivating Congress*, pp. 136–142.

37. Robert H. Salisbury, "The Paradox of Interests in Washington, D.C.: More Groups and Less Clout," in Anthony King, ed., *The New American Political System*, 2d ed. (Washington, DC: American Enterprise Institute, 1990), pp. 203–230.

38. Browne, *Cultivating Congress*, pp. 143–144.

39. Josephson, *The Politicos*, p. 531.

40. James Sterling Young, *The Washington Community, 1800–1828* (New York: Harcourt, Brace and World, 1966).

41. Jane J. Mansbridge, *Beyond Adversary Democracy* (Chicago: University of Chicago Press, 1983); and Jane J. Mansbridge, "A Deliberative Theory of Interest Representation," in Mark P. Petracca, ed., *The Politics of Interests: Interest Groups Transformed* (Boulder, CO: Westview, 1992), pp. 32–57.

42. Clemens, *The People's Lobby.*

43. Robert A. Dahl, *A Preface to Democratic Theory* (Chicago: University of Chicago Press, 1956).

44. Schlozman and Tierney, *Organized Interests and American Democracy,* pp. 164–169.

45. Frank R. Baumgartner and Beth L. Leech, *Basic Interests: The Importance of Groups in Politics and in Political Science* (Princeton, NJ: Princeton University Press, 1998), chap. 8.

46. Milbrath, *The Washington Lobbyists;* Zeigler and Baer, *Lobbying;* and Schlozman and Tierney, *Organized Interests and American Democracy.* These studies include, in addition, Jeffrey M. Berry, *Lobbying for the People: The Political Behavior of Public Interest Groups* (Princeton: Princeton University Press, 1977); David Knoke, *Organizing for Collective Action: The Political Economies of Associations* (Hawthorne, NY: Aldine de Gruyter, 1990); Jack L. Walker, Jr., *Mobilizing Interest Groups in America: Patrons, Professions, and Social Movements* (Ann Arbor: University of Michigan Press, 1991); and John P. Heinz, Edward O. Laumann, Robert L. Nelson, and Robert H. Salisbury, *The Hollow Core: Private Interests in National Policymaking* (Cambridge, MA: Harvard University Press, 1993).

47. Heinz, et al., *The Hollow Core,* p. 348.

48. John R. Wright, *Interest Groups and Congress: Lobbying Contributions and Influence* (Boston: Allyn and Bacon, 1996).

CHAPTER 4

1. Burdett A. Loomis, "A New Era: Groups and the Grass Roots," in Allan J. Cigler and Burdett A. Loomis, eds., *Interest Group Politics* (Washington, DC: Congressional Quarterly Press, 1983), pp. 169–190.

2. Sidney Verba, Kay Lehman Schlozman, and Henry E. Brady, *Voice and Equality: Civic Voluntarism in American Politics* (Cambridge, MA: Harvard University Press, 1995), pp. 391–415.

3. V. O. Key, Jr., *Politics, Parties, and Pressure Groups,* 5th ed. (New York: Crowell, 1964), pp. 130–132.

4. Robert Presthus, in his theory of social determinism set in motion by elite interaction, is the best example. See his *Elites in the Policy Process* (London: Cambridge University Press, 1974). But this tendency can be seen in the commentary of all those cited previously who extensively surveyed group techniques.

5. Murray R. Benedict, *Farm Policies of the United States, 1790–1950* (New York: Twentieth Century Fund, 1950).

6. Willard W. Cochrane, *The Development of American Agriculture: A Historical Analysis* (Minneapolis: University of Minnesota Press, 1979).

7. Joseph S. Davis, "Agricultural Fundamentalism," in Norman E. Hines, ed., *Economics, Sociology, and the Modern World* (Cambridge, MA: Harvard University Press, 1935), pp. 3–22; A. Whitney Griswold, *Farming and Democracy* (New York: Harcourt, Brace, 1948).

8. Kenneth W. Rowe, *Mathew Carey: A Study in American Economic Development* (Baltimore: Johns Hopkins University Press, 1933).

9. James T. Bonnen and William P. Browne, "Why Is Agricultural Policy So Difficult to Reform?" in Carol S. Kramer, ed., *The Political Economy of U.S. Agriculture: Challenges for the 1990s* (Washington, DC: Resources for the Future, National Center for Food and Agricultural Policy, 1989), p. 15.

10. Peter Odegard, *Pressure Politics: The Story of the Anti-Saloon League* (New York: Columbia University Press, 1928), p. 76.

11. E. Pendleton Herring, *Group Representation before Congress* (Baltimore: Johns Hopkins University Press, 1929).

12. John Mueller, *Policy and Opinion in the Gulf War* (Chicago: University of Chicago Press, 1994), p. 138.

13. Robert C. Paehlke, *Environmentalism and the Future of Progressive Politics* (New Haven: Yale University Press, 1989), pp. 14–22; Christopher J. Bosso, "Adaptation and Change in the Environmental Movement," in Allan J. Cigler and Burdett A. Loomis, eds., *Interest Group Politics*, 3d ed. (Washington, DC: Congressional Quarterly Press, 1991), pp. 151–176.

14. Carroll Pursell, ed., *From Conservation to Ecology: The Development of Environmental Concern* (New York: Crowell, 1973); Bob Pepperman Taylor, *Our Limits Transgressed: Environmental Political Thought in America* (Lawrence: University Press of Kansas, 1992), pp. 51–80.

15. William P. Browne and Kenneth VerBurg, eds., *Michigan Politics and Government: Facing Change in a Complex State* (Lincoln: University of Nebraska Press, 1995), pp. 276–282.

16. J. Clarence Davies III and Barbara S. Davies, *The Politics of Pollution*, 2d ed. (Indianapolis: Pegasus, 1975).

17. William A. Gamson, *Talking Politics* (New York: Cambridge University Press, 1992); Theodore Sasson, *Crime Talk: How Citizens Construct a Social Problem* (New York: Aldine de Gruyter, 1995), pp. 149–150.

18. Bernard C. Cohen, *Democracies and Foreign Policy: Public Participation in the United States and the Netherlands* (Madison: University of Wisconsin Press, 1995), pp. 128–152.

19. Andrew S. McFarland, *Common Cause: Lobbying in the Public Interest* (Chatham, NJ: Chatham House, 1984); Browne and VerBurg, *Michigan Politics and Government*, pp. 223–226; Mark J. Rozell and Clyde Wilcox, *Second Coming: The New Christian Right in Virginia Politics* (Baltimore: Johns Hopkins University Press, 1996).

20. Reo M. Christenson, "The Power of the Press: The Case of *The Toledo Blade*," *Midwest Journal of Political Science* 3 (August 1959): 227–240.

21. Stephen Hess, *The Washington Reporters* (Washington, DC: Brookings, 1981), pp.18–21.

22. Richard Davis, *The Press and American Politics: The New Mediator* (New York: Longman, 1982), pp. 18–21.

23. Ibid., pp. 16–17.

24. Edward Jay Epstein, *News from Nowhere: Television and the News* (New York: Random House, 1973), pp. 258–273.

25. Edward Jay Epstein, *Between Fact and Fiction: The Problem of Journalism* (New York: Random House, 1967).

26. Larry J. Sabato, *Feeding Frenzy: How Attack Journalism Has Transformed American Politics* (New York: Free Press, 1991), especially pp. 208–212.

27. Delmar D. Dunn, *Public Officials and the Press* (Reading, MA: Addison-Wesley, 1969); Leon V. Sigal, *Reporters and Officials: The Organization and Politics of Newsmaking* (Lexington, MA: D.C. Heath, 1973).

28. David L. Paletz and Robert M. Entman, *Media Power Politics* (New York: Free Press, 1981), pp. 124–146.

29. Kay Lehman Schlozman and John T. Tierney, *Organized Interests and American Democracy* (New York: Harper and Row, 1986), pp. 178–182.

30. Dan Nimmo and James E. Combs, *Mediated Political Realities*, 2d ed. (New York: Longman, 1990).

31. Doris A. Graber, *Mass Media and American Politics* (Washington, DC: Congressional Quarterly Press, 1980), pp. 148–150.

32. James E. Combs and Dan Nimmo, *The New Propaganda: The Dictatorship of Palaver in Contemporary Politics* (New York: Longman, 1993), pp. 18–20.

33. Schlozman and Tierney, *Organized Interests and American Democracy*, pp. 179–180.

34. Murray Edelman, *The Symbolic Uses of Politics* (Urbana: University of Illinois Press, 1964); Murray Edelman, *Constructing the Political Spectacle* (Chicago: University of Chicago Press, 1988).

35. Charles D. Elder and Roger W. Cobb, *The Political Uses of Symbols* (New York: Longman, 1983).

36. Jeffrey J. Mondak, *Nothing to Read: Newspapers and Elections in a Social Experiment* (Ann Arbor: University of Michigan Press, 1995).

37. Mircea Eliade, *Myth and Reality* (New York: Harper and Row, 1963), pp. 5–8.

CHAPTER 5

1. Alan Rosenthal, *The Third House: Lobbyists and Lobbying in the States* (Washington, DC: Congressional Quarterly Press, 1993).

2. Ibid., pp. 62–206.

3. Jeffrey H. Birnbaum, *The Lobbyists: How Influence Peddlers Get Their Way in Washington* (New York: Times Books, 1992).

4. James Deakin, *The Lobbyists* (Washington, DC: Public Affairs Press, 1956), p. 28.

5. It's been a modestly debated truism of the literature since Lester W. Milbrath, *The Washington Lobbyists* (Chicago: Rand McNally, 1963), pp.

186–189. Milbrath was influenced by Norbert Weiner, *Cybernetics* (New York: Wiley, 1948).

6. Deakin covers this ground in *The Lobbyists*, pp. 54–60.

7. James Sterling Young, *The Washington Community, 1800–1828* (New York: Harcourt, Brace and World, 1968), pp. 213–228.

8. Thurlow Weed, *Life: Including His Autobiography*, two vols. (New York: Houghton Mifflin, 1883–1884).

9. Deakin, *The Lobbyists*, p. 59.

10. Elbert B. Smith, *The Death of Slavery: The United States, 1837–1865* (Chicago: University of Chicago Press, 1967), pp. 12–33.

11. Kenneth M. Stampp, *The Era of Reconstruction, 1865–1877* (New York: Knopf, 1966), pp. 83–118.

12. Herbert Croly, *Marcus Alonzo Hanna* (New York: Macmillan, 1909).

13. Stampp, *The Era of Reconstruction*.

14. John H. Aldrich, *Why Parties? The Origin and Transformation of Party Politics in America* (Chicago: University of Chicago Press, 1995).

15. David Loth, *Public Plunder: A History of Graft in America* (New York: Carrick and Evans, 1938).

16. Deakin, *The Lobbyists*, p. 75.

17. Roberta Ash, *Social Movements in America* (Chicago: Markham, 1972), pp. 87–88, 119–121.

18. David R. Szatmary, *Shays' Rebellion: The Making of an Agrarian Insurrection* (Amherst: University of Massachusetts Press, 1980).

19. Kenneth G. Crawford, *The Pressure Boys: The Inside Story of Lobbying in America* (New York: Julian Messner, 1939).

20. Ernest S. Griffith, *The Impasse of Democracy* (New York: Harrison-Wilton, 1939).

21. For reviews, see James E. Anderson, *Public Policymaking*, 3d ed. (New York: Holt, Rinehart and Winston, 1984), pp. 40–41; and Keith E. Hamm, "Patterns of Influence among Committees, Agencies, and Interest Groups," *Legislative Studies Quarterly* 8 (August 1983): 379–426.

22. For "the classics" that show narrow policy, see Douglass Cater, *Power in Washington* (New York: Random House, 1964); J. Leiper Freeman, *The Political Process: Executive Bureau-Legislative Committee Relations*, rev. ed. (original edition 1955; New York: Random House, 1965); A. Lee Fritschler, *Smoking and Politics: Policymaking and the Federal Bureaucracy* (Englewood Cliffs, NJ: Prentice-Hall, 1969), revised in four later editions; and John A. Ferejohn, *Pork Barrel Politics: Rivers and Harbors Legislation, 1947–1968* (Stanford: Stanford University Press, 1974).

23. Randall B. Ripley and Grace A. Franklin, *Congress, the Bureaucracy, and Public Policy*, 5th ed. (Pacific Grove, CA: Brooks/Cole, 1991), pp. 76–101.

24. Arthur A. Maass, *Muddy Waters: The Army Engineers and the Nation's Rivers* (Cambridge: Harvard University Press, 1951).

25. Theodore J. Lowi, *The End of Liberalism: Ideology, Policy, and the Crisis of Public Authority* (New York: Norton, 1969).

26. For the best statement, see Lawrence C. Dodd and Richard L. Schott, *Congress and the Administrative State* (New York: Wiley, 1979), especially pp. 151–154.

27. Morris Ogul, *Congress Oversees the Bureaucracy: Studies in Legislative Supervision* (Pittsburgh: University of Pittsburgh Press, 1976), pp. 81–90.

28. James T. Bonnen, William P. Browne, and David B. Schweikhardt, "Further Observations on the Changing Nature of National Agricultural Policy Decision Processes, 1946–1995," *Agricultural History* 70 (Spring 1996): 130–152.

29. It's the story everyone knows to be true, at least in its barebones essentials. See Robert H. Salisbury, John P. Heinz, Robert L. Nelson, and Edward O. Laumann, "Triangles, Networks, and Hollow Cores: The Complex Geometry of Washington Interest Representation," in Mark P. Petracca, ed., *The Politics of Interests: Interest Groups Transformed* (Boulder, CO: Westview, 1992), p. 131.

30. Thomas L. Gais, Mark A. Peterson, and Jack L. Walker, Jr., "Interest Groups, Iron Triangles, and Representative Institutions in American National Government," *British Journal of Political Science* 14 (April 1984): 161–185.

31. John Mark Hansen, *Gaining Access: Congress and the Farm Lobby, 1919–1981* (Chicago: University of Chicago Press, 1991), p. 77.

32. William P. Browne, *Cultivating Congress: Constituents, Issues, and Interests in Agricultural Policymaking* (Lawrence: University Press of Kansas, 1995), pp. 142–150.

33. Mark A. Peterson, "How Health Policy Information Is Used in Congress," in Thomas E. Mann and Norman J. Ornstein, eds., *Intensive Care: How Congress Shapes Health Policy* (Washington, DC: American Enterprise Institute and Brookings, 1995), pp. 79–125.

34. Gary Mucciaroni, *Reversal of Fortune: Public Policy and Private Interests* (Washington, DC: Brookings, 1995).

35. Deakin, *The Lobbyists*, pp. 73–77.

36. George D. Webster and Frederick J. Krebs, *Associations and Lobbying Regulation*, rev. ed. (Washington, DC: U.S. Chamber of Commerce, 1985).

37. Peter H. Stone, "Lobbyists on a Leash?" *National Journal* 28 (February 3, 1996): 242–246.

38. Ibid., p. 246.

39. Hugh Heclo, "Issue Networks and the Executive Establishment," in Anthony King, ed., *The New American Political System* (Washington, DC: American Enterprise Institute, 1978), pp. 87–124.

40. Ibid., p. 103.

41. Charles O. Jones, "American Politics and the Organization of Energy Decision Making," *Annual Review of Energy* 4 (1978): 99–121.

42. Andrew S. McFarland, *Public Interest Lobbies: Decision Making on Energy* (Washington, DC: American Enterprise Institute, 1976).

43. Jeffrey M. Berry, *The Interest Group Society*, 3d ed. (New York: Longman, 1997), pp. 17–43.

44. Kay Lehman Schlozman and John T. Tierney, *Organized Interests and American Democracy* (New York: Harper and Row, 1986), pp. 75–76.

45. Jeffrey M. Berry, *Lobbying for the People* (Princeton, NJ: Princeton University Press, 1977), pp. 212–252; William P. Browne, *Private Interests, Public Policy, and American Agriculture* (Lawrence: University Press of Kansas, 1988), pp. 138–146.

46. Richard Flacks, *Making History: The American Left and the American Mind* (New York: Columbia University Press, 1988).

47. Clement E. Vose, *Caucasians Only: The Supreme Court, the NAACP, and the Restrictive Covenant Cases* (Berkeley: University of California Press, 1959); Stuart A. Scheingold, *The Politics of Rights: Lawyers, Public Policy, and Political Change* (New Haven, CT: Yale University Press, 1974), p. 17.

48. Gais, et al., "Interest Groups, Iron Triangles, and Representative Institutions in American National Government"; John P. Heinz, Edward O. Laumann, Robert L. Nelson, and Robert H. Salisbury, *The Hollow Core: Private Interests in National Policy Making* (Cambridge, MA: Harvard University Press, 1993), pp. 193–217.

49. See the articles in John E. Chubb and Paul E. Peterson, eds., *Can the Government Govern?* (Washington, DC: Brookings, 1989).

50. Rosenthal, *The Third House*, pp. 121–23.

51. Lisa Zagaroli, "For Lobbyists, Game Stays Same," *Detroit News* (February 3, 1997): 8A.

52. Elaine K. Swift, *The Making of an American Senate: Reconstitutive Change in Congress, 1787–1841* (Ann Arbor: University of Michigan Press, 1997).

53. Daniel J. Elazar, *The American Mosaic: The Impact of Space, Time, and Culture on American Politics* (Boulder, CO: Westview, 1994).

54. Even in Illinois, as evidenced in Samuel K. Gove and James D. Nowland, *Illinois Politics and Government: The Expanding Metropolitan Frontier* (Lincoln: University of Nebraska Press, 1996), pp. 1–20.

55. Samuel C. Patterson, "Legislative Politics in the States," in Virginia Gray and Herbert Jacob, eds., *Politics and the American States: A Comparative Analysis*, 6th ed. (Washington DC: Congressional Quarterly Press, 1996), pp. 159–206.

56. Woodrow Wilson, *Congressional Government* (Boston: Houghton Mifflin, 1885); Joseph Cooper and David W. Brady, "Institutional Context and Leadership Style: The House from Cannon to Rayburn," *American Political Science Review* 75 (March 1981): 411–425.

57. Barbara Sinclair, *The Transformation of the U.S. Senate* (Baltimore: Johns Hopkins University Press, 1989); David W. Rohde, *Parties and Leaders in the Postreform Congress* (Chicago: University of Chicago Press, 1991).

58. Heinz, et al., *The Hollow Core*, p. 348.

59. Michael T. Hayes, *Lobbyists and Legislators: A Theory of Political Markets* (New Brunswick, NJ: Rutgers University Press, 1981).

60. Birnbaum, *The Lobbyists*, pp. 297–300.

61. Heinz Eulau, "Lobbyists: The Wasted Profession," *Public Opinion Quarterly* 28 (Spring 1964): 27–38. For a reaffirming view of the importance of multiple tasks, see Elisabeth S. Clemens, *The People's Lobby: Organizational Innovation and the Rise of Interest Group Politics in the United States, 1890–1925* (Chicago: University of Chicago Press, 1997).

62. See three illustrations: Charles Peters, *How Washington Really Works* (Reading, MA: Addison-Wesley, 1980); A. Lee Fritschler and Bernard H. Ross, *Business Regulation and Government Decision-Making* (Cambridge, MA: Winthrop, 1980); and A. Lee Fritschler and Bernard H. Ross, *How Washington Really Works: The Executive's Guide to Government* (Cambridge, MA: Ballinger, 1987). Peters writes of insider networking. The others emphasize insider decision processes.

CHAPTER 6

1. Frank R. Baumgartner and Bryan D. Jones, *Agendas and Instability in American Politics* (Chicago: University of Chicago Press, 1993), pp. 175–192.

2. Lisa Zagaroli, "Ex-Michigan Lawmakers Turn Political Expertise into Lucrative Jobs," *Detroit News* (February 2, 1997): 8A.

3. Marie Hojnacki, "Interest Groups' Decisions to Join Alliances or Work Alone," *American Journal of Political Science* 41 (January 1997): 83.

4. John P. Heinz, Edward O. Laumann, Robert L. Nelson, and Robert H. Salisbury, *The Hollow Core: Private Interests in National Policy Making* (Cambridge, MA: Harvard University Press, 1993), pp. 252–253.

5. William P. Browne, *Private Interests, Public Policy, and American Agriculture* (Lawrence: University Press of Kansas, 1988), p. 188.

6. Ibid., p. 158.

7. William P. Browne, *Cultivating Congress: Constituents, Issues, and Interests in Agricultural Policymaking* (Lawrence: University Press of Kansas, 1995), pp. 109–130.

8. Don F. Hadwiger and Ross B. Talbot, *Pressures and Protests: The Kennedy Farm Program and the Wheat Referendum of 1963* (San Francisco: Chandler, 1965).

9. Kevin Hula, "Rounding Up the Usual Suspects: Forging Interest Group Coalitions in Washington," in Allen J. Cigler and Burdett A. Loomis, eds., *Interest Group Politics*, 4th ed. (Washington, DC: Congressional Quarterly Press), p. 239.

10. Burdett A. Loomis, "Coalitions of Interests: Building Bridges in the Balkanized State," in Allen J. Cigler and Burdett A. Loomis, eds., *Interest Group Politics*, 2d ed. (Washington, DC: Congressional Quarterly Press), pp. 258–274.

11. Robert H. Salisbury, "The Paradox of Interest Groups in Washington—More Groups, Less Clout," in Anthony King, ed., *The New American Political System*, 2d ed. (Washington, DC: American Enterprise Institute, 1990), pp. 203–229.

12. Jeffrey M. Berry, *The Interest Group Society*, 3d ed. (New York: Longman, 1997), pp. 190–192.

13. Hula, "Rounding Up the Usual Suspects," pp. 250–252.

14. Browne, *Private Interests, Public Policy, and American Agriculture*, pp. 177–179.

15. Virginia Gray and David Lowery, "To Lobby Alone or in a Flock: Foraging Behavior among Organized Interests," *American Politics Quarterly* (forthcoming).

16. Hojnacki, "Interest Groups' Decisions to Join Alliances or Work Alone," pp. 84–85.

17. For example, public interest groups are seen as the biggest coalition players. Loree Bykerk and Ardith Maney, "Consumer Groups and Coalition Politics on Capitol Hill," in *Interest Group Politics*, 4th ed., pp. 259–279. E. E. Schattschneider, as a more historical figure, suggested the same in *The Semisovereign People: A Realist's View of Democracy in America* (New York: Holt, Rinehart and Winston, 1960), pp. 20–43.

18. Loomis, "Coalitions of Interests," pp. 267–270.

19. Timothy H. Breen, *Tobacco Culture: The Mentality of the Great Tidewater Planters on the Eve of Revolution* (Princeton, NJ: Princeton University Press, 1985).

20. Claude Bowers, *The Tragic Era: The Revolution after Lincoln* (New York: Houghton Mifflin, 1929).

21. Charles Lindblom, *Politics and Markets: The World's Political–Economic Systems* (New York: Basic Books, 1977).

22. Jo Freeman, *The Politics of Women's Liberation* (New York: David McKay, 1975); Jane J. Mansbridge, *Why We Lost the Era* (Chicago: University of Chicago Press, 1986).

23. John P. Heinz cited fears of this impasse in "The Political Impasse in Farm Support Legislation," *Yale Law Journal* 71 (April 1962): 954–970. Garth Youngberg, "The National Farm Coalition and the Politics of Food," paper prepared for the Fourth Annual Hendricks Public Policy Symposium (Lincoln, NE, 1979).

24. Henry J. Pratt, *Gray Agendas: Interest Groups and Public Pensions in Canada, Britain, and the United States* (Ann Arbor: University of Michigan Press, 1993), pp. 178–200.

25. Browne, *Private Interests, Public Policy, and American Agriculture*, pp. 167–190.

26. Bykerk and Maney, "Consumer Groups and Coalition Politics on Capitol Hill," pp. 269–272.

27. Christopher J. Bosso, in four articles, has done a superb job of dealing with the nuances of the environmental groups and their coalition politics: "Adaptation and Change in the Environmental Movement," in Allan J. Cigler and Burdett A. Loomis, eds., *Interest Group Politics*, 3d ed. (Washington, DC: Congressional Quarterly Press, 1991), pp. 151–176; "After the Movement: Environmental Activism in the 1990s," in Norman J. Vig and Michael E. Kraft, eds., *Environmental Policy in the 1990s*, 2d ed. (Washington, DC: Congressional Quarterly Press, 1994), pp. 31–50; "The

Color of Money: Environmental Groups and the Pathologies of Fund Raising," in *Interest Group Politics*, 4th ed., pp. 101–130; and "Seizing Back the Day: The Challenge to Environmental Activism in the 1990s," in Norman J. Vig and Michael E. Kraft, eds., *Environmental Policy in the 1990s*, 3d ed. (Washington, DC: Congressional Quarterly Press, 1997), pp. 53–74.

28. William H. Riker, *The Theory of Political Coalitions* (New Haven, CT: Yale University Press, 1962), pp. 32–42.

29. Loomis, "Coalitions of Interests," pp. 258–259.

30. Paul R. Dommel, *The Politics of Revenue Sharing* (Bloomington: Indiana University Press, 1974), pp. 89–91.

31. D. W. Brogan, *Politics in America* (Garden City, NY: Doubleday, 1960), p. 64.

32. Browne, *Private Interests, Public Policy, and American Agriculture*, p. 171.

33. Alan Rosenthal, *The Third House: Lobbyists and Lobbying in the States* (Washington, DC: Congressional Quarterly Press, 1993), p. 151.

34. Ibid.

35. Paul Light, *Still Artful Work: The Continuing Politics of Social Security Reform* (New York: McGraw-Hill, 1995), p. 71.

36. Robert H. Salisbury, "Interest Representation: The Dominance of Institutions," *American Political Science Review* 78 (March 1984): 64–76.

37. David B. Truman, *The Governmental Process: Political Interests and Public Opinion* (New York: Knopf, 1951), pp. 28–33.

38. A. Lee Fritschler and James M. Hoefler, *Smoking and Politics: Policy Making and the Federal Bureaucracy*, 5th ed. (Upper Saddle River, NJ: Prentice Hall, 1996), p. 51.

39. Browne, *Private Interests, Public Policy, and American Agriculture*, pp. 12–123, 186–190.

40. Richard E. Cohen, *Washington at Work: Back Rooms and Clean Air* (New York: Macmillan, 1992), pp. 151–166.

41. Charles W. Wiggins and William P. Browne, "Interest Groups and Public Policy within a State Legislative System," *Polity* 24 (Spring 1982): 548–558; Charles W. Wiggins, Keith H. Hamm, and Charles G. Bell, "Interest-Group and Party Influence Agents in the Legislative Process: A Comparative State Analysis," *Journal of Politics* 54 (February 1992): 82–100.

42. James Q. Wilson, *Political Organizations* (New York: Basic Books, 1973), p. 263; William P. Browne, "Organized Interests and Their Issue Niches: A Search for Pluralism in a Policy Domain," *Journal of Politics* 52 (May 1990): 477–509; Virginia Gray and David Lowery, *The Population Ecology of Interest Representation: Lobbying Communities in the American States* (Ann Arbor: University of Michigan Press, 1996), pp. 210–215.

43. Rosenthal, *The Third House*, pp. 178, 199–201.

44. Andrew S. McFarland, "Interviewing Interest Group Personnel: The Little Village in the World," in William Crotty, Mildred A. Swartz, and John C. Green, eds., *Representing Interests and Interest Group Representation* (Lanham, NY: University Press of America, 1994), pp. 46–47.

45. Rosenthal, *The Third House*, pp. 198–201.

46. Gray and Lowery, *The Population Ecology of Interest Representation*.

47. Andrew S. McFarland, *Cooperative Pluralism: The National Coal Policy Experiment* (Lawrence: University Press of Kansas, 1993).

48. Steven S. Smith, *Call to Order: Floor Politics in the House and Senate* (Washington, DC: Brookings, 1989), pp. 55–59.

49. Browne, *Private Interests, Public Policy, and American Agriculture*, pp. 233–236.

50. Jonathan Rauch, *Demosclerosis: The Silent Killer of American Government* (New York: Times Books, 1994); William P. Browne and David B. Schweikhardt, "Demosclerosis: Implications for Agricultural Policy," *American Journal of Agricultural Economics* 77 (December 1995): 1128–1134.

51. Browne and Schweikhardt, "Demosclerosis," p. 1133.

52. Gray and Lowery, *The Population Ecology of Interest Representation*, p. 254.

53. Gray and Lowery, "To Lobby Alone or in a Flock."

CHAPTER 7

1. Harold Wolman and Fred Teitelbaum, "Interest Groups and the Reagan Presidency," in Lester M. Salamon and Michael S. Lund, eds., *The Reagan Presidency and the Governing of America* (Washington, DC: Urban Institute Press, 1985), p. 324.

2. William P. Browne, Kristen Allen, and David B. Schweikhardt, "Never Say Never Again: Why the Road to Agricultural Policy Reform Has a Long Way to Go," *Choices* 12 (Fourth Quarter): 4–9.

3. William P. Browne, *Cultivating Congress: Constituents, Issues, and Interests in Agricultural Policymaking* (Lawrence: University Press of Kansas, 1995), pp. 186–205.

4. Kenneth A. Shepsle, "Institutional Equilibrium and Equilibrium Institutions," in Herbert Weisberg, ed., *Political Science: The Science of Politics* (New York: Agathon, 1986), pp. 51–82.

5. Robert H. Salisbury and John P. Heinz, "A Theory of Policy Analysis and Some Preliminary Applications," in Ira Sharkansky, ed., *Policy Analysis in Political Science* (Chicago: Markham, 1970), pp. 39–60.

6. Clive S. Thomas and Ronald J. Hrebener, "Interest Groups in the States," in Virginia Gray and Herbert Jacob, eds., *Politics in the American States: A Comparative Analysis*, 6th ed. (Washington, DC: Congressional Quarterly Press, 1996), pp. 147–153.

7. Jeffrey M. Berry, *The Interest Group Society*, 3d ed. (New York: Longman, 1997), pp. 225–229.

8. John Mark Hansen, *Gaining Access: Congress and the Farm Lobby, 1919–1981* (Chicago: University of Chicago Press, 1991).

9. David Hamilton, *From New Day to New Deal: American Farm Policy from Hoover to Roosevelt, 1928–1933* (Chapel Hill: University of North Carolina Press, 1991), pp. 170–194.

10. Theda Skocpol and Kenneth Finegold, "State Capacity and Economic Intervention in the Early New Deal," *Political Science Quarterly* 97 (Summer 1982): 255–278.

11. Hansen, *Gaining Access*, pp. 45–75.

12. Murray R. Benedict, "Agriculture as a Commercial Industry Comparable to Other Branches of the Economy," *Journal of Farm Economics* 24 (May 1942): 476–496.

13. Jess Gilbert and Carolyn Howe, "Beyond 'State vs. Society': Theories of the State and New Deal Agricultural Policies," *American Sociological Review* 56 (April 1991): 218.

14. Patrick J. Akard, "Corporate Mobilization and Political Power: The Transformation of U.S. Economic Policy in the 1970s," *American Sociological Review* 57 (October 1992): 605.

15. Mark Green and Andrew Buchsbaum, *The Corporate Lobbies: Political Profiles of the Business Roundtable and the Chamber of Commerce* (Washington, DC: Public Citizen, 1980).

16. Sar Levitan and Mary Cooper, *Business Lobbies: The Public Good and the Bottom Line* (Baltimore: Johns Hopkins University Press, 1984).

17. William Greider, *The Education of David Stockman and Other Americans* (New York: Dutton, 1982), p. 49.

18. Akard, "Corporate Mobilization and Political Power," p. 607.

19. For a distinctly different analytical view of the advantages, see Daniel W. Bromley, *Environment and Economy: Property Rights and Public Policy* (Oxford: Basil Blackwell, 1991), pp. 204–231.

20. Charles E. Lindblom, *Politics and Markets: The World's Political-Economic Systems* (New York: Basic, 1977), especially p. 356.

21. James Q. Wilson, "Democracy and the Corporation," in Ronald Hessen, ed., *Does Big Business Rule America?* (Washington, DC: Ethics and Public Policy Center, 1981), p. 37. See also his *Political Organizations* (New York: Basic, 1973).

22. Kenneth J. Meier, in many places, writes especially well about the several dimensions of gatekeeping. See, for example, his *Politics and the Bureaucracy: Policymaking in the Fourth Branch of Government*, 2d ed. (Belmont, CA: Brooks/Cole, 1987), pp. 114–130.

23. Bromley, *Environment and Economy*, pp. 218–222.

24. On learning by interests, see Louis Galambos, *Competition and Cooperation: The Emergence of a National Trade Association* (Baltimore, MD: Johns Hopkins University Press, 1966).

25. Hansen, *Gaining Access*, pp. 73–75.

26. Frederic N. Cleaveland and associates, ed., *Congress and Urban Problems* (Washington, DC: Brookings, 1969).

27. Suzanne Farkas, *Urban Lobbying: Mayors in the Federal Arena* (New York: New York University Press, 1971), pp. 35–68; Beverly A. Cigler, "Not Just Another Special Interest: Intergovernmental Representation," in Allan J. Cigler and Burdett A. Loomis, *Interest Group Politics*, 4th ed. (Washington, DC: Congressional Quarterly Press, 1995), pp. 131–153.

28. For an eloquent statement, see James A. Morone, *The Democratic Wish: Popular Participation and the Limits of American Government* (New York: Basic, 1990).

29. The idea of American politics being driven by political ambition among public officials is well-developed and complementary to this view, but it doesn't say much about organized interests. Joseph A. Schlesinger, *Ambitions and Politics: Political Careers in the United States* (Chicago: Rand McNally, 1966); Alan Ehrenhalt, *The United States of Ambition: Politicians, Power, and the Pursuit of Office* (New York: Random House, 1991).

30. Stephen Skowronek, *Building a New American State: The Expansion of National Administrative Capacities, 1877–1920* (Cambridge: Cambridge University Press, 1982).

31. John P. Heinz, Edward O. Laumann, Robert L. Nelson, and Robert H. Salisbury, *The Hollow Core: Private Interests in National Policy Making* (Cambridge, MA: Harvard University Press, 1993), pp. 384–391.

32. Douglass C. North, *Institutions, Institutional Change, and Economic Performance* (Cambridge: Cambridge University Press, 1990), pp. 135–137.

33. Oliver E. Williamson, *The Economic Institutions of Capitalism* (New York: Free Press, 1985), pp. 18–19.

34. North, *Institutions, Institutional Change, and Economic Performance*, pp. 3–4.

35. Virginia Gray and David Lowery raise this point about public-over-lobbyist influence in *The Population Ecology of Interest Representation: Lobbying Communities in the American States* (Ann Arbor: University of Michigan Press, 1996), p. 253.

36. Hansen, *Gaining Access*, pp. 61–75.

37. David J. Webber, "Analyzing Political Feasibility: Political Scientists' Unique Contribution to Policy Analysis," *Policy Studies Journal* 14 (June 1986): 545–553.

38. Wilson, *Political Organizations*, pp. 337–340.

39. Arthur F. Bentley, *The Process of Government: A Study of Social Pressures* (Chicago: University of Chicago Press, 1908).

40. Myron Q. Hale, "The Cosmology of Arthur F. Bentley," *American Political Science Review* 54 (December 1960): 957.

41. John Dewey and Arthur F. Bentley, *Knowing and the Known* (Boston: Beacon Press, 1949), p. 108.

42. Robert H. Salisbury emphasizes the importance of selectively received benefits to interest group members. That's not necessarily the case here. Robert H. Salisbury, "An Exchange Theory of Interest Groups," *Midwest Journal of Political Science* 13 (February 1969): 1–32.

43. Shepsle, "Institutional Equilibrium and Equilibrium Institutions."

44. North, *Institutions, Institutional Change, and Economic Performance*, p. 3.

45. Ibid., p. 140.

CHAPTER 8

1. An exceptional refuting of conventional wisdom on lobbying is done by Gary Mucciaroni in *Reversals of Fortune: Public Policy and Private Interests* (Washington, DC: Brookings, 1995), pp. 1–27. He pretty well settles it.

2. Frederick H. Buttel, et al. "The State, Rural Policy, and Rural Poverty," in Rural Sociological Society Task Force on Persistent Rural Poverty, ed., *Persistent Poverty in Rural America* (Boulder, CO: Westview Press, 1990), pp. 292–326.

3. *Report of the Country Life Commission.* Senate Document 705, 60th Cong., 2d sess. Washington, DC: U.S. Government Printing Office, 1909.

4. Sandra S. Osbourn, *Rural Policy in the United States: A History* (Washington, DC: Congressional Research Service, The Library of Congress, 1988).

5. Willard W. Cochrane, *The Development of American Agriculture: An Historical Analysis* (Minneapolis: University of Minnesota Press, 1979).

6. Harold F. Breimyer, "Conceptualization and Climate for New Deal Farm Laws of the 1930s," *American Journal of Agricultural Economics* 65 (December 1983): 1153–1157.

7. John D. Black, *Agricultural Reform in the United States* (New York: McGraw-Hill, 1929); L. C. Gray, "Disadvantaged Rural Classes," *Journal of Farm Economics* 20 (February 1938): 71–85; M. L. Wilson, "Problem of Poverty in Agriculture," *Journal of Farm Economics* 22 (February 1940): 10–33.

8. Richard S. Kirkendall, *Social Scientists and Farm Politics in the Age of Roosevelt* (Columbia: University of Missouri Press, 1966).

9. Kevin Gross, Richard Rodefeld, and Frederick H. Buttel, "The Political Economy of Class Structure in U.S. Agriculture," in Frederick H. Buttel and Howard Newby, eds., *The Rural Sociology of Advanced Societies* (Montclair, NJ: Allanheld Osun, 1980), pp. 83–132.

10. Leonard S. White, *The Republican Era: A Study in Administrative Management* (New York: Macmillan, 1958).

11. John M. Gaus and Leon O. Wolcott, *Public Administration and the United States Department of Agriculture* (Chicago: Public Service Administration, 1940).

12. Wayne B. Rasmussen and Gladys L. Baker, *The Department of Agriculture* (New York: Praeger, 1972).

13. Gladys L. Baker, *The County Agent* (Chicago: University of Chicago Press, 1939).

14. Murray R. Benedict, *Farm Policies of the United States, 1790–1950* (New York: Twentieth Century Fund, 1950).

15. Theodore W. Schultz, *Redirecting Farm Policy* (New York: Macmillan, 1943); Theodore W. Schultz, *Agriculture in an Unstable Economy* (New York: McGraw-Hill, 1945).

16. Cochrane, *The Development of American Agriculture*, pp. 378–395.

17. Osbourn, *Rural Policy in the United States*.

18. Richard S. Kirkendall, "Farm Politics and the New Deal," in Louis H. Douglas, ed., *Agrarianism in American History* (Lexington, MA: D.C. Heath, 1969), pp. 148–153.

19. James H. Shideler, *Farm Crisis: 1919–1929* (Berkeley: University of California Press, 1957).

20. Theda Skocpol and Kenneth Finegold, "State Capacity and Economic Intervention in the Early New Deal," *Political Science Quarterly* 97 (Summer 1982): 255–278.

21. Douglas E. Bowers, Wayne D. Rasmussen, and Gladys L. Baker, *History of Agricultural Price Support and Adjustment Programs* (Washington, DC: Economic Research Service, U.S. Department of Agriculture, December 1984).

22. James T. Bonnen and William P. Browne, "Why Is Agricultural Policy So Difficult to Reform?" in Carol S. Kramer, ed., *The Political Economy of U.S. Agriculture: Challenges for the 1990s* (Washington, DC: Resources for the Future, 1989), pp. 7–33.

23. Benedict, *Farm Policies of the United States*.

24. John Mark Hansen, "Taxation and the Political Economy of the Tariff," *International Organization* 44 (Autumn 1990): 527–551.

25. Arthur Capper, *The Agriculture Bloc* (New York: Harcourt Brace, 1922); Orville M. Kile, *The Farm Bureau through Three Decades* (Baltimore, MD: Waverly Press, 1948).

26. Theodore J. Lowi, *The End of Liberalism: Ideology, Policy, and the Crisis of Public Authority* (New York: W.W. Norton, 1969).

27. Grant McConnell, *The Decline of Agrarian Democracy* (Berkeley: University of California Press, 1953); Grant McConnell, *Private Power and American Democracy* (New York: Knopf, 1966), chap. 7.

28. William P. Browne and Won K. Paik, "Initiating Home-Style Issues in a Postreform Congress," *Agriculture and Human Values* 14 (March 1997): 81–95.

29. William P. Browne and J. Norman Reid, "Misconceptions, Institutional Impediments, and the Problems of Rural Governments," *Public Administration Quarterly* 14 (Fall 1990): 265–284.

30. William P. Browne, *Private Interests, Public Policy, and American Agriculture* (Lawrence: University Press of Kansas, 1988), pp. 89–108.

31. John Mark Hansen, *Gaining Access: Congress and the Farm Lobby, 1919–1981* (Chicago: University of Chicago Press, 1991), pp. 26–31.

32. Patrick H. Mooney and Theo J. Majka, *Farmers' and Farm Workers' Movements: Social Protest in American Agriculture* (New York: Twayne, 1995).

33. Hansen, *Gaining Access*, pp. 61–72.

34. Arthur L. Stinchcombe, "Agricultural Enterprise and Rural Class Relations," *American Journal of Sociology* 67 (September 1961): 165–176.

35. James T. Bonnen, "Why Is There No Coherent U.S. Rural Policy?" *Policy Studies Journal* 20 (No. 2, 1992): 190–201.

36. William J. Nagel, "Federal Organization for Rural Policy," in *Towards Rural Development Policy for the 1990's: Enhancing Income and Employment Opportunities.* Symposium Proceedings of the Congressional Research Service and Joint Economic Committee of Congress, Washington, DC: 101st Cong., 1st sess., S. Print 101–50, 1990.

37. Kevin Hula, "Rounding Up the Usual Suspects: Forging Interest Group Coalitions in Washington," in Allan J. Cigler and Burdett A. Loomis, eds., *Interest Group Politics*, 4th ed. (Washington, DC: Congressional Quarterly Press, 1995), pp. 250–255.

38. Jonathan Rauch, *Demosclerosis: The Silent Killer of American Government* (New York: Times Books, 1994).

39. William P. Browne and Louis E. Swanson, "Living with the Minimum: Rural Public Policy," in Emery N. Castle, ed., *The Changing American Countryside: Rural People and Places* (Lawrence: University Press of Kansas, 1995), pp. 481–492.

CHAPTER 9

1. Arthur F. Bentley, *The Process of Government: A Study of Social Pressures* (Chicago: University of Chicago Press, 1908).

2. Kenneth G. Crawford, *The Pressure Boys: The Inside Story of Lobbying in America* (New York: Julian Messner, 1939).

3. Ernest S. Griffith, *The Impasse of Democracy* (New York: Harrison-Wilton, 1939).

4. James Madison, *The Federalist Papers*, no. 10.

5. For an insightful commentary, see Melvin Steinfield, ed., *Cracks in the Melting Pot: Racism and Discrimination in American History*, 2d ed. (Glencoe, IL: Glenco Press, 1973), pp. xix–xxiv.

6. John Dewey and Arthur F. Bentley, *Knowing and the Known* (Boston: Beacon Press, 1949).

7. William P. Browne, *Private Interests, Public Policy, and American Agriculture* (Lawrence: University Press of Kansas, 1988), p. 134.

8. Kenneth A. Shepsle, *The Changing Textbook Congress*, in John E. Chubb and Paul Peterson, eds., *Can the Government Govern?* (Washington, DC: Brookings, 1989), pp. 250–256.

9. John Mark Hansen illustrates this best in *Gaining Access: Congress and the Farm Lobby, 1919–1981* (Chicago: University of Chicago Press, 1991). So does Elisabeth S. Clemens in *The People's Lobby: Organizational Innovation and the Rise of Interest Group Politics in the United States, 1890–1925* (Chicago: University of Chicago Press, 1997).

10. Hugh Heclo is an excellent example. Hugh Heclo, "Issue Networks and the Executive Establishment," in Anthony King, ed., *The New American Political System* (Washington, DC: American Enterprise Institute, 1978), pp. 87–89.

11. Charles O. Jones has sloppy hexagons. Charles O. Jones, "American Politics and the Organization of Energy Decision Making," *Annual Review of Energy* 4 (1978): 99–121.

12. Jeffrey M. Berry, *The Interest Group Society*, 3d ed. (New York: Longman, 1997), pp. 194–202.

13. William P. Browne, *Cultivating Congress: Constituents, Issues, and Interests in Agricultural Policymaking* (Lawrence: University Press of Kansas, 1995), pp. 207–213.

14. A very nice study guesses this to be true: Thomas L. Gais, Mark A. Peterson, and Jack L. Walker, Jr., "Interest Groups, Iron Triangles, and Representative Institutions in American National Government," *British Journal of Political Science* 14 (April 1984): 161–185.

15. Randall B. Ripley and Grace A. Franklin, *Congress, the Bureaucracy, and Public Policy*, 5th ed. (Pacific Grove, CA: Brooks/Cole 1991), p. 184.

16. Robert H. Salisbury, "The Paradox of Interest Groups in Washington—More Groups, Less Clout," in Anthony King, ed. *The New American Political System*, 2d ed. (Washington, DC: American Enterprise Institute, 1990), pp. 208–212.

17. Browne, *Cultivating Congress*, pp. 31–34.

18. Constance Ewing Cook, *Lobbying for Higher Education: How Colleges and Universities Influence Federal Policy* (Nashville, TN: Vanderbilt University Press, 1998).

19. William P. Browne, "Organized Interests and Their Issue Niches: A Search for Pluralism in a Policy Domain," *Journal of Politics* 52 (May 1990): 502.

20. Virginia Gray and David Lowery, *The Population Ecology of Interest Representation: Lobbying Communities in the American States* (Ann Arbor: University of Michigan Press, 1996), p. 251.

21. William P. Browne, "Issue Niches and the Limits of Interest Group Influence," in Allan J. Cigler and Burdett A. Loomis, eds., *Interest Group Politics*, 3d ed. (Washington, DC: Congressional Quarterly Press, 1991), pp. 362–366. See also his earlier "Variations in the Behavior and Style of State Lobbyists and Interest Groups," *Journal of Politics* 47 (May 1985): 450–468. Style matters.

22. For an environmental explanation, see Gray and Lowery, *The Population Ecology of Interest Representation*, pp. 75–79.

23. Hansen, *Gaining Access*. Ken Kollman's analysis helps sort this out, too, in "Inviting Friends to Lobby: Interest Groups, Ideological Bias, and Congressional Committees," *American Journal of Political Science* 41 (April 1997): 519–544.

24. Browne, *Private Interests, Public Policy, and American Agriculture*, p. 38.

25. Gray and Lowery, *The Population Ecology of Interest Representation*.

26. Ibid., pp. 46–49.

27. Christopher J. Bosso shows this especially well in *Pesticides and Politics: The Life Cycle of a Public Issue* (Pittsburgh: University of Pittsburgh Press, 1987).

28. Browne, *Private Interests, Public Policy, and American Agriculture,* pp. 233–236.

29. Michael T. Hayes, *Lobbyists and Legislators: A Theory of Political Markets* (New Brunswick, NJ: Rutgers University Press, 1981).

30. Gray and Lowery, *The Population Ecology of Interest Representation,* p. 38.

31. Raymond A. Bauer, Ithiel de Sola Pool, and Lewis Anthony Dexter, *American Business and Public Policy: The Politics of Foreign Trade* (Chicago: Aldine-Atherton, 1963).

32. Terry M. Moe, "The New Economics of Organization," *American Journal of Political Science* 28 (November 1984): 739–777.

33. Ronald Coase, "The Nature of the Firm," *Economica* 4 (November 1937): 386–405.

34. Oliver E. Williamson, *The Economic Institutions of Capitalism* (New York: Free Press, 1985).

35. Douglass C. North, *Institutions, Institutional Change, and Economic Performance* (Cambridge: Cambridge University Press, 1990).

36. Browne, "Organized Interests and Their Issue Niches," pp. 499–503.

37. Glenn L. Johnson deals with asset fixity. See, for example, his comments throughout Glenn L. Johnson and C. Leroy Quance, eds., *The Overproduction Trap in U.S. Agriculture: A Study of Resource Allocation from World War I to the Late 1960s* (Baltimore: Johns Hopkins University Press, 1972), pp. 22–40.

38. John P. Heinz, Edward O. Laumann, Robert L. Nelson, and Robert H. Salisbury, *The Hollow Core: Private Interests in National Policy Making* (Cambridge, MA: Harvard University Press, 1993), pp. 262–312.

39. Gray and Lowery, *The Population Ecology of Interest Representation,* pp. 251–252.

40. Robert H. Salisbury was getting at this in "The Paradox of Interest Groups in Washington," pp. 203–229.

CHAPTER 10

1. E. E. Schattschneider, *The Semisovereign People: A Realist's View of Democracy in America* (New York: Holt, Rinehart and Winston, 1960).

2. Most recently, there's Haynes Johnson and David S. Broder, *The System: The American Way of Politics at the Breaking Point* (Boston: Little, Brown, 1996).

3. Jane J. Mansbridge, *Beyond Adversary Democracy* (Chicago: University of Chicago Press, 1983).

4. Jeffrey H. Birnbaum and Alan S. Murray, *Showdown at Gucci Gulch: Lawmakers, Lobbyists, and the Unlikely Triumph of Tax Reform* (New York: Random House, 1987).

5. Johnson and Broder, *The System.*

6. Robert A. Dahl gives the most cogent statement of pluralism in both *A Preface to Democratic Theory* (New Haven, CT: Yale University Press, 1956) and *Dilemmas of Pluralist Democracy* (New Haven, CT: Yale University Press, 1982). Another book of his that should also be read is *Who Governs? Democracy and Power In an American City* (New Haven, CT: Yale University Press, 1961).

7. Theodore J. Lowi, *The End of Liberalism: The Second Republic of the United States* (New York: Norton, 1979).

8. Allan J. Cigler and Burdett A. Loomis, "Contemporary Interest Group Politics: More Than 'More of the Same,'" in Allan J. Cigler and Burdett A. Loomis, *Interest Group Politics*, 4th ed. (Washington, DC: Congressional Quarterly Press, 1995), pp. 393–406.

9. Constance Ewing Cook, *Lobbying for Higher Education: How Colleges and Universities Influence Federal Policy* (Nashville, TN: Vanderbilt University Press, 1998).

10. Alan Rosenthal, *The Third House: Lobbyists and Lobbying in the States* (Washington, DC: Congressional Quarterly Press, 1993), pp. 19–28.

11. Steven S. Smith, *Call to Order: Floor Politics in the House and Senate* (Washington, DC: Brookings, 1989), pp. 55–59.

12. This is the real everyday lesson of Virginia Gray and David Lowery, *The Population Ecology of Interest Representation: Lobbying Communities in the American States* (Ann Arbor: University of Michigan Press, 1996).

13. Ibid.

14. Johnson and Broder, *The System*, pp. 622–635.

15. Ibid., p. 629.

16. Ibid., p. 635.

17. James Q. Wilson, "Interests and Deliberations in the American Republic, or, Why James Madison Would Never Have Received the James Madison Award," *PS: Political Science and Politics* 23 (December 1990): 558–562.

18. James Madison, *The Federalist Papers*, no. 51.

19. Fred S. McChesney, *Money for Nothing: Politicians, Rent Extraction, and Political Extortion* (Cambridge, MA: Harvard University Press, 1997).

20. But, after raising a media fuss, they did get their money back.

21. William P. Browne, *Cultivating Congress: Constituents, Issues, and Interests in Agricultural Policymaking* (Lawrence: University Press of Kansas, 1995), pp. 18–19.

22. Robert H. Salisbury, "Putting Interests Back into Interest Groups," in Allan J. Cigler and Burdett A. Loomis, eds., *Interest Group Politics*, 3d ed. (Washington, DC: Congressional Quarterly Press, 1991), pp. 383–389.

23. Schattschneider, *The Semisovereign People*, pp. 102, 141.

Index